NO
WOMAN
TENDERFOOT

NO
WOMAN
TENDERFOOT

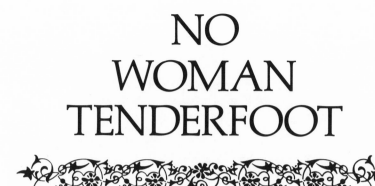

FLORENCE MERRIAM BAILEY,
PIONEER NATURALIST

By Harriet Kofalk

TEXAS A&M UNIVERSITY PRESS
COLLEGE STATION

Frontispiece: A familiar bird near Paradise Lake at Smith College,
this kingfisher was pictured in Florence's first book,
Birds through an Opera Glass.

The paper used in this book meets the minimum requirements of the
American National Standard for Permanence of Paper for Printed
Library Materials, Z39.48984. Binding materials have been
chosen for durability.

Library of Congress Cataloging-in-Publication Data

Kofalk, Harriet, 1937–
　　No woman tenderfoot : Florence Merriam Bailey,
pioneer naturalist / by Harriet Kofalk.
　　　　p.　　cm. —
　　Bibliography: p.
　　Includes index.
　　ISBN 0-89096-378-9 :
　　1. Bailey, Florence Merriam, b. 1863.　2. Bird
watchers—United States—Biography.　3. Bird
watching—United States—History.　4. Birds,
Protection of—United States—History.　I. Title.
II. Series.
QL31.B24K63　1989
598'.092'4—dc19
[B]　　　　　　　　　　　　　　　　　88-24758
　　　　　　　　　　　　　　　　　　　　CIP

Some women writers found in bird study
a model for tranquility within a turbulent world.
DEBORAH STROM, *Birdwatching with American Women*

And at night, the peace of the star-filled canopy
of the heavens. Is that not what we need to remember
above all in these terrible days of man-made disasters?
Let us raise our eyes to the heavens above us.
FLORENCE MERRIAM BAILEY, letter written during World War II

Contents

Illustrations

xi

Acknowledgment

I WISH TO THANK all those along the way who have shared my enthusiasm and added their own, especially the librarians who enhance
research because they share in the discovery. Without them a book like
this cannot be written. It is people like these who make the pleasures
of research a lifelong satisfaction. Through our joint efforts we can
better help the larger community we all serve.

Introduction

WE HAVE AN ASTONISHING CAPACITY to forget our history, one historian remarked recently. And so you may well ask, "Who was Florence Merriam Bailey?" Although she was one of the most important women nature writers of the nineteenth century, few today have ever heard her name, unless you read old ornithology magazines or study the history of birding. I certainly hadn't when I read a chance remark in a book review about bird artist Louis Agassiz Fuertes. His art was first published in one of her early books, described as "a charming work by an intrepid young woman who refused to believe that (in the words of an early ornithologist) the female sex could not 'without some eccentricity of conduct follow birds and quadrupeds to the woods.'"[1]

As a birder and freelance writer myself, I wanted to know more about that intrepid lady and set out to find her. What I found was a role model for values that are as important today as they were then, if not more so—a woman with the determination to follow her study wherever it led her and to enjoy life enthusiastically along the way. She combined the qualities of a real Victorian lady and an adventuresome pioneer. During winters in Washington, D.C., she served elegant dinners to her husband's coworkers at the U.S. Biological Survey, where he served as chief naturalist for most of his forty-six-year career. For fifty years, primarily during the summers, she traveled the American Southwest seeking out the life stories of the birds she found there, riding horseback across the desert and to many of the West's highest mountains, always with her field notebook handy.

Florence Merriam Bailey was one of the first to study live birds in the field. Scientists of her early days shot birds first and asked questions later, but her main concern then was the millinery fashion for feathers. She wanted to save her "bird friends" from sure extinction at the hands of unscrupulous hunters, although she admired the sportsmen who established societies for game protection. Despite protests of purist friends, she even wrote occasionally for hunting magazines, always with the aim of teaching people to love live birds.

The parallel today bears a familiar challenge. Now we face threats to the planet itself, and it is time to teach more people to love the living planet. We no longer have the option of shooting first and asking questions later. Florence shows us the way by reminding us of that era in which she lived so fully.

One writer called Florence the greatest woman ornithologist of the nineteenth century. No college degree was available then in that science, and the term was used to define anyone who elected to study birds seriously — and few did. The definition of a scientist has changed dramatically from the years when Florence was first active. Nevertheless, our changing the definition makes her no less a scientist. If we choose to identify her by a changed definition, it is our loss. She had a dedication and enthusiasm for life that many seek in today's more defined world, and time cannot steal that from her.

Two hundred years ago Gilbert White, the first natural history writer, saw that classifying animals with "bare descriptions" could be done in one's study, but investigating "the life and conversation of animals" required being active and inquisitive and spending much time in the country.[2] Florence had all of these investigative qualities and few of the classifier's. She was never satisfied with bare descriptions.

One hundred years ago birds were used as examples of virtues for humans to emulate. Then, by the end of the last century, birds were romanticized, like everything else, and a controversy raged over whether they could be thought of as "human," with human traits. At the same time, in its effort to become legitimized, science was swinging the pendulum to the opposite extreme. By the 1940s the pendulum had reached the far end, but today it has swung back toward the middle. Birds once again can be described with attributes like those of humans without fear of offending scientists or the general public.

Writers like Florence pioneered new ways of viewing and describing birds. Her work continues to "leaven the lump," as she would have termed it. Studying birds, like other wildlife, moved from shooting them to keeping them in zoos, and then to observing them in their natural habitats. Even now, however, "this more enlightened approach is, alas, not yet general," James Lovelock mourned in *Gaia: A New Look at Life on Earth.*[3] So we still have much to learn from those early pioneers, as well as the challenge to extend their insights to the larger picture we see today.

Florence had an inherent love of nature that deepened during her daily childhood excursions into the woods with her family. Her brother, C. Hart Merriam, approached the world of nature as if it were a laboratory and sought to identify and classify everything in it. Thus brother and sister represent two divergent views of nature. By viewing nature through Florence's eyes we can better appreciate the synthesis today as we complete the circle, experiencing both an intuitive love for the wholeness of nature and a scientific knowledge of its intricate workings.

Her path through the garden of life was to her a model of the universe. To Florence birds were winged messengers of heaven — a time and place of happiness. Hart would not have described them that way. Yet now that we have taken birds apart feather by feather and bone by bone, many long to see them whole, as part of a larger nature. Birds are each unique, as we each are, and yet a part of the whole. As we began in the twentieth century to concentrate more on birds' feathers, we tended to lose sight of their role as messengers, an equally valid role that birds play in our lives.

Writing has swung on the same pendulum as bird study. Those who loved nature in the nineteenth century necessarily expressed it poetically, even if they wrote in prose. The essence of that thought will always remain poetic, one writer suggested, because *as thought* it is extralogical, that is, beyond and greater than the scope of logic.[4] Stephen Jay Gould has characterized conventional prose of this century as lean and spare, whereas our Victorian predecessors delighted in leisurely detail.[5] Rachel Carson found science and literature identical in discovering and illuminating truth, and she defined her aim as correcting an imbalance between the two. She responded to the dehumanizing of the animal world by arguing that in order to understand the behavior of animals we must describe their physical responses in words that belong to human psychological states. To use her example, it's not that we — or Florence — believe that fish fear their enemies, but that they behave as though they were frightened.[6]

The nature-writing pendulum also continues to swing. Today poets generally include birds incidentally and no longer dwell on their larger value or symbolic images. Yet city dwellers increasingly seek respite in the woods, as they did at the turn of this century, although they have to go farther now to find them than in Florence's day. So perhaps both poet and scientist can once again share their experiences in nature for the benefit of those who seek its joy as well as its definitions. Victorian romanticism has a role to play in the 1980s. I quote Florence often, because I feel that her form of expression has been forgotten and yet speaks loudly to that need we have today to see things whole.

Florence was an explorer in the true sense, for she *sought* discoveries. Yet the records of the explorers of this land, often overlooked, are almost as important as the discoveries they made while on their journeys, as William Goetzmann has commented. We remember the Darwins and Pasteurs, but not the many who followed. One of Florence's contemporaries, in applauding the concept of this biography, pointed out that science is not all breakthroughs, but depends on setting solid foundations and laying bricks, one by one, to build the structure of knowledge.[7] Florence claimed no breakthroughs, but in the firm foundation for studying live birds in the field she certainly laid bricks that lasted for half a century before others refined the study to its present terms.

Yes, Florence was an explorer. She traveled, like many women of her era, first as a health cure. Considering the health risks involved then, such as contracting other diseases, encountering hostile Indians, and suffering physical discomfort, travel seems an unlikely cure, but it was more advantageous than staying inside the damp, poorly heated city homes of the times. The Victorian women relished the opportunity to get away, as many women still do. The risks remain, although the houses have improved — and some would question even that. Most of those traveling women blazed no trail and set no fashion; nor were they imitating men, as some have claimed.[8] They simply enjoyed the exploration of life beyond the boundaries they had lived within, and they took full advantage of the new freedom they were discovering, under the guise of improving their health. Of course, being outdoors generally did improve their health, so they felt justified in their travels.

Florence always spoke out *for* life, rather than against injustice. It wasn't that she ignored or denied problems, but she simply chose to focus elsewhere. In this respect she was like her artist friend Fuertes, whose passion was birds of prey, by definition violent animals. He rarely depicted violence in his art, preferring to focus instead on the harmonies of the universe. In the same way, Florence chose to speak for the benefits of living outdoors. Doing so required that she develop and live with a strength of character that comes across not only in what she did or said, but in how she lived her life. In her story can be found the secrets, for those who choose to see them, of how one can live life fully, as she most certainly believed in doing. She lived by her principles of moving humanity forward, not as we usually think of progress but as "upliftment" — one of her favorite words — which is the most powerful way one can speak out for life.

This book is not meant to be a critical biography. Rather, it is primarily a chronicle of her life. Following the scientific principle of discovery, it leaves the readers to work out for themselves the meaning of her life to them.

Orlando Romero, a young philosopher in New Mexico, has spoken out for the importance of remembering the past. "Today will be the past, and, since the future seems uncertain, we derive our strength to face each new day from the lingering warmth of what has gone by. Each one of us lives in his own time. Each one of us lives in his own world. It is the health of our own past and the health of our own world that will determine our future."[9]

Before we forget our past entirely, it is important to learn what we can from it to guide us on our way. Who was Florence Merriam Bailey? In learning the answer to that, if you catch her enthusiasm for living, you will be the winner, as she was.

NO
WOMAN
TENDERFOOT

Homewood, near Leyden, New York. It stood on a hilltop above the homestead Florence's grandparents had developed and called Locust Grove. (From the collection of Florence Merriam Youngberg.)

Babe in the Woods, 1863–1882

R UTH SAT DRESSED in her red wool coat with the black braid trim, her china head lighted by the sun coming through the bay window. Outside, young Florence noticed how closely some of the autumn maple leaves matched the red wool as she waved to her friend in the window. Then she turned away from the house and toward the call of a woodpecker coming from the hill. Her father was starting on his favorite walk, circling the family woods around Homewood, their large home in upstate New York, near Leyden. She hurried to catch up with him. She loved to share these walks, for she never knew what she might find—a new kind of bird to ask her brother Hart about, or the tracks of a weasel if she were especially watchful. All their small neighbors, whether two- or four-footed, interested Florence and her family.

Autumn meant the end of the haying season, the most fascinating time for children on the farm. As she and her father returned from their walk, Florence was already planning a game of hide-and-seek among the haycocks with her cousins who lived down the road. Then she thought ahead to the next day. The men would load the hay high onto the wagons, and at midday she would take them a drink of cold well water flavored with ginger and molasses. Then she would have the happy task of tidying the meadow with the long-handled rake. So tonight was their last chance for a game.

These were special years.[1] She and Ruth enjoyed them from morning until "golden lanterned fireflies peopled the grass" at night, sometimes even into the night. Florence remembered one night, after she had put Ruth to bed in her little spindle-sided cradle and even after her mother had heard her prayers and tucked her in. Suddenly she woke up and found herself being bundled into a warm blanket. Up the stairs they climbed to the little glassed-in cupola on the roof. A sun parlor by day, at night this was the observatory where her mother often studied the constellations through a telescope, her mythological star atlas by her side.

Caroline Merriam, a Rutgers College graduate, especially loved astronomy. She gave prayerful thanks that this subject was now being taught to women and that she had had the opportunity to learn it so that she could share the wonders of the heavens with her children. Besides the study, as her contemporary, astronomer Maria Mitchell, described it, "There is the same enjoyment in a night upon the housetop, with the stars, as in the midst of other grand scenery . . . a call to the troubled spirit, and a hope to the desponding."[2] This night was a special treat that Mrs. Merriam didn't want her daughter to miss. She excitedly described the eclipse of the moon to Florence, who watched its progress through the telescope and listened sleepily from the folds of the blanket. Clinton Merriam shared the inspiration of the stars with his wife. He later wrote to his daughter Florence that "everyone should become acquainted with all visible constellations, so that when the soul takes wings and flies into illimitable space it would know the roads and not get lost."

Soon it was the holiday season, and the smells and sights brought Christmas closer and closer. Mother's songs now included the familiar carols as well as her favorite hymns, and cousins and aunts and uncles arrived for family parties. Florence thought back to the joy of an earlier Christmas and her surprise when the dining-room door was thrown open. A great lighted Christmas tree filled the bay window from floor to ceiling. On the floor at its foot sat the large china-headed doll she named Ruth.

Winter had other joys for a child in rural New York state in the 1870s, and Florence loved to describe them for her grandnieces in later years. Frost pictures iced the windows, and Florence and her mother enjoyed their pointed stars. At night they identified the winter constellations in the star-filled sky, and on one special night the whole family hurried outside "to see the sky flaming with the aurora borealis — a spectacle of glory never to be forgotten." There were sleigh rides, with bells jangling, down the hill to their grandparents' home. Once, when driving home in the cutter, Florence remembered being "unceremoniously tipped over into a snowdrift."

On the quieter side, a special pleasure was watching the birds and squirrels that came for food outside the dining-room bay window. "The woodpeckers were quiet eaters of suet, the bluejays dashed around showing their handsome colors, and the ruffed grouse — we called them partridges — excited us by strutting around on the snow with black ruffs and banded tail spread." On the garden side of the house one special day, she ran to call the family to come see a partridge jumping up from the snow to pick berries off the high bush cranberry.

Florence's father, Clinton Levi Merriam, ca. 1890. (From the collection of Mr. and Mrs. Sheldon Gustavus Merriam.)

Florence's mother, Caroline Hart Merriam, ca. 1890. (From the collection of Mr. and Mrs. Sheldon Gustavus Merriam.)

It was hard to keep the driveway plowed for the quarter-mile down to the road, so travel often started on snowshoes. Best of all were the times when they circled the woods just for the fun of it. Icicles fringed her father's moustache, but the air was so dry that they didn't feel the below-zero cold. "What fun to bundle up for it — to pull on pair over pair of thick woolen stockings and add moccasins or high felt boots with rubber feet for extra protection. Then to strap on our oval, webbed snowshoes and start out in procession with our two dogs — big black Balder and small yellow Scrap — bringing up the rear in dignified silence. When a fresh snow had covered our trail, Father would lead the way and I would follow, stepping carefully in the spaces between his webbed tracks to make a continuous pathway for dear Mother."

One morning when she and her father were exploring by themselves, they found an open space in the woods where a little surface water had been frozen over and the ice broken. "A red fox has been here to drink," her father pronounced, and the discovery delighted her. Off they went through the woods, following his tracks. They ended at a great boulder, the largest in the woods, which she had often climbed, happy at the success of reaching the top. Another discovery — the fox had been on top, using the boulder as a lookout for "small woodland beasties that might furnish him with a comfortable meal. How did we know? The prints of his front feet and the streak made by his long brush lying on the snow behind told the story."

Those happy childhood times at Homewood were not confined to winter, however. "What choice days those were when we discovered the first spring flowers in the woods! There was the first gentle pink spring beauty that I remember dear sorrowing Father had me kiss tenderly in memory of the little lost sister who had loved it." Florence never forgot her father's association of that flower with Ella Gertrude. Gertie, five years old, had died the day before Florence was born. It was there in the woods that she first found out that her dear doll Ruth had once belonged to Gertie. Ruth and the spring beauty became lifelong special friends to Florence. One year for the family Christmas play, Florence played the part of a spring beauty. Others in the cast included Hart as an Indian, grandfather Ela as Snow and Winter, and Father as Santa Claus.

Florence found joy as well as memories of sorrow around Homewood. She especially loved the residents of her mother's carefully tended gardens. "Then came the filmy-leafed ladies and gentlemen — real persons to me — the lordly yellow adder's tongue, the dark red trillium, and many more which later made a gay flowery carpet over parts of the woods. These, together with uncurling ferns, red-cupped mosses, vari-tinted lichens that came to life after a rain, toadstools and fairy tree shelves made the woods rare treasure houses to wander in . . . Especially dear to my child heart were the snow-drops, babies' breath, the sweet-faced little violets and the small sweet-smelling pinks. The tall, handsome tiger lilies belonged to a different clan. Rarest of all — I

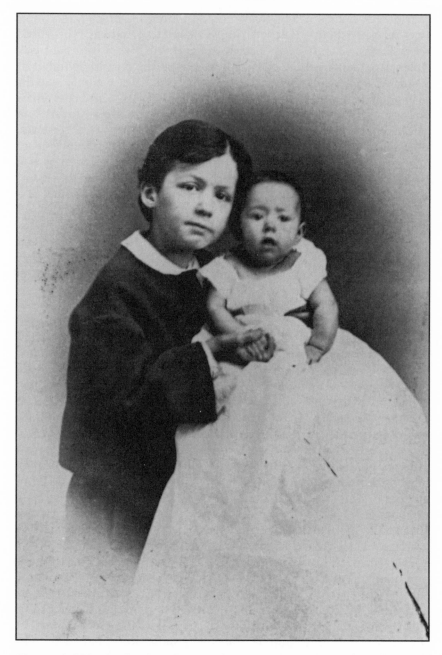

Florence held by her brother, C. Hart Merriam, in 1863. (From the collection of Florence Merriam Youngberg.)

remember standing and looking at it wonderingly — was a large moccasin plant, a pink and white pouched lady slipper brought from its woodland privacy by dear Aunt Helen, our family botanist — she called it *Cypripedium.*"

Aunt Helen Bagg, her father's sister, lived nearby and was always wandering in the woods looking for new specimens for her large herbarium. She taught her own children and her brother's to know and love the plants, and she actively encouraged both Florence and her brother Hart toward their careers as naturalists. Their family standard defined a naturalist as one who knew not only plants and animals, but stars, rocks, birds, and all of nature's wonders. With Aunt Helen's encouragement as well as his own family's, Hart became an ornithologist while still in his teens. Little formal study was available or required to achieve that title. It was also used to describe those who studied birds seriously, and Hart soon had to his credit the largest collection of bird skins in the country. There was never any doubt about the seriousness of his study. Born Clinton Hart Merriam, he was known as C. Hart to distinguish him from his father, also Clinton.

Florence tagged happily behind, admiring Hart and vowing to do just what he did. It never occurred to her that being a woman made any difference, and her educated mother and aunt nodded approvingly. She didn't hear — and they didn't listen to — the prevalent opinion about education for women. Repeated endlessly in sermons by people like the Reverend Morgan Dix at Trinity Church in New York, it held that education for women should be solely for womanly purposes, "in order to be to the man all that he needs."[3]

The year she was seven, Florence's father took a trip to California on the newly opened transcontinental railroad. His strong interest in natural history and in literature had led him to the writings of John Muir, who had recently begun to explore the magnificent Yosemite Valley. Clinton Merriam wanted to see it and to meet Muir. It was a momentous occasion for both men. When Merriam later sent him a question about glacial activity, Muir responded with a long letter. It was one of his first attempts to explain his new theory of glaciation, a theory then unacceptable to men of science. Muir persisted, and his explanation eventually became a standard for defining the erosion of valleys like the Yosemite. Florence and Hart later found glacial scratches on the lower Black River level near Homewood, which stimulated their own geological interests. Hart and Muir remained lifelong friends.

Florence's other brother, Collins, was thirteen years her senior. When she was quite young, he left home to establish himself in business. He shared his father's interest in travel and shortly after this made a trip

Florence's older brother Collins. (From the collection of Mr. and Mrs. Sheldon Gustavus Merriam.)

around the world, returning with many gifts from foreign ports for friends and relatives. The family was glad to have him close by again, especially his mother, for he shared her talent for singing and she missed their duets. One of Collie's gifts might well have been the Chinese fan that has turned up at an Australian auction.[4] It had been used for autographs, and the determined new owner traced it through one signer who identified his town as Locust Grove. Florence and two other cousins had also signed the fan, more than a hundred years ago.

Like Collie and their father, Hart also loved to travel, but his scientific interests led him in other directions. The business world held no interest for him as it did for his brother. Attracted by the abundant wildlife around their home, by the age of twelve he was already collecting mammals and birds and making his first novice's attempts at taxidermy, encouraged by Aunt Helen. Her son Clint was his closest friend, and Florence, eight years younger than Hart, toddled along and listened as the two cousins planned to run away and hunt lions in Africa.

While Hart trapped the small mammals of the area, Florence learned from him how to identify the local birds, happily following him through the woods when he went to collect specimens. Afterward she watched him try to prepare bird skins as you would clean a fish, before he learned to use powdered arsenic to preserve them. Hart soon had so many specimens that his father eventually built a three-story building to serve as a museum.[5] Here is where Florence first decided that she preferred *live* birds over stuffed specimens. Whenever she went into the woods, she tucked some seeds in the pocket of her dress, and often a chickadee or other woods bird would come close enough to feed without being frightened away.[6] She soon learned the benefits of being quiet so she could watch the birds in their home grounds.

Only a few years before, her family had moved to Clinton Merriam's family homestead in the mountains of northern New York. Both of her parents had been raised in this area, and they had always loved its natural beauty. So they had returned here after living in the city for some years, before Florence was born and when Hart was still a baby, to build a home for themselves at the edge of the woods near Florence's grandparents.

The elder Merriams still lived in the farmhouse that they had enlarged early in the century. Here all their children, including son Clinton, had been born. They called it Locust Grove for the tall trees that gave it shade and sweet-smelling white blooms in the spring, and the community that built up around it eventually took on that name as well. It was fitting, since the Merriams had helped to develop this country. For years Ela Merriam had been part-owner of the stagecoach line that carried the mail before the railroads were built. He had also run a tavern, or inn, for stage travelers. It was later used as a play school and as a Sunday school by generations of Merriam children until it burned down, despite efforts to save it by the whole family, including young Florence and all the neighbors and thrashers and farmhands.

Ela was known as General Merriam, having been an officer of the militia. The meadow near his home had been a training ground, where he once drilled a thousand men, riding his spirited black charger. Tradition and history live on in Lewis County, where memories people the meadows like Florence's golden-lanterned fireflies.

Mr. Merriam selected a homesite on the top of the hill above Locust Grove. Like his own father, who also loved the wilderness, Clinton Merriam was always pained by the loss of any of the grand old trees and carefully cut only enough to provide views of the homestead below and of the blue Adirondacks on the horizon. Then he designed a long drive curving up the hill, with bridle paths and carriage roads encircling the woods. Along the edges of the woods Mrs. Merriam planted lilies of the valley, as her husband's grandfather had once done on the homestead below. Here, too, they naturalized and scented the spring air. For years afterward they were gathered to make Memorial Day bouquets.

When the large house was finished, the Merriams called it Homewood. Here they spent happy times with their two boys and little Gertie, whenever Father could leave his business in New York City — first a mercantile house and later a brokerage firm he founded on Wall Street. Mother played the guitar, and she loved to sing lullabies of old hymns to its strumming. On August 7, 1863, there was no singing, no strumming. The next morning Mr. Merriam wrote a brief note to a friend: "With yesterday evening's twilight, passed away, as gently as has been her life, the spirit of our little daughter. Our hearts go out, after her, with deep sadness. God was pleased to take her yesterday, and this morning, has been pleased to give us another daughter. Mrs. Merriam and child are doing well."[7] Gertie had left them, and Florence had arrived.

The following spring, Mr. Merriam awoke one morning in their New York City home to the tune of a robin singing outside his window. It reminded him so of nature's peace and the deep satisfaction of country life that he determined that very day to retire from business and return to Homewood to live permanently. And they did. Florence heard him tell the story of that robin many times, and from it began her interest in birds. The Civil War was just ending, and their new life was just beginning.

But "retirement," to Father at the age of forty, meant managing the family farm, with the help of a farmer and his family whom he employed. It also meant helping his aging parents on the old homestead below Homewood. In 1869 they celebrated their golden wedding anniversary, a gala occasion in any family. Their nine children and all of their grandchildren came home to Locust Grove. A booklet was pub-

Ela Merriam, grandfather of Florence, and his homestead, shown at his golden wedding anniversary in 1869. The banner of flowers reads "Come Haste to the Wedding." He is seated in the rocker in the foreground. Florence, age six, is among the children pictured. (From the collection of Florence Merriam Youngberg.)

lished for the occasion, with a long poem by their cousin Anna Halliday. In it she described each member of the family in verse.

Grandfather Ela was then seventy-five. He posed for the photographer by sitting in his rocking chair on the front lawn of Locust Grove, surrounded by his wife Lydia and the entire family. Florence, then six, and the other younger children sat prominently in the front to one side. A large banner of summer flowers hung across the width of all four pillars on the front veranda, inviting one and all to "Come Haste to the Wedding."

Young Florence and her brothers formed part of the procession of grandchildren that preceded the bride and groom. Then a judge and long-time friend again pronounced them man and wife. The celebration continued far into the night in the ballroom built on as a wing to the house, a frequent addition to houses in that era. It was two stories high with pine woodwork, cornices, pillars, and mantel. The walls were covered with gold-and-white French flocked paper.[8] Florence especially remembered her grandfather's dancing that evening. "He cut the pigeon-wing, greatly to the delight of the assembled children, grandchildren and guests."

Grandfather also insisted on continuing to ride horseback, much to the consternation of his son Clinton. But he would not be dissuaded and exclaimed indignantly, "Right in the prime of life — right in the prime of life!"

Clinton Merriam was also right in the prime of life, and he stayed active in community affairs as well as on the farm. The next year he was elected to Congress, where he served two terms.[9] History remembers him for his successful crusade for legislation to prohibit sending obscene literature through the mails, but Florence remembered the simple piece of paper that hung in his study for years afterward. While in Congress he voted against the "Salary Grab" bill, believing it was neither right nor honorable. When it passed anyway and a check was sent to him for several thousand dollars, he returned it to the U.S. Treasurer and received in return a receipt. He framed and hung it in Homewood, "where it bore testimony to the family principles."

When he wasn't in Washington, Father took Hart into the nearby Adirondacks every spring on fishing trips. Florence always listened eagerly to their discussions when they returned, especially to Hart's enthusiasm as he compared the plants and animals he saw there with those at home. He recognized that they differed mainly because of the cooler climate in the mountains, and his father supported this with books from his large library, especially Humboldt's *Views of Nature*.[10] Observing these differences was one of the most thrilling events of Hart's early life, and anything that thrilled him affected Florence as well. She was especially fascinated with what this idea meant for the birds.

While he was in Washington, Congressman Merriam had the opportunity to further Hart's budding career as a naturalist, which would have far-reaching effects on Florence as well. He arranged a meeting with Spencer Fullerton Baird, assistant secretary of the Smithsonian Institution, who soon afterward appointed Hart, then age sixteen, as the ornithologist with the last of the Hayden Expeditions to study the geography and geology of the Rocky Mountains. Baird was not disappointed in his choice. Hart returned with 313 bird skins and 67 nests with eggs, all of which were classified and stored at the Smithsonian.[11]

While Hart was gone for that summer of 1872, Florence wrote letters to him about the wild pigeons she had tamed and about two hawks that their cousin Clint had sent to Central Park. An eight-year-old can't ask for every word to be spelled, and so she raced onward with her important news. "I have three Fliing Squirles not counting the mother . . . we have not received the rattlesnakes tail yet. We have a little cousin in Kansas. . . . I wish you were here." The new cousin was Anna Theresa Merriam, daughter of Florence's uncle Gustavus, whose family was to play a major role in her future work in the West.

Hart's mother was more concerned about his welfare in the unknown West of the moment, however, as she added to the back of Florence's letter, "We have felt great solicitude on your account of late. Your father particularly has been distressed beyond measure lest the Indians should take possession of you." In answer to Hart's next letter home, Florence replied, "I would not like to have an Indian in the family but I would like to see the little boy you spoke of." Though neither was aware of it yet, he was gently leading her to share his interest in what would become the object of another of his lifelong studies, the American Indian.

The results of the first Hayden Expeditions were directly responsible for the naming of Yellowstone as the first national park in the world, and the experience was unsurpassed as a training ground for the country's upcoming scientific leaders. Until this period, science had been an attempt to comprehend, in Louis Agassiz' terms, a vast system that was the mind of God. Now that the West was filling up so rapidly, the earth was becoming more important than the cosmos.[12] That first trip west certainly had a deep effect on young Hart and his relationship with the earth, as he continued to express it in his theory of distribution of plants and animals by life zones. Her brother's accomplishment only served to increase Florence's admiration. The geographical exploration of the West may have been nearing an end, but many scientific frontiers were just opening. Both brother and sister were attracted to the possibilities.

Evenings in the Merriam household usually consisted of sitting around the lamp at various tasks. Balder, the great black Newfoundland dog who was often Florence's comrade in the woods, dozed at their feet on the hearth rug near the fire. Father read aloud from Shakespeare or some other literary or historical classic. Hart already had a well-deserved reputation as a storyteller. The winter after he returned from Wyoming, he varied the evening routine by sitting before the fireplace and telling his wide-eyed little sister tales of the West.

After listening to Hart's stories, Florence had trouble going to bed,

Evenings at Homewood were often spent by the fire. This evening in 1887 Mrs. Merriam attends to some handwork while Florence reads and Mr. Merriam listens. Over the mantel is the portrait of his grandfather, Judge Nathaniel Merriam. The portrait was lost when Homewood burned. The artist was Gilbert Stuart, who painted the famous portrait of George Washington. (From the collection of Florence Merriam Youngberg.)

thinking about seeing antelope and other discoveries of the frontiers. But she obediently made her way from the warmth of the fire and past the portrait of her great-grandfather Nathaniel Merriam, which hung over the mantel. He had been a judge, who was remembered as "not much on law but great on equity." She paused to look up at him shyly with the feeling she always had when met by the "grave, compelling eyes of the noble man" that followed her wherever she turned. As she studied the portrait, she also felt the strength of his personality, strength she knew was shared by her brother. On her way to bed, she shivered with excitement for the future that lay ahead of them both.

One day, however, excitement lay nearer by. Collins was home for a visit and as he stood looking out of the front window, he calmly

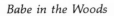

Florence, walking the woods of Homewood with her beloved dog, Balder. (From the collection of Florence Merriam Youngberg.)

announced, "Why, Merriam, you have bears here." Their father rushed to the window to watch a big black bear walking deliberately across the meadow toward the house on his way to the woods. Florence was in the kitchen washing dishes. Her surprise at seeing such large wildlife so close to the house was tempered with her natural talent for analyzing the situation. "Although exciting at the time, the appearance of the bear was easily understood, for during the berry season bears occasionally crossed from the Adirondacks on the east to the low Tug Hill range on the west, doubtless to favorite pastures of their own."

From one of the smaller local mammals she learned another early nature lesson. The Merriam children often "taught school" for the neighbor youngsters in the summer house, formerly the tavern run by her grandfather. As she walked in one day, Florence was surprised by a weasel popping up through a knothole in the floorboard of the old building. When she told Hart about the incident, he described that though brown now, the weasel would be white in winter, giving her one of her first hints of nature's adaptations through protective coloration. By then Hart's interest in science was well beyond the stage of hints. One summer he spayed one of Florence's cats, as well as Balder.[13] Everything was grist for the mill of his scientific mind, and Florence was never far behind.

In that Victorian era, the only member of the opposite sex a girl knew well was her brother.[14] By the time Florence was fourteen, she was deeply in love with Hart, addressing her letters to "My Precious Brother Hartie." She wrote him about how lonely she was while he was away at medical school, and she dutifully told him how she spent her days at home. "In the morning I have been occupied with studying and reciting Geography, Arithmetic, and Spelling, and reading Hitchcock's Anatomy, also having my Music lesson, and as much of my hour's practice as I can get in. In the afternoons, I finish practice, go to see Grandma, write letters, and read Hiawatha. Is it not beautiful? Today I have finished it, and will take up Tennyson next, I guess. Next week I am to try studying *all* day . . . adding for afternoon study Latin and History, and if we find time for more, French." On the back of the letter was a question from Mother, who wanted to know "what you want done with the skeleton you left on the kitchen stove."

By then Hart had already published his first book, *The Birds of Connecticut* — the first book on the subject in thirty years.[15] In letters, Florence poured out her love and admiration, painfully wishing "I was more worthy of being your sister." When Hart sent some human bones to Clint, who was also heading for a medical career, Florence was ready to follow her brother and take part. "I wish I might have the opportunity of seeing some dissections. One can learn so much more about Anatomy that way than through books although it would seem rather out-of-place for a girl to be cutting up a corpse. I don't think but what if I had a very good chance I should improve it."

She soon had her wish, at least on a rabbit. She found Clint dissecting one, "so I had a real nice time, and when I went away he gave me the three ear bones." On the other hand, she was glad to hear from Hart that he now had little time for collecting animal and bird specimens. "You have gotten enough Arsenic in you now to last for a while." Soon he graduated to studying surgery, and she was so happy that she sent him a box of flowers in celebration, "lilies of the valley, as they are *so* sweet." And she sprinkled a few of them with the spring beauties on Gertie's grave.

When Hart completed his training in 1879, he returned home to practice medicine, using Homewood as his base for serving the rural area by then becoming known as Locust Grove. At the same time, he carried on extensive correspondence with naturalists and collectors, building up his museum of study material and developing friendships with some of his correspondents. One was a young farm boy in Elk River, Minnesota, named Vernon Bailey. Vernon's parents had hewed a farm out of the wilderness. When the fields were finally planted, it was his task to catch gophers so they wouldn't destroy the crops.[16] To do this he made tiny traps, modeled after the box traps he set for rabbits, thus beginning a lifelong fascination with humane ways to trap animals.[17] One day he would be able to distinguish 125 species of pocket gophers.

Vernon was eager for scientific information, and so he wrote to Hart, whose reputation had already reached Minnesota, asking if he would identify animals if some prepared specimens were sent to him. Hart not only agreed but also offered to buy specimens from Vernon of the different species found in Minnesota. The prices he offered seemed fabulous to the young farm boy — twenty-five cents apiece for mice and a dollar for woodchucks and skunks — and he envisioned the joint wealth of scientific knowledge and money. He soon had a box packed for shipment, which Hart received eagerly, with Florence peering over his shoulder as he unpacked it.

A lifelong friendship had begun. Hart supplied the names Vernon had requested and much more, including instructions on preparing specimens and skeletons for museum use.[18] Three years later Vernon would become one of Hart's first field agents.

Between writing letters and unpacking field specimens, Hart continued his medical practice. Florence was glad to have him close again, especially since the medical demands did not fill his time, so he could help her brush up on her anatomy studies and prepare her for school. Hart also spent many hours working on papers about his research and designing scientific and surgical instruments, some of which are still in use.[19] But Florence could usually persuade him to join scientific picnics to interesting places with their Aunt Helen. They studied not only the plants and birds and mammals — his growing interest — but developed a keen eye for trilobites, which they hunted in the shale ravine near the house. On one memorable outing they had a guest, the eminent trilobite specialist Dr. Charles Wolcott. But what made it most memorable for Florence was the goshawk that attacked Dr. Wolcott so violently that he had to kill the bird with his geological hammer.

Florence also loved to go on trips with her brother and father, from the time they had shared a two-month vacation and collecting trip to Florida when she was nine.[20] Travel was rugged in those days, and Caroline Merriam, never a rugged woman, stayed home. But now Florence was busy with her studies, and Hart went alone on collecting trips, usually to the southern states and sometimes as far as the Bahamas. He continued to bring home tales of the new country he had seen, as well as specimens, which only served to whet Florence's interest both in travel and in *live* birds.

Hart roused her enthusiasm for birds, but he was a careful teacher. Her questions in the field were usually answered with "the wise but somewhat undervalued advice" to look it up, and she would head off for the Homewood library to check Elliott Coues's key to the birds or another of the minimal resource books then available.[21]

Time together for brother and sister was limited, however. Florence's health had always been somewhat fragile, although in typical Victorian manner no definitive description was recorded. With his newly acquired medical knowledge, Hart insisted one year that she spend most of the winter in Syracuse, New York, undergoing medical treatment with a specialist there. She sent Hart a special letter for his birthday, apologizing that her gift had to be so small. "I was very anxious to have it just the opposite, but as you were so far off, and things break, by travelling, I was obliged to put up with this little offering."

She lived with her physician's family while recuperating, which gave her her first chance to attend public school, half-days, with his daughter. Florence was very anxious about doing well, especially when she realized that she was far behind others of her age. She fell prey briefly to the then-current theory that perhaps her female mind was not up to it, but Hart continued to encourage and reassure her.

While in Syracuse she also had a chance to help the doctor perform minor surgery, since he recognized her interest in medicine. The first occasion went well, and she wrote Hart a bubbling letter with all the details. A week later she had a different experience and fainted. She then felt it her duty to tell Hart what a "dreadful little dunce" she had made of herself, although the doctor assured her that she would "overcome the ridiculous practice." A medical career seemed further away.

In their younger years the Merriam children had been tutored at home. Florence later described her early education as coming mainly from the woods and fields where, like Thoreau, she found Shakespeare's "books in trees, sermons in stones, and good in everything."[22] Her discoveries were then "wisely interpreted by scientific members of my family but not interfered with by the hard and fast requirements of school life. Taught sporadically at home, my doctor brother opened my eyes to the marvelous in anatomy as well as the delights of ornithology; a visiting relative opened my mind to the rich stores to be found in music, and my father aroused my interest in literature."

In addition to her short stint at school in Syracuse, Florence attended school when the family wintered in New York City. Because of the difficulties of keeping the Homewood driveway passable in the snow — commonly two or three feet deep — Father usually took his family to live in the city for a few months. In school Florence discovered grammar, which she loved, especially, she wrote Hart, "as our lessons are all oral, it is great sport."

She continued to bombard Hart with medical and bird questions, and once asked him "for my happiness, always keep a little place in one of your auricles or ventricals, for the little sister who loves you more than a little." She still looked forward to being his medical assistant and wondered how many operations he expected to perform weekly.

Florence was later sent away to school at Mrs. Piatt's in Utica, New York. Following in her mother's footsteps, she was preparing for college, and the one recently begun for women by Sophia Smith in Northampton, Massachusetts, had been selected. Mrs. Piatt approved of the choice and agreed to help her, for she thought it was the best college for girls in the country. Unlike the Reverend Mr. Dix's opinion that a woman should be educated only to be all that a man needs, the aim of Smith College was "to perfect her intellect . . . so that she may be better qualified to enjoy and to do well her work in life, whatever that work may be."[23]

One evening just before she left home for college, the family took one of their favorite walks across the woods. On the way, Mother sang familiar old ballads and soft eventide hymns. Soon they reached a neighbor's clearing, the perfect setting for an experience that would be repeated many times in many places throughout Florence's life. "As we looked off over the valley and the sunset light slanted in, reddening the tree trunks, we would listen spellbound to the serene song of the hermit thrush, voicing the peace and beauty of evening."

Just before dark they walked back through the woods to Homewood, where Florence packed Ruth away in a trunk to be stored while she was at college. As she wrapped Ruth's red wool coat around her carefully, but absentmindedly, she thought ahead to the future, at the moment forgetting about the maple leaves that would soon be turning as red outside the bay window.

College-bound Special, 1882–1885

A SPECIAL STUDENT was not so special, Florence found soon after she arrived with her trunks in Northampton, Massachusetts, in the autumn of 1882. She was nineteen. Her older brother Collins had expressed such urgency about her further education, and Hart had so wholeheartedly supported him, that she had enrolled in Smith College in spite of her lack of sufficient formal education to qualify as a regular student. But, as her mentor Emerson had written in his essay on compensation, for everything you have missed, you have gained something else. As a Special, Florence could choose the upper-level subjects she was most interested in, rather than freshman classes, an option rare today that many might envy. Smith College was too young to have developed a science course yet, so she worked mainly in writing, English literature, geology (taught by an Amherst professor), ethics, comparative religions, and philosophy, with additional lectures on music and art.

Choosing subject matter is only one aspect of college life, as anyone who has been there can wryly attest. Florence soon found herself enmeshed in campus politics. She and a sympathetic friend balked at the attempts of a few to run the freshman class. She wrote Hart that when they walked into the first class meeting a few minutes late, they found "a self appointed committee of two, handing round blank papers for votes to elect the class officers. We had been here less than a week, and probably none of us knew more than half a dozen girls by name — and we were indignant — it was so utterly silly." After "fussing a long time," the two innocents succeeded in having a temporary chairman elected and thereby gained an opportunity to learn the qualifications of the girls they were voting for, Florence's first lesson in practical politics.

Like many freshmen before or since, they also quickly learned how un-special freshmen are but also what their futures as sophomores held. Although her mother had been extremely religious, Florence resisted

As she began studies at Smith College in 1882, Florence already wore the set chin that marked her determination to succeed at everything she did. (From the collection of Eithne Golden Sax.)

formal religion from an early age, as did her brother. Now, in addition to being treated as a freshman, she had to endure chapel as well. Florence complained to Hart, "Isn't it horrid—we have to wait until the other classes have left chapel, before we get up! My! Won't we laud it over the poor Freshs next year though!"

Her doctor brother came in handy in providing quinine for the girls to take to ward off the threat of malaria. Hart also cautioned her about studying too hard, but she replied indignantly that she didn't work five hours a day on chemistry, as he had heard. "I never spend more than four hours a day on it, including recitation — that is, very rarely . . . French usually takes 2-½ to 3 hours of study, and the rest of the time I spend on Macaulay, which can't come under the head of work . . . From 12–1 I try to walk, and from 5 to 6 we are exercising, changing our clothes, walking over and back, and at the gym. We get to bed, as a rule, about 10, or a little before, so you see we have plenty of sleep, plenty of exercise, and work enough to keep us from being lazy."

One can almost feel her mind opening up in her first year at Smith, as she expressed to her brother her criticisms of the literature of the day, questions on the effects of liquor and of opium on habitual users, tales of her botanical discoveries, the thrill of watching Halley's comet coming up over nearby Mount Tom, and comments on the silliness she observed in some girls — "Just as if boys were such wonderful things that they deserved being made a fuss over! Not but what you are well enough, my dear, in your places, but I don't think flirtation is very womanly, or manly either, and it makes me sick."

Florence watched the birds in Northampton as she had always done elsewhere, and she regularly told Hart of the species she had seen. The next fall was the first meeting of the American Ornithologists' Union (AOU), but the date conflicted with her college work. As one of the founders, Hart would be there, and she urged him to write and tell her all about it. Meanwhile, she spent as much time outdoors as possible, at his urging and because she too was convinced that it was the only way for her to keep well in every way.

While her own college life proceeded rather quietly, Florence had the vicarious pleasure of watching her brother's accomplishments. In addition to his medical practice and his work with the AOU, by working nights he had completed most of a book on the mammals of the Adirondacks. He spent some time traveling each year, once as physician on an expedition to Labrador and Greenland so he could study and collect seals. Another year he went to Germany to work and to visit the great natural history museums. Clearly Hart's first love was still nature and not the practice of medicine. Florence looked forward to the day when they might go to Europe together, but meanwhile she sent him off with a volume of Emerson's essays as "a spiritual tonic."

With Hart's activity in the new AOU, prominent ornithologists began to make their way to the welcoming doorway of Homewood. Many of them became lifelong friends. Henry Henshaw, noted ornithologist of the Wheeler Survey and later a coworker, wrote that the location of the Merriam house had inspired Hart's notable book on the mammals, and that the character of the surroundings was "also well calculated to stimulate and gratify a love of nature, and to afford unlimited opportunities to the naturalist." Florence was at home during Henshaw's visit, and he later recalled that, although her "footsteps were not yet fully set in the path which later was to bring her fame," she was familiar with the local bird species and always ready to act as guide to the haunt of any desired bird. Although Florence was interested in Hart's collections, it was obvious to Henshaw that she already preferred to study birds live in the field.[1]

One spring vacation Florence was home from Smith when her brother had a new visitor. Hart was planning to write a comprehensive book on the mammals of North America, and a young artist and naturalist came in hopes of supplying him with the drawings he would need.[2] Ernest Seton Thompson (later he changed his name to Ernest Thompson Seton) recorded in his journal that he had met Hart's "charming mother and his father" as well as "his beautiful sister Florence."[3] Photographs of the young Smith undergraduate bear out his description.

Florence listened eagerly as her brother and their visitor discussed the artwork Thompson proposed. "So far," Hart told the young artist, "I haven't found an artist who can make a correct drawing of an animal." When Thompson assured him he could, Hart replied, "Very well. Then prove it." To test his skill, Hart gave the young artist pen and ink and a shrew pickled in alcohol. From the impressive sketch that resulted in the next few hours, another career began. Thompson would succeed not only as a writer but also as an artist. Both Florence and Hart made extensive use of his artistic talents in illustrating their writings. In describing this episode, conservationist writer Paul Brooks commented that "seldom has a shrew cast so long a shadow."[4]

Thompson/Seton became well known for his own nature books later in the century, but they were to bring violent reactions — and support — because he humanized animals. Florence saw some merit in his approach, for it offered her a way out of the scientific method of shooting birds first and asking questions later. Instead, it encouraged her preference for studying them live, as friends.

Shrews were of particular interest to Florence's brother in his quest for information on the geographic distribution of mammals, because they were nocturnal and secretive and thought to be rare. He once asked his collector-correspondent Vernon Bailey for some specimens, to which Bailey replied, "How many do you want?" As one coworker described the ensuing interchange, "At that time specimens of shrews were derived mainly from something the cat brought in, something that fell in the well, or something found dead and decayed in the road, so Merriam then wrote Bailey, 'all you can get.' Some time later, Bailey sent him no fewer than 60 shrews and it is not unlikely that then and there [Merriam] envisioned the possibilities of a continental campaign of mammal collecting." The friendship between Hart and Vernon Bailey extended rather naturally to Florence, but in this early part of the 1880s she had other things on her mind. She continued her college studies, while her adoration of her brother grew, both for his accomplishments and for his dreams.

Florence felt so drawn into Hart's life that she was ready to give up her own to be part of his. At one point she wanted to leave college because she thought that he needed her help. "When we are working together, neither of us will have so much drudgery to do for we'll divide it between us, and we'll both have more time for genuine work. . . . Our firm will be Merriam and Sister, won't it—bright and early tomorrow morning; but it won't be long, and I only wish that I knew enough to begin sooner." He tried to dissuade her, and she retorted, "When I've made up my mind to a thing I'm not to be turned aside by a small child of your avoirdupois!" But she did turn aside, recognizing that at Smith she could best learn how to help him better.

As she discussed with Hart her own developing philosophy of life, she realized how closely it paralleled his. "You and I have that basis of sympathy, we think alike on the cardinal points, our religion is almost identical . . . and the principles that govern our lives, the most prominent part of that religion, are the same. . . . But it is so much easier to think than to live. . . . Life is our constant struggle to Be, as Emerson says."

Florence was keeping records for Hart on bird migration at the same time, and she was glad to be doing that to take her outside "into the heart of things, and I see and feel what I never would otherwise. Sometimes I think I love the woods the best of all, but it is hard to tell—it is a part of the whole." About this time she began to voice what was to become a cardinal principle of her life. "It doesn't make any difference what a person believes—however superstitious they may be— if they live as they should." Two years later she refined that principle: "The longer I live the more it seems to me that all men think alike. Fundamentally we all believe the same things, though we call them by different names. . . . Infinite goodness is the underlying thought in every case."

By the next spring, 1885, the world of Florence Augusta Merriam had changed. Hart was no longer "a small child of your avoirdupois." At twenty-six he had given up the practice of medicine and life at Homewood in favor of moving to Washington, D.C., to head a newly created division of the U.S. Department of Agriculture, later separated as the U.S. Biological Survey. Florence suddenly found that she didn't need to prepare to give her life to help in his work, as she had been so ready and willing to do. Having been brought up among naturalists, it had always seemed merely a question of which form of nature study to follow. But that decision was now suddenly up in the air.

Summers between college terms were usually spent at the ocean, for the health-giving qualities of the sea air that she and her mother both benefited from and needed. At 'Sconset on Nantucket Island, she picked flowers and identified them after dinner. The driver of the one-horse wagon amused them with whaling stories as they passed "all the curiosities of the fishermen's cottages." They also stopped to see the local bird collection and to watch some "funny little birds here that look like sandpipers that the people call pickies." Florence was already focusing on birds as her life's work, although she didn't yet realize it.

Knowing that Hart had a growing interest in the American Indians as well, Florence told him about the new book, *Ramona*, by Helen Hunt Jackson. The author was inspired by Harriet Beecher Stowe's work for the blacks and wanted to do the same for the Indians. Her descriptions of western scenery served as a vision for Florence, who found the "golden mustard as high as the horse's head" so appealing when she later met it firsthand in Utah and California.

As school opened in September of 1885, her last year in college, Florence was becoming more engrossed in birds. Her letters to Hart reflected her growing curiosity about them. She quoted him Shakespeare's *King Lear* and wanted to know about cuckoos laying their eggs in the nests of hedge-sparrows — "and what is the latter?" — and why kingfishers kept their bills turned toward the wind: "Renege, affirm, and turn their halcyon beaks / With every gale and vary of their masters." Halcyon was the Greek word for a bird associated with the kingfisher, one thought to calm the ocean waves. Florence's fascination with the kingfisher would keep her trying to calm the murderous waves destroying many species of birds, so the legend of the halcyon lived on.

She asked Hart for a copy of the new nomenclature list published by the AOU, and she expressed concern about a moth that flew out of one of the drawers in his museum at Homewood when she was looking for a specimen of a warbler that she had seen. She delighted in hearing the bluejays from her cottage windows at Smith. "They are so happy in Paradise," as the end of the campus by the lake was called.

Her interest peaked when she was assigned to write an article for the college Science Association, but her self-conscious attitude about her Special status still haunted her. She wrote to Hart, "After casting about in my mind for the one thing in my incapacitating ignorance that was less staggering than the others, and for which I had a present interest, I thought of — now don't laugh, just wait till I explain — birds. Of course I know as well as you do how absolute my real ignorance of the subject is, but you see the girls here know less about it than I do, and I thought that by reading up I might write an article that would serve to interest or at least call their attention to the common birds we have here, and at the same time give them a few points on general habits, etc. that they have failed to notice."

The meeting was only ten days away, which shows how much more one could trust the mails then than now, for she asked Hart to send her some articles to read and some data on the destruction of birds for millinery purposes. Seldom has a bird cast so long a shadow.

When she presented her article, she concluded with a "preach on the subject of birds for millinery purposes," and two local newspapers reprinted the main part of it. Most writers, budding or established, have rationalized as she did, "I thought as long as I had it on hand the least I could do was to use it." One editor "took the unwarranted liberty of printing my private letter to him," a hard lesson to learn but one best learned early if you devote yourself to writing: Never write anything you don't want to see in print.

By December the die was being cast. Florence met Fannie Hardy, the daughter of bird collector Manly Hardy, who for the past eight years had been "keeping his book, making up his skins" — a kindred soul. They were already planning ahead to observe birds together in the spring, and Florence knew that she had to build her strength by then because "Miss Hardy can walk as far as she wants to — doesn't know what it is to get tired." Florence did.

Florence's parents were spending the winter in New York and she looked forward to a family reunion there, but the AOU meeting didn't bring Hart there as she had hoped. She sent him another book of Emerson and urged him to make Miss Hardy an associate member of the AOU. Instead, he nominated his sister, and Florence became the first woman associate of the AOU. During the holidays she saw New York City through a haze of snow, as her contemporary, novelist Edith Wharton, described it: "It seemed to snow more often in those New York winters, and the snow seemed to lie in cleaner heaps on the sidewalks than in later years. One of the regular diversions was to walk along Fifth Avenue or Broadway, well muffled, while snow swept down silently onto the roofs of the horsecars and the steps of the basement entryways." Like the snow, New York life was quiet and leisurely, made up of "little

dinner parties of ritualistic solemnity."⁵ As she walked and dined in
the snowy city, Florence thought about the coming springtime and bird
observations with Miss Hardy.

On Christmas Day Florence wrote to Hart that she was planning
a biological-philosophical thesis on evolution and asked to borrow his
copy of Darwin, whose famous paper on evolution had first been presented in London a mere twenty-seven years earlier, in fact the summer before Hart was born, during that "golden age of the amateur naturalist in England." Early reaction to Darwin had included vituperative
comments in the press on evolution. "Things must keep their proper
places if they are to work together for any good. If our glorious maidens and matrons may not soil their fingers with the dirty knife of the
anatomist, neither may they poison the springs of joyous thought and
modest feeling, by listening to the seductions of this author."⁶ But the
theories of evolution had already changed the world, and Florence and
her brother were in at the beginning of a new golden age of amateur
naturalists in America.

Back at school in late January, Florence was horrified to find that
Fannie Hardy wore feathers on her hats. She gave her new friend some
articles to read so that she would think the matter over more seriously.
But her horror was tempered with the good news from her favorite college teacher, Miss Jordan, that her article and "preach" on birds had
encouraged more students to enroll in science that term. Miss Jordan
taught rhetoric and Anglo-Saxon and had read reams of Florence's manuscripts as she gained experience and self-confidence in her writing. Even
more valuable, Miss Jordan encouraged her to believe that she could
succeed with it.

Florence recognized Emerson's lesson in compensation again, for the
loss of a college degree had gained her the opportunity to concentrate
on science and writing. She moved into the last spring term listening
to the bluebirds in plain view of her window and wondering how best
to help them. The answer lay close at hand.

Bonnets and Burroughs, 1886–1887

At supper the conversation turned to clothes, as it often does among college girls, now as well as in 1886. Florence winced inwardly as a classmate exclaimed, "I saw the most beautiful hat in the city last weekend. It had thirteen blue birds on it, each with a white collar and a curious topnotch. Thirteen — I counted them!" Kingfishers, Florence thought to herself in horror. She tried to smile and to stay calm at the same time, for in her mind's eye she was picturing a live bird sitting on a dry limb over a waterfall, watching the water below and ready to dive through the air instantly for any fish that came near the surface.

Florence turned back to the supper table more determined than ever to do something about this craze for birds on women's hats that her classmates found so attractive. But she knew that this wasn't the place to speak out in favor of birds instead of fashion. She would bide her time. If only the girls could observe *live* birds as she had, she mused, they would no longer wear dead ones on their heads. But how?

She recalled "Each and All," the poem she had just memorized for the Emerson Club —

> I thought the sparrow's note from heaven,
> Singing at dawn on the alder bough;
> I brought him home, in his nest, at even;
> He sings his song, but it cheers not now,
> For I did not bring home the river and sky; —
> He sang to my ear,— they sang to my eye.

This reminded her of John Burroughs, whose well-thumbed book of nature essays, *Wake-Robin*, was one of her favorites. In the preface he had written, "I have reaped my harvest more in the woods than in the study; . . . what has interested me most in Ornithology is the pursuit, the chase, the discovery; . . . I have done what I could to bring home the 'river and sky' with the sparrow I heard 'singing at dawn on the alder bough.' In other words, I have tried to present a live bird,— a bird in the woods or the fields,— with the atmosphere and associations of the place, and not merely a stuffed and labeled specimen."[1]

Florence often thought of Mr. Burroughs, a friend of her dear brother Hart, as an ideal observer who was content to sit and watch birds for hours to know their habits and behavior.[2] He had discovered the fascination of birds the year before Florence was born, in 1862 when he happened upon a copy of Audubon in a library and "went into the woods with new interest, new enthusiasm." He began to write nature essays, but not for the purpose of teaching children, for to do that he believed in going into nature rather than to books. Florence would follow in his footsteps in that regard. Burroughs was also a student of Emerson, who appealed to his "spiritual side," another link between the young woman and the sage.[3]

Florence also admired Burroughs's comment that "the writing of the book was only a second and finer enjoyment of my holiday in the fields or woods. Not til the writing did it really seem to strike in and become part of me."[4] Writing — and birds — were also striking in and becoming part of her life.

In 1885 Florence was already the first woman associate member of the AOU. Among other purposes, it had been organized to protect birds from extinction, especially by the demands for feathers such as those her classmates admired. Hart had told her about the first AOU meeting two years before, when his friend William Brewster raised the alarm about the killing of birds for millinery ornaments and urged them to form a Committee on the Protection of North American Birds.[5]

Although Florence saw only the small local picture at the college supper table, on the larger scene the destruction of birds had reached crisis proportions. Concerned scientists reported that five million birds a year were being sacrificed for ladies' hats. In attempting to bring back the romance of antebellum years, dresses had become more voluminous and soon hats grew to match. Milliners used feathers to make hats larger and more elegant without undue weight, and the call went out worldwide. Hunters, and then exploiters, responded; the harder the bird was to obtain, the higher the price. Some were literally worth their weight in gold.[6]

At the same time, the whole country was experiencing an awakening of interest in nature, and Smith College girls were no exception. They read Henry David Thoreau, gone only twenty years and already a folk hero. Emerson, highly revered in his own time, had just died. Certainly his words, which so strongly influenced writers like Thoreau and Burroughs, did not fall on deaf ears. Florence read him eagerly

Florence, shown in 1886, the year she finished college, having already begun her life's work of studying birds. (From the Archives, Smith College. Portrait by Notman Photographic Co.)

and later identified him as the person who meant the most to her developing philosophy. The power of nature was strong in both her upbringing and in her own intellect, and she intuitively knew that live birds were the most inspiring study she could undertake and share.

Now at college Florence found herself among three hundred girls, only a handful of whom had ever heard of protecting birds or knew anything at all about them except as hat ornaments. Walking back to her cottage along the flower-lined path after dinner, Florence listened to the sparrows chipping in the elms, but she kept her ear tuned for the kingfisher down by Paradise Lake, flying with his noisy rattling call as he sought out good fishing spots.[7]

Soon after this incident Florence learned of a new effort to protect the birds, being launched by another friend of her brother, fellow AOU member Dr. George Bird Grinnell. He was the editor of the best out-door journal of that decade, *Forest and Stream* (later *Field and Stream*), whose readers had recognized the decline in game their hobby depended on. Both the passenger pigeon and the bison were nearly extinct. The myth of nature's superabundance had ended, and sportsmen became among the most vociferous and active in the fight to conserve species.[8] One of his readers was Theodore Roosevelt, who was already incor-porating Grinnell's views into his own philosophy. Grinnell, who was both a sportsman and an ornithologist, used *Forest and Stream* to start the Audubon Society for the Protection of Birds.[9] He named it for the famous bird man and for his wife, who had tutored Grinnell as a young man, and aimed it not at scientists but at educating the general public in her memory.[10]

When Florence heard about Grinnell's new society, she quickly real-ized that this could be the key to reaching her Smith College class-mates. By now Fannie Hardy had stopped wearing feathers, to Flor-ence's great relief, so she told her friend about the new organization. The two girls "laid deep, wily schemes" to create a similar bird group at Smith. They did not want it to be an organization of "dry bones tied with red tape," but one that would remain active and last be-yond the time when birds were temporarily protected by a change of fashion. Spring hats would soon be appearing, so they knew they had to act quickly.[11]

The enthusiasm of the two schemers was contagious, and they capi-talized on it. They cut articles on bird destruction from newspapers, choosing the most graphic ones they could find. Although written later, T. Gilbert Pearson's recollections of his Florida boyhood tell of events that predated 1886 and exemplify why the girls felt the urgency to act: "A few miles north of Waldo, in the flat pine region, our party came one day upon a little swamp where we had been told herons breed in numbers. Upon approaching the place the screams of young birds reached our ears. The cause of this soon became apparent by the buzz-ing of green-flies and the heaps of dead herons festering in the sun, with the back of each bird raw and bleeding. . . . Young herons had been left by scores in the nests to perish from exposure and starvation."[12]

The girls distributed their articles with telling effect among their friends, who were urged to pass them along to other friends. They raised the question in Science Association meetings and discussed it in the biological laboratory. Each new mention engendered new enthusiasm for the cause, and their list of friends increased, including faculty members. Little groups of students met to read each other the startling statistics. That year only a dozen breeding herons were left near the outlying Florida keys, where sailors had reported thousands only six years before. By 1890 there would be *no* heron rookeries left on the bayous or outer keys.[13]

The two organizers recognized that the time for action had arrived. They arranged a mass meeting and posted notices inviting all the college. Their hopes were more than realized when seventy girls and five faculty showed up to hear papers by the best speakers they could find, who all emphasized bird *life*. Florence had learned a lot about politics since the time she stumbled late into her first freshman class meeting. The technique for engineering an election that had seemed so wicked to her then she now used successfully to help the vanishing birds. Today we call it railroading, and it often still works. "We even went so far as to select the chairman, and those who should move her appointment. The result was that everything went off without a hitch or a pause."[14]

Afterward, so many girls took their hats to town to be retrimmed that a milliner inquired anxiously if the college had banned the use of birds. The wily schemers smiled knowingly at this tangible evidence of their classmates' conversion.

Dr. Grinnell assured the new group that they could be perfectly independent, so they rejected names like "The Pterodactyl" in favor of becoming a branch of his organization. The Smith College Audubon Society (SCAS) was formally constituted on March 17, "scarcely three weeks from the beginning of our work, and, as we prided ourselves, some time before the establishment of the Wellesley Society."[15] It was also barely a month after Grinnell had formally established his society.

Florence knew that this was just the beginning and that the girls needed to get outdoors themselves — for something besides tennis. She wanted to "take them into the fields and let them see how the birds look, what they have to say, how they spend their time, what sort of houses they build, and what are their family secrets."[16] Led at first by her own enthusiasm, she later realized that field work was what had made their new society a success.

It was then April, and the birds were filling the fields — chipping sparrows, pewees, waxwings, kingfishers, and the earlier birds, with an occasional junco and chickadee left behind. The ground was blooming with hepaticas, bloodroot, adder-tongue, and arbutus. She thought again of John Burroughs and the purpose for which he had written *Wake-Robin* — to awaken others to study the living bird. This was already the basis of her own interest, as his words sang in her head, "I have reaped my harvest more in the woods than in the study."

Although other schoolwork was jealously claiming her attention with the approaching end of the spring term, Florence took time to write to Mr. Burroughs, inviting him to come for a visit after the spring break. She explained that since his visit and their field work would be outside of the regular curriculum, one walk could be scheduled for early in the morning, so they would be back in time for breakfast at half-past seven. After recitations and study, they could go again in the midafternoon, for as many days as he could stay. She promised to see that he had a pleasant room in one of the cottages, with a view of the woods and hills and a glimpse of Paradise Lake at the western end of the campus.

As Easter approached, Florence's thoughts turned more often to her own personal philosophy. She wrote to Hart, ostensibly to analyze a lecture he had given, but more deeply to philosophically compare science and religion. "Ultimately we recognize the same principles that govern the orthodox man . . . we do not bow before the man Christ, but the best part of our nature responds to the grand thought for which he stands — self-sacrifice and devotion to the good of the world."

She went on to tell him about an interpretation of Easter that she had just heard as "the resurrection of all that we had ever known of noble aspiration, of noble living, of our highest, truest selves. Thinking of it afterwards in connection with the meadow lark's song, it seemed as if nature at this Easter-tide would, perhaps more than ever, help us to do that."

Somehow she made it through crams and exams, checking the letterbox in the main building every day for some word from Mr. Burroughs. Then one day his reply was there, and she eagerly tore open the envelope. He agreed to come in the first week of May! The word spread quickly, his name acting like magic, and fifty girls excitedly discussed plans for their outings with the famous nature writer. Meanwhile, their enthusiasm grew measurably for the small walks Florence and Fannie led.

Suddenly it was May. The first morning of his visit, about forty girls started out at half-past five, and the same afternoon thirty climbed nearby Mount Tom with him. "It was early in the spring for birds, and our numbers were enough to have frightened back to the South the few that had ventured North; but the strong influence of Mr. Burroughs's personality and quiet enthusiasm gave just the inspiration that was needed. We all caught the contagion of the woods."[17] Not only did the girls find eyes and ears outdoors with Burroughs, but Florence found, she wrote to Hart, that "a new world opened to them with a gain in spirituality, which realized my highest hopes for the influence of the work."

"With gossamers and raised umbrellas we would gather about him under the trees, while he stood leaning against a stump, utterly indifferent to the rain, absorbed in incidents from the life of some goldfinch or sparrow, interpreting the chippering of the swift as it darted about overhead, or answering the questions put to him, with the simplicity and kindliness of a beneficent sage."[18]

Burroughs also recorded the event in his journal, delighting in the great enthusiasm among the college girls. When he returned home, Burroughs wrote to a friend, dangling the experience before his active imagination. "My walks and talks with the Smith College girls would set every old bachelor like you fairly wild. Twice a day I walked with fifty of them, and every night I was surrounded by them; never was a wolf so overwhelmed by the lambs before. One of the lambs gave up her room to me, and I am not certain but a lamb blacked my shoes in the morning. It was all very pretty and charming, and I have half promised to go again."[19]

He kept the promise, for this outing marked the first of many years' mutual enjoyment of bird walks with college girls. Burroughs later recalled that first one again, when a great pool of girls had gathered on his cottage doorstep. "When I heard them whispering and moving around, out I came, and we began our ramble. They were so anxious to hear everything I said, that they crowded close after me. In fact, they were stepping on my heels all along the way. But that didn't matter. I had stout shoes on."[20] And a lamb to black them in the morning.

Supper conversations at the college changed considerably after Burroughs's visit. Instead of talking about kingfishers on hats, the girls began to report on the live birds they had observed in the orchard or in the backyard on the way to the lake. Spring field work went into high gear. Each participant had a pocket notebook in which to note bird characteristics. Florence obtained blank migration schedules for them from her brother at the new Ornithological Division of the U.S. Department of Agriculture. As soon as Grinnell published Audubon Society materials, she and her classmates also distributed those to all the college houses.

Florence was by then leading several groups a week into the fields, and she and Fannie both had to work hard to keep ahead of their eager students. She peppered Hart with questions: "Does a redstart ever put pitch on the outside of her nest? What relation does the song of a hermit thrush bear to that of the Wilson? How late would hermits probably stay here? Is the red tail of the hermit unique? Would a young thrasher sing so like the adult as to be identified by his song? How many birds hang their nests? How many birds walk? Do birds often desert their nests after they have begun building? What birds lay in others' nests? What is the average period of incubation? Do birds begin setting before their eggs are all laid? Do chipmunks eat eggs as much as red squirrels? What key or book is best for western or middle state girls? Is there any ornithology primer, or book for the use of beginners?"

Within three months almost a hundred girls — a third of the campus — had become members of the SCAS, and half had been out into the field with leaders whom Florence and her committee had trained. After all, she wrote later, "A list of species is good to have, but without a knowledge of the birds themselves, it is like Emerson's sparrow brought home without the river and sky."

During the summer her favorite teacher, Miss Jordan, had another special visitor.[21] Her cousin, naturalist David Starr Jordan, was actively studying the effects of Darwin's theory of evolution, and Miss Jordan would later encourage Florence to study with him in California.

The Class of '86 was graduated in June, but SCAS had firmly begun. "The summer vacation, bringing with it the attempt to force the fashion of feather millinery back again, called for the best efforts of our workers, and 10,000 circulars were sent out by a few of the most zealous, while letters and newspaper protests were used to spread the opposition." The circulars included material like poet Celia Thaxter's article on woman's heartlessness. In it she decried the lack of interest in the minds of "bird-wearing women" who went around like one with "a charnel house of beaks and claws and bones and feathers and glass eyes upon her fatuous head." Thaxter endowed the blessings of heaven on those who dared to turn their backs on Fashion — "how refreshing is the sight of the birdless bonnet!"[22]

Another Audubon circular included letters on the subject of bird protection from such eminent people as poet John Greenleaf Whittier, minister Henry Ward Beecher, and John Burroughs, who wrote, "It is a barbarous taste which prompts our women and girls to appear upon the street with their head gear adorned with the scalps of our songsters."[23]

The Smith College Class of '86 stayed in touch for many years through class letters. Each year the bits and pieces told what each member thought was momentous in her life. Florence usually contributed, even though she had been a Special student who received a certificate but was not officially graduated that June.

In November she wrote in their first class letter, "I have been doing Audubon work combined with that most abhorred and *abhorrable* occupation of plain sewing, with house-keeping and book-keeping, and am taking a course in business with my father." A foot of snow was already on the ground at Homewood, and it was storming hard. Clinton Merriam was having eye trouble, and Florence was feeling more family responsibility. When she was not busy with housekeeping or business — or Audubon work — they played chess and whist. This also helped her mother, who was sleeping poorly. Florence's own state of health was also becoming more precarious, and an uncharacteristic depression seeped into her letters to Hart. Working on family affairs she found "discouraging, because business requires so much actual experience, and neither you nor I have had a great deal of that kind."

She wanted to attend the AOU meeting, but her old feelings of inadequacy held sway: "I suppose the papers would be so technical that I couldn't profit by them much." Although she wished she could have done more, few at that meeting could report doing as much as Florence had for the cause of bird protection. In addition to the 10,000 circulars she had helped to distribute, she had "sent articles to about 15 newspapers, organized 6 Local Secretaryships, 3 of which are doing active work, distributed papers in all the neighboring towns, stirred the College girls up to renew the battle, and written letters to everyone I ever heard of. My list of Audubon members is now 72."

Florence continued her bird work into the winter, when her hometown newspaper, the *Boonville Herald*, published "Why Not Have a Christmas Tree?" In it she urged adults to think of the joy a Christmas tree gives to children and how inexpensive it is to provide. "The father or older brother can get the tree, or if that is too much work, a couple of evergreen branches left from the Sunday school tree, tied back to back, and stuck into a flower pot, will give just as much pleasure in fact." By suggesting the alternative of using branches, she was working to protect the trees that housed the birds, showing her growing awareness of habitat as an important part of her bird study. Although she was never to have children of her own, Florence always encouraged young people and thought of herself as "The Children's Friend," as she signed that article.

In early December Collins's home burned to the ground, and he and his family came to stay at Homewood during the rebuilding. By New Year's 1887 the weather was at its worst. When the thermometer hit −26 degrees, she wrote to Hart that "we are gradually congealing." So

Florissante, Collins Merriam's sixteen-room family home in Lyons Falls, New York, shown here as rebuilt after it burned in 1886. (From the collection of Mr. and Mrs. Sheldon Gustavus Merriam.)

the family again moved into New York City to spend the rest of the winter. The presence of other family members to help care for her parents freed Florence to think of studying literature. Later she planned to travel to Europe with her parents, but neither plan materialized. Instead, she wrote her Smith College class, she worked at "a spiritual life-saving station for the Brooklyn starvation-wage working girls."

When spring arrived, she returned to Homewood and the birds. With a good deal more humor than she was capable of when it was −26 degrees, Florence wrote in her next Smith College class letter how she "spent three or four months sitting on a stump in the woods staring through my opera glass at the 'bipeds with feathers' that we heard about in our logical days. The wisdom accumulated, by the help of mosquitoes and punkies, in that process was too great to withhold from the world, and so it is appearing in homeopathic quantities (the poor world couldn't bear much of such highly concentrated knowledge at once) in that far-famed journal, *The Audubon Magazine,*—'Hints to Audubon Workers: Fifty Common Birds and How to Know Them.' If you want to know what a wonderful classmate you have, just send for the series! It will be finished sometime next year, if the compositor and I don't get to throwing dynamite bombs at each other before that."

Grinnell had his hands full trying to keep in contact with the fast-growing Audubon membership, then numbering 20,000, so he had just started the *Audubon Magazine.* Florence immediately started to write the series she mentioned to her classmates. Even before it was published, she obtained Hart's help to copyright it and of course to review her manuscript. They argued good-humoredly over details such as whether a black-and-white creeper is "much nearer the color of the gray moss and bark, than the brown one." Although Hart always insisted on scientific accuracy, Florence held out for including as many common names as possible since one of her helpers at Smith had said, "It is perplexing when one is studying alone to have your book give one name, your father another, and your farmer a third."

The first segment appeared in the June issue, a year after Florence finished college and just before she spotted a kingfisher's nest on Leyden Hill near Homewood. She wrote the series from her heart, a style she later tempered with more scientific knowledge; but the simplicity of her prose won eager admirers among the women and young people whom she addressed. Even her handwriting showed her different approach to life. When she first entered Smith, Florence's girlish penmanship had taken on a look of rushing to keep up with the world. But by the time she left college, she had settled into a more relaxed handwriting that she would use the rest of her life.

Throughout the series for the *Audubon Magazine,* she relied heavily on Burroughs's descriptions of bird habits and behavior. She quoted Emerson and Thoreau, as well as contemporary ornithologists, showing the broad study she had already done among her favorite authors and mentors. Florence's description of the hermit thrush is a good example of the approach she used throughout her lifetime of writing. Because this bird's song is based on musical thirds, the basis of our modern music system, it is especially pleasing to the human ear and is a favorite among many nature writers. Florence wrote, "This is probably the most beautiful song of our woods. Mr. Burroughs says to him it is the finest sound in nature. In the Adirondack region the retiring hermit is appropriately known as the 'swamp angel.' Comparing his song with that of the wood thrush, Mr. Burroughs says 'the song of the hermit is in a higher key, and is more mild and ethereal. His instrument is a silver horn which he winds in the most solitary places. . . . It is very simple, and I can hardly tell the secret of its charm. 'O, spheral, spheral!' he seems to say; 'O holy, holy!' . . . [It] seems to be the voice of that calm sweet solemnity one attains to in his best moments. It realizes a peace and a deep solemn joy that only the finest souls may know.'"24

The series of articles went on for almost a year, finishing with a summary of bird characteristics, best studied in spring when birds give the best excuse for getting out. "Spring! — let the poets sing of it, and listen to them if you will, but you can never know what they mean or what spring is until you have felt the first tremulous warble of the bluebird, and picked wild flowers in the hermitage of the 'swamp angel.'"25 Florence predicted to Hart the possibility of revising the series and publishing it as a much-needed pocket guide to field work, but for the moment, "it is a perfect spring day, too lovely to stay in the house."

Meanwhile, in the *Audubon Magazine* Florence also described the founding of the Smith College Audubon Society and stressed the importance of field work to encourage interest in live birds. The editor called attention to her article, urging his readers to go and do likewise. "To all such who have opportunities for field work the example of the Smith College Society may be followed with profit."26

Although she wrote in her annual Smith College letter about her articles and social work and bird activities, to her these seemed insignificant compared with the accomplishments of her classmates. At twenty-four, Florence found herself akin to writer and socialite Edith Wharton, who thought of herself as "dangerously close to the age beyond which the young women of her set became steadily less marriageable."27 The standards of the day for young women dictated home and marriage and children, of which many of Florence's classmates were already writing.

They had all come a long way from the supper table discussions of hats adorned with kingfishers. Florence had told them of spending the summer watching the bipeds with feathers, but now she apologized. "Girls, this seems a very flippant letter, but I have done so little this year, and you have done so much, that I have to take refuge in nonsense. One thing I have learned, the *need* there is for *doing*, and I am glad in my heart when I think that I am one of '86, that sisterhood of earnest *doers*."

She needn't have worried; she was always certainly one of the most earnest of the doers.

Easing the Burden, 1886–1893

W HAT'S A YOUNG LADY TO DO when she finishes college and no young man is courting her? Florence did what was expected in 1886: She resigned herself to her unmarried fate, she helped her parents, and she did social work. When she was well enough, she continued her bird work and writing. Before she left Smith, with Miss Jordan's encouragement she had determined to make writing her life's work. But she had said nothing about her decision to Hart, nor to anyone else, until she had proved that she could do it. By the next winter her philosophy had matured and she was ready to write Hart. "'To ease the burden of the world,' and help others to the truer higher living . . . this is my aim and to leave the world better for my having lived, and I feel that I can fulfill it better through my pen than in any other way."

She envisioned writing at home, so she could also fulfill her family obligations to her parents. First she thought of writing fiction, and then of creating "articles of the Burroughs' stamp, on the theory that the world is made better for having its attention called to the best things, which I most firmly believe."

At the same time, her mother's devotion to philanthropic work gave her a different role model. Faced with a choice between a life in social service or in studying nature, with the wisdom of a Solomon Florence determined to combine the two. "For what better form of philanthropic work could anyone choose, with my background, instincts and training, than to write of nature with birds as my text, to open closed eyes to the uplifting, ennobling influences of nature?" But for the moment, she had to guard her health, so she put aside thoughts of field work and settled into following her mother's example.

While her mother helped to establish circulating libraries in neighboring New England villages during the summers, Florence did her share at Grace Dodge's Working Girls' Clubs during their winters in New York City.[1] Inspired by Jane Addams, who had started Hull House in Chicago to provide self-help for the needy, Miss Dodge had begun a similar program in New York. The idea struck a chord with the earnest doer from Smith.

But every time she saw a woman on the street with feathers on her hat—and there were many who continued that fashion—Florence resolved anew to discourage the killing of birds by putting her energy into educating people about live birds. *Auk*, the journal of the AOU, reported atrocities like the 400,000 hummingbird skins sold in *one week* in London, which kindled her resolve all the more.[2] Since her family was spending more time in the city, she saw more feathered hats wherever she went. Although she could take out some of her frustration in doing social work at Miss Dodge's, she had an overpowering need to do more.

She continued to study live birds and to keep extensive field notes about them, especially when she was in Locust Grove. She even pinned feathers into her journals for reference. She tried to arrive home in the spring in time for the best birding of the year, as she had advised fellow bird workers in the *Audubon Magazine*. Out of the city and back in the Adirondacks, she could again feel "the first tremulous warble of the bluebird" and visit the hermitage of the "swamp angel"—the hermit thrush whose song inspired her, as it did her idol John Burroughs, as the finest in nature.

The spring of 1887 was suddenly different in one major respect for Florence. Hart had married the previous fall and was now firmly established in Washington, both in house and office. Although Florence saw him on visits to one home or the other, it wasn't the same. The woods developed new importance to her as her own sphere for studying live birds. Hart continued to tell her of the threats to birds, not only by new demands from milliners, but increasingly by farmers who shot birds they thought were damaging their crops. One of the major reasons why the federal government had established the Biological Survey that he headed was to educate farmers about beneficial birds. Since education was a personal priority for Florence and since she adored Hart, she still wanted to help him. After all, she reasoned, Congress had not seen fit to give her brother an adequate budget, and he needed her help.

In addition to helping the farmers, Hart continued his larger vision of a systematic nationwide collection of bird and mammal specimens. He called on outside help—today we call them consultants—since he couldn't finance a large enough staff. One of his most active collectors, his correspondent Vernon Bailey, was sending in previously unknown species of mammals with every shipment. Hart was so impressed that

By 1890, when this photograph was taken, Hart Merriam headed the U.S. Biological Survey in Washington. (From the collection of Florence Merriam Youngberg.)

as one of his first official acts he offered Vernon a job as a special field agent. The pay, forty dollars a month, gave Vernon a chance to do what he loved best. He accepted the offer and spent the next forty-six years working for the survey.[3]

While Hart and his collectors were enthusiastically active in field work to help the farmers, Florence struggled to maintain her health. Her mother was not well either, and Florence may have contracted tuberculosis from her. Their illness was never defined as such, and Florence had such a horror of the disease that she avoided any mention of it at all. Hart was concerned about both of them, and he began to plan a family journey. They would consider it an exploration, but he knew the curative benefits of "western air." Father was not well himself, but he agreed to take them. Clinton Merriam already knew the beauties of California from his visit there and from the occasional long letters he received from his brother Gustavus, who had homesteaded there.

When the Civil War had ended, Major Gustavus French Merriam had moved west with his new bride, Nina, and their young son, Edwin. His wife's health was poor, and they went first to Kansas, where they thought the climate would help her. Three more children were born: Helen, Harry, and then Anna Theresa. Florence remembered when Anna was born, while Hart was on his first trip west; she had written him about their new little cousin in Kansas. Mrs. Merriam's health did not improve there, so Gustavus had gone on to California to establish a homestead in the dry, rolling hills of northern San Diego County. He named the area Twin Oaks for the ancient live oak there with two separate trunks. Today it measures 125 feet across at the crown.

The next summer the rest of the family prepared to join him, packing all their worldly belongings, including the family Bible that dated back to 1769, when Gustavus's grandfather was born. Just before they left Topeka, sad news came from the east, where little Anna had been sent until her mother's health improved. Major Merriam opened that Bible to the family records in the center, turning to the page headed Deaths. There he added little Anna Theresa's name and the notation, "We loved this sweet flower but it faded." His brother Clinton wrote him a letter of sympathy, remembering the death of his own "dear Gertie," Florence's sister.

The early years at Twin Oaks were lean ones for Gustavus and his family, and Clinton Merriam sometimes helped out by sending a little money to tide them over. There was no year-round water supply in the Twin Oaks valley, and dry farming is always difficult. Drought years took cattle and the few crops the major attempted, and beehives

Gustavus Merriam, Clinton's brother, homesteaded in northern San Diego County, California, naming the area Twin Oaks after this ancient tree, which still stands. (From the collection of Mr. and Mrs. Sheldon Gustavus Merriam.)

sometimes provided the only cash crop. Wild flowers were plentiful, and dry as it was, "very little of it is desert in the eyes of a bee," one early reporter extolled.[4] They lined oak barrels with beeswax and filled them with honey. Some of it they shipped north to the gold-mining camps but most of it went to Australia, easier to reach in those days than the East Coast, which required sailing around the Horn.

Major Merriam began a school for his and the neighbors' children, and seventeen were enrolled by the spring of 1891. Gertrude Smith was the teacher that term. We might consider her experience a bit limited today: "a few weeks as substitute in New York Public School," but the bureaucracy was clearly already at work, for the bottom of her school form was rubber-stamped: "Teachers will take notice that salaries will not be paid until this report is completed and filed in my office."[5] Florence was grateful not to be teaching, for she always preferred birds to bureaucrats.

Although Major Merriam was justly proud of the development of his homestead, the climate was not enough to restore Nina's health. She never quite adjusted to the rough life after her southern plantation upbringing, and in 1888 she died. Alone with his young children, the major wrote to his brother, and Clinton decided to go to California, taking his wife and their daughter Florence in hopes that the good air might improve their health.

In order to experience Mardi Gras in New Orleans on the way, they left Homewood in February with sleigh bells jangling and snowdrifts above the horses' heads. "But in driving to our hotel in Pasadena, to our bewilderment we looked out on green grass and blooming fruit trees and our ears were filled with the rapturous song of the western meadowlark. Such was my introduction to California."[6]

Florence and her parents arrived at Twin Oaks in March, 1889, just as "all San Diego is afire for gold, the whole male population going off" to Ensenada, Mexico, a hundred miles south.[7] In southern California Florence found her own jewels, as the hills were blooming with forget-me-nots, wild heliotrope, and shooting stars, with hummingbirds everywhere. Her enthusiasm for the West and its birds never waned.

Her father purchased the land south of his brother's homestead and arranged to have Gustavus build a house on it, which he called La Mesita. They stayed at Twin Oaks to attend the wedding of Florence's cousin Edwin on June 6 to Kitty Keyes, daughter of another early settler in nearby Lilac. The major and his family had come of age in California, and the fifth generation of Merriams today lives on part of the original homestead. Clinton's house is still called La Mesita.

All three in Clinton's family felt so much better after spending the spring at Twin Oaks that they then traveled north by coastal steamer to San Francisco, where Florence continued her bird study. She found the scientific library there woefully inadequate, complaining that the librarian knew nothing about Olive Thorne Miller nor entomologist Mary Treat, "but," he told her, "we have Thoreau."[8]

After a bout with typhoid fever, Florence headed north again to Oregon to meet Hart, "as hale and handsome as ever," for a trip along the coast of Washington to the country's northwesternmost corner at Neah Bay. From the piazza of the house where they stayed, Florence could see the Indians' "big canoes with beaks to the ocean drawn up to strew the beach."[9]

From Washington they returned to the East Coast to join their parents, who had taken an earlier train back with Gustavus's daughter Helen, so that she could finish school in New York. Once home, and able to consider writing again, Florence began to reach out to the general public. She felt more than ever that people needed education on the vital part birds played in their lives.

Since the serious study of live birds was new, few aids — and many hindrances — were involved. The opera glass, imperfect as it was and with its small magnification, had only recently come into use as such an aid. For women, the style of long cumbersome dresses of the period was hardly a help. However, since guns were not involved, the pursuit of birds was more seemly for women, and young people could be brought into the study as well. So these groups for the first time went comfortably — using the term loosely — into the field, and Florence was in the forefront of helping them do so.

By now the *Audubon Magazine*, for which she had written the series on common birds, had ceased publication. The publisher, *Forest and Stream*, had taken an initial commercial interest in developing public support, but it wasn't paying off.[10] Thanks to people like Florence, the relapse was temporary, and others would soon redouble those beginning efforts. In the meantime, she gathered her fifty common birds and revised the series, then added some new birds that she had studied since the articles were originally written. She published them all as her first book, *Birds Through an Opera Glass*, an accomplishment of some note for a young woman of twenty-six, especially in 1889. It was directed at women and young people and was the first bird book that did not presuppose shooting.[11]

In the preface to her book she reassured her audience, who were more used to reading Shakespeare than pursuing a hobby like birdwatching: "Like Snug the Joiner, in Midsummer Night's Dream, I would explain to the ladies at the outset that this little book is no real lion, and that they have nothing to fear. It is not an ornithological treatise . . . but is 'a very gentle beast, and of a good conscience.'" She furnished only hints, nothing more, that would enable readers to know the common birds that they saw. Thinking of the working girls she met at Miss Dodge's, she directed her book not merely to those who can get outdoors themselves, but "it is above all the careworn indoor workers to whom I would bring a breath of the woods, pictures of sunlit fields, and a hint of the simple, childlike gladness, the peace and comfort that is offered us every day by these blessed winged messengers of nature."

Although she knew that many would never get beyond reading about the birds, she trusted that a breath of the woods in words would at least discourage them from wearing feathers on their hats. But she knew that the real benefit was to those who could take her hints and go out to see the birds themselves. They would certainly never wear feathers again, once they met the live birds as friends. The hints she offered the ladies serve as well today as they did then, for all observers regardless of age or sex:

"To guard against scaring the wary, you should make yourself as much as possible a part of the landscape. Most birds are not afraid of man as a figure, but as an aggressive object. 1) Avoid light or bright-colored clothing. . . . 2) Walk slowly and noiselessly. Among the crisp rattling leaves of the woods, a bit of moss or an old log will often deaden your step at the critical moment. 3) Avoid all quick, jerky motions. How many birds I have scared away by raising my glass too suddenly! 4) Avoid all talking, or speak only in an undertone — a most obnoxious but important rule to young observers. 5) If the bird was singing, but stops on your approach, stand still a moment and encourage him by answering his call. If he gets interested he will often let you creep up within opera-glass distance. . . . 6) Make a practice of stopping often and standing perfectly still. In that way you hear voices that would be lost if you were walking, and the birds come to the spot without noticing you when they would fly away in advance if they were to see or hear you coming toward them. 7) Conceal yourself by leaning against a tree, or pulling a branch down in front of you. The best way of all is to select a good place and sit there quietly for several hours, to see what will come. Then you get at the home life of the birds, not merely seeing them when they are on their guard."

In addition to these hints, Florence advised consideration of the time of day and of the weather. "Birds usually follow the sun. In spring and fall you will find them in the fields and orchards early in the morning, but when the sun has warmed the south side of the woods they go there; and in the afternoon they follow it across to the north side. During heavy winds and storms you are most likely to find birds well under cover of the woods, no matter at what time of day; and then, often on the side opposite that from which the wind comes."

Continuing her "preach," Florence suggested three general rules for careful observation of birds: "1) In clear weather be sure to get between the sun and your bird. In the wrong light a scarlet tanager or a blue-bird will look as black as a crow. 2) Gaze. Let your eyes rest on the trees before you, and if a leaf stirs, or a twig sways, you will soon discover your bird. At a little distance, it is well to gaze through your glass. 3) Beware of the besetting sin of observers. Never jump at conclusions. Prove all your conjectures." As she had learned so well from Hart, carrying a notebook in which to jot observations was the best way to capture detail on the spot.

Florence continued to believe in showing others the best in life and inserted a message about maintaining high principles wherever she could, even in bird descriptions. "Like other ladies, the little feathered brides have to bear their husbands' names, however inappropriate. What injustice! Here an innocent creature with an olive-green back and yellowish breast has to go about all her days known as the black-throated blue warbler, just because that happens to describe the dress of her spouse!"[12] The year was 1889, and the few women who even dared to publish their writings generally did so under a pen name. Florence not only used her own name throughout her publications, but she spoke out for injustice in her own way and in her own style. Both warblers and women benefited from her work.

Inside the covers of his copy of *Birds Through an Opera Glass* her father pasted a half-dozen newspaper reviews, including one from Pasadena, California, where one of his brothers lived. The *Atlantic Monthly* called the book a "collection of bird portraits tossed off with a deft and vivid touch." In *Auk* (October, 1889) William Brewster complimented her talent both in field work and in writing, comparing her work favorably with that of Thoreau and Burroughs. As an ornithologist, he separated her from the ranks of professional scientists by noting that "her sole weapon has been not a gun, but an opera glass." Brewster also found fault with her layman's interest in bird songs and suggested that "it may well be doubted if it is really worth while to attempt anything definite of this kind," but he finished his review with more words of encouragement. "As an observer, Miss Merriam is unmistakably keen, discriminating, and accurate; as a writer, always simple and true, at times highly vigorous and original. Her attractive little book may be cordially recommended to all who wish to study our familiar birds, either with or without an opera glass."

This was high praise by a professional for an unknown young woman writer publishing her first book. But to reverse today's cliché, in the late 1800s behind many a good woman stood a man, at least for her to gain a place among scientists. Brewster was a close friend of her brother's, and Hart always took an active interest in his sister's writing.

Regardless of speculations about the politics behind the scenes, Florence was off to a good start with her first book. It had developed her skills in writing and publishing, and it led her to consider doing more. These in turn would lead future historians like Robert Welker to class her as one of the four most important woman authors of bird books in the nineteenth century.[13] The others were Olive Thorne Miller, Mabel Osgood Wright, and Neltje Blanchan. These women served as an inspiration to one another and helped to develop their own eventual network with others for politics within the scientific field.

Florence was especially fond of Mrs. Miller, also an early associate member of the AOU, who had been writing books for children for some years. Only recently she had published bird books for adults as well. The two met when Florence was fresh from college, and Mrs. Miller made an immediate impression on the earnest young doer from Smith. "Her hair was nearly white, but the discrepancy in our ages never seemed to occur to me, for she had the spirit and enthusiasm of youth, and we worked side by side as sisters."[14]

Florence had no living sisters, and her closer brother was now totally involved in his own life, with his bride expecting their first child in a few months. Mrs. Miller gave Florence confidence and encouragement in bird protection activities; and Mrs. Miller, whose own children were now grown, found equal comfort in the idealism and enthusiasm of her new young friend. The friendship flourished. They shared many common beliefs and goals, and at times their expressions are so similar that it is difficult to distinguish between the two writers.

At the time, Florence was writing mostly articles, some for children and some for the general public. They were published in periodicals like *St. Nicholas, Our Animal Friends,* the *American Agriculturist,* and the *Observer.* She also started to contribute to *Auk,* the only major birding magazine then being published. At first she wrote general notes for their field studies section. In one, "Was He a Philanthropist?" (October, 1890), she provided exacting descriptions based on her own habit of sitting quietly for several hours to observe bird behavior in detail. These field notes helped to establish her reliability with the scientific AOU members who read *Auk.* In addition, by mentioning the presence of her friend Mrs. Miller, whose reputation was already established, she increased the acceptability of the observations, such as the strange behavior of a chestnut-sided warbler feeding another species' young, not only once (a redstart) but twice (an unidentified ground bird).

Florence ended that field note with her typical philosophical comment about birds being symbolic of humans in behavior. "If he was the same bird [as they had watched before], he certainly deserves a position at the head of an orphanage, for perhaps his combination with 'fresh air' work is a bit of warbler wisdom that might be imitated."

Florence had watched warblers from the time she could walk and had written about them since college days. On the other hand, Olive Thorne Miller had followed the traditional family role for a woman of her day, raising four children before thinking about a career for herself, and then writing under a pen name. Florence's own sense of independence and her Smith College class of earnest doers had given her new ideas about a woman's role. She may not have discussed these feelings with Mrs. Miller in respect for the difference in their ages, despite her protestation that the difference never seemed to occur to her. But after Mrs. Miller died some years later, Florence commented in a memorial that "in her conscientious effort to be a model wife and to master domestic arts to which she had never been trained, she sacrificed herself unnecessarily."[15]

Their approach to birding was different, but Mrs. Miller provided a technique that Florence used through all her years of birding: to keep the birds unaware that she was watching them. Usually when they went to the woods, Mrs. Miller "would steal in through the bushes in her leaf-colored gown, open her camp-stool cautiously at the foot of a tree whose dark trunk would help conceal her, pull down a branch before her and, with note-book ready, carefully raise her opera-glass and focus it upon the nest she wanted to study. And there she would sit in silence, stoically defying tormenting gnats and mosquitoes, patiently waiting and watching to see what might befall."[16] Olive Thorne Miller might well have used the same description for Florence in the field.

The song of the hermit thrush especially intrigued Mrs. Miller, so Florence invited her to Locust Grove to study the bird on its breeding grounds there. Board was secured for her in the only farmhouse near the woods. Although her quarters were cramped, she was enthusiastic about the opportunities to watch from behind a closed blind "the unsuspecting birds promenading up and down the fence and feeding in the bushes outside. . . . No beauty of forest or meadow, sky, cloud, or mountain escaped her, and she loved birds as she did nature."[17]

After Mrs. Miller's visit, Florence traveled to Illinois to conduct a field bird class at the Hull House summer school at Rockford. She found the factory girls she taught surprisingly full of enthusiasm, but her own inspiration came from being associated with Jane Addams in such uplifting work. "Uplifting" had already become an important word in Florence's vocabulary and was to remain so throughout her life. To her, it signified aspiration, and she lived by her belief that the highest aim is always the most worthwhile.

Although summers in Locust Grove were pleasant, winters were not, and the Merriam family still moved to its New York City home for the cold months. Florence continued to work with Miss Dodge, "another of the strong, inspiring women of the day," in spite of her recurring spells of ill health. She was under the care of her cousin Clint, by now an established physician in New York, whose childhood vision of African safaris with Hart she had shared. As soon as the weather warmed, Clint advised her to get outdoors, though closer to home than the settings of their childhood dreams.

Florence enlisted Hart's help to accomplish this without alarming their parents, neither of whom was in good health either. So she packed her trunks again, this time for Lake Placid, New York, to rest in the sunshine and balsam-saturated air. Her coughing lessened, and she immediately felt better there, looking forward to the end of the summer when "I hope not to know I even had a chest." She kept an eye on the local birds while she rested, and she noted one kingfisher, who responded to her quiet respect. While moored in a boat near shore, he perched directly overhead and then dived so near that the water spattered her paddle. She also enjoyed the nesting hermit thrushes, but she missed the anticipated opportunity to share field work with Hart. The struggle for health was depressing her, and by fall all she wanted was to get cured. "I've had years enough of being miserable and unable to work. I haven't courage for any more of them."

After a short time back in the miserably cold and damp winter climate of Locust Grove, the family again went to New York. Florence took her typewriter in hopes of spending the time writing up her bird notes. "That, with two walks a day and an occasional Philharmonic and interspersed relatives and friends is my present programme."

Neither Florence nor her mother was doing well. They turned to another popular cure of the time, southern air. In February the family traveled to Florida. At first, Florence felt stronger, but it was too early in the year for much field work, although she noted the good observing grounds that would be accessible when migration time approached. Meanwhile, she spent her time caring for her mother and playing whist with her father.

Victorians had a passion for improvement—of themselves and others —that found an outlet in travel.[18] Mrs. Miller was planning a trip to Utah to study flowers, and Florence wrote to Hart to see what he and Mr. Bailey thought of her going along for the summer, since both men had been there and knew the country. Florence was growing weak again and still not up to field work, as she had hoped to be. She told him that she needed to get away and preferred "to go quietly with Mrs. Miller," rather than to vegetate again at Lake Placid; she wanted to be "where there are birds and I can work." In Utah she thought she would have the perfect combination of her most delightful field companion and her favorite subject for study.

At the end of March, after lingering at the edge for some weeks with Florence in attendance, Caroline Merriam died in Florida. Florence's dread of consumption was certainly not lessened by the experience. Her mother was buried as she had wished, at Homewood by the large rock that marked Gertie's grave. There would be two to put spring beauties on now, with the addition of the Queen of Homewood, as Father called his wife. He penned in his journal, "Our lovely home trio broken forever. The birds sing but a sweeter voice is silent to us, but not to our sad hearts — circle the woods alone!"[19] Hart arranged to spend the summer at Homewood with their father, and Florence left for a western cure — for her body and her psyche.

The result of that trip was her second book, *My Summer in a Mormon Village*. It was such an unusual trip for a woman to make in 1893 that in the book's preface she felt she had to explain why she went. Not only was she joining another enthusiastic student of birds looking for new worlds to conquer, but she also added the reason of climate, since Arizona and Utah are "the natural sanitariums of our continent."

Florence also found new worlds to conquer, for this book was her first (and only) attempt at a travel narrative rather than a book specifically to educate readers about birds. She included personal descriptions of nature at its best and also brought in her aspiration, as always, to uplift with her writings by adding some social commentary about polygamy, recently outlawed but still a common practice. The original manuscript does not survive, but relatives still remember her brother's horror when he first read it, in his habit of reviewing all her manuscripts. "I'll never be able to show my face in Utah again if you publish this!"[20] The cleaned-up version speaks more of her growing philosophy about meaningful work for women in any environment than it does about the religious practices of the Mormons.

Florence and Mrs. Miller stayed at the only boardinghouse in town, run, to their relief, by "only mother and daughters." With her abhorrence of plain sewing, it was no wonder that Florence was appalled by one daughter, who liked to make rag carpets simply because it took up her time. "All that I had known of the meagreness and wasted energy of farm and village life came back to me with fresh force . . . And I recalled with a shudder the statistics I had known about the number of farmers' wives who go insane. . . . I wanted to start out on a village crusade, to put to use the young strong life of our countrywomen, so full of the common sense and simple goodness that our civilization is in need of, and, in turn, to save them from stagnation, from the bare dreary lives whose drudgery ends with the asylum. It seemed such an easy matter to bring farm and village life into touch with the centres of intelligence, in this age of circulating libraries, Channing Auxiliaries,

Home Culture Clubs, Chautauqua Circles, and Boston Home Study Societies."[21] It was obvious that she was writing for the members of those circles and societies, whom she also hoped to educate.

Florence rested in the sunshine and warm, dry air. When she first arrived, she had recognized the poor state of her health, both of mind and body. "The feverish longing one has for the country in spring had possessed my blood before I left the city. The brick horizons and squares of sky had irritated my tired spirit."[22] Soon she was responding to the change in climate. She began to keep field notes on the many pleasures in nature she found in Utah, including the birds, but for the book she shortened their descriptions:

"High from above, a bird of prey came sailing down the mountain, projecting its shadow ahead. Now it would swoop close over a rocky ledge or sweep low over the side of canyon wall,—a mere seam to me,— then slowly sail across the face of the range, rising upward till it soared beyond the lofty crags at the summit. It rested me to follow up and down the mountain with my eye."[23]

"The meadow road was so little frequented that the birds of the neighborhood gathered on its fences, flying up as [my horse] cantered by. We often scared up noisy flocks of blackbirds from the cattails, the old birds anxiously bustling their young out of the way. Once we passed close by to a big baby dove, trying to balance himself on the top wire of the fence, and bewildered him greatly, for his mother had evidently told him to stay right there till she came back. At one point in the road, for some days, we were met by patrolling kildeer, who escorted us safely past the hiding-places of their young."[24]

"One day I startled a small brown heron standing in the road, making him strike such an attitude that I wanted to laugh in his face. He raised his long neck, fixing his gaze upon the zenith, like an abstracted philosopher rather than the reed he would have me take him for."[25]

In late June Mr. Bailey stopped for a few hours on his way through to spend the summer field season in Nevada. He arrived on the train from Ogden after tea and stayed only until the eleven o'clock train back, so he could catch the midnight train west. Even that short visit gave them a chance to talk of Hart's anticipated visit, ostensibly so Florence could join him briefly in the field, but more likely so he could observe the health of his sister. Vernon reassured Florence that the field trip wouldn't be rougher than the one he planned to take his sister on. She lived on a ranch in Fallon, Nevada, a handy stopping place for the government naturalist to stretch his fifty-cent daily allotment.

Meanwhile, Florence spent most of her time near town observing the birds. On occasion, she accompanied Mrs. Miller on botanical outings, once in the company of a local botanist. When a sudden mountain shower opened up, "I resigned myself to a wetting while the botanists loitered gathering new flowers, oblivious of the drizzle; and amused myself watching the chipmunks playing among the rocks, and the hummingbirds whizzing around the flowers — the hillsides seemed to whirr with them."[26] She remembered back to a similar afternoon a few years before, with her "gossamer and raised umbrella" when John Burroughs had been equally oblivious to the rain while describing sparrows and goldfinches to the eager young Smith College girls who crowded close around him.

Since Florence and Mrs. Miller were both still actively working to protect birds, Florence also used the pages of her book as an opportunity to express their horror of killing for sport. "We met a party of summer hotel young men, calling for a gun — they saw grouse in the trees. I heard them recalling their recent achievements — they had killed a badger, a deer, and an eagle within a few days. It was a rude shock to me, and I thought bitterly that even these wild grand mountains would soon be 'civilized' by the pleasure-seekers who destroy all they can of the nature they have come to enjoy . . . I could only reflect thankfully that though the mountains might be made patent-medicine advertisers, and the deer that drank from the lakes at their feet and the eagles that soared over their heads might be killed to gratify man's lust of power, the cloudless blue sky above us was beyond their reach."[27] A hundred years later, the deer populations today are encouraged by the sportsmen themselves, as they have helped to protect the birds, although the lakes at their feet are certainly suspect and the eagle is barely out of danger. But the cloudless blue sky is no longer beyond reach and is the most threatened of all.

On the sunnier side, Florence shared her observations of summer in the West and their meaning in her own life. "As I gazed dreamily into the blue sky, a beautiful butterfly, red against the sun, flew over my head straight on as if it would storm the mountain wall,— frail, airy flutterer, strong with the joy of climbing to heaven. I followed it with my eye . . . My spirit rose exultant, catching inspiration from nature in its purity, strength, and radiant joy."[28]

She especially admired the yellow mustard, taller than her horse's head, that she had read about in *Ramona*. Helen Hunt Jackson had written her book from a part of southern California where Florence's uncle Gustavus lived, so the novel and its setting were as close to her heart as was the mustard — "whole fields were yellow with it, reflecting back the sunshine of the sky."[29]

But *My Summer in a Mormon Village* is mostly about travel, human travel, written for easterners who had not had the opportunity to go west but who would be encouraged to go there by books like this one. And she wrote about the travelers, who were a constant curiosity in the little town where she stayed. "The sound of galloping hoofs was as common as that of wheels. . . . But more striking than the horseback riders were the frequently passing emigrant wagons. The whole family were often seen looking out from under the white wagon cover; while the team was flanked by colts. The people usually looked tired and disheveled, huddled in with their household gods. . . . Traveling men from the South told us exciting bits of war history; but more of our visitors discussed living history; the silver question was the excitement of the summer. . . . But all these discussions were like the whistle of the express train passing us on its way from New York to San Francisco,—a mere echo of the outside life of the world. Our swiftest currents ran through beds of brooks—still a long distance from the sea."[30] She could not resist adding a touch of nature even when writing about travelers.

Another traveler who passed her doorstep was the returning Mr. Bailey, now seeking a chipmunk species he had missed collecting. "He was so breezy he did us good," she wrote Hart. But her health interfered with her hostess duties, and she had to let Mrs. Miller's daughter Minnie entertain him much of the day.

Although Florence felt stronger in the western air, her health was still so much on her mind that she decided not to return east with Minnie but to stay in the West for the winter. Hart's friend David Starr Jordan, cousin to her favorite Smith instructor, Miss Jordan, had been named as the first president of the new Stanford University in California. She asked Hart to write him to see about accommodations and attending informally "anything I choose to take without regard to classes, etc." College entrance has changed a bit since then.

August was approaching, and she eagerly awaited Hart's visit and a last horseback outing to Mary's Lake. "The fresh mountain air came cool over our faces, the morning sunlight silted through the silent firs, giving a green gleam to the mountain side and touching with a tender vivid light a bit of meadow on the border of the lake. No sound broke the stillness, no ripple stirred the smooth pure face of the lake, over which arched the deep blue sky. A hush had fallen upon our spirits. It seemed as if the noble mountains under whose great shadow we had passed the summer had at last admitted us to their Holy of Holies."[31] Whether she realized it or not, a great shadow was passing from her own life as well.

Minnie Miller followed her mother back east, and both Florence and

Mrs. Miller continued to write. When Mrs. Miller published another book, as a nonprofessional like Florence, she received a scolding in *Auk* (October, 1893) from William Brewster for not reporting discoveries "in some accredited scientific journal, instead of scattering them broadcast over the pages of popular magazines or newspapers, or ambushing them in books with titles such as [*Little Brothers of the Air*]." He was a bit sensitive about this, he admitted, because he had published in *Auk* what he thought was a new discovery, only to learn that Mrs. Miller had previously written it up in an essay in the *Atlantic Monthly* that she later incorporated into her book.

Mrs. Miller replied in a letter to the *Auk* (January, 1894) editors within a week. She defended her writing, and in so doing she spoke for others like Florence, with her longstanding reputation adding weight to her argument. With polite, ladylike reference to Brewster's "gentle admonition," she listed her reasons for writing in a literary rather than a scientific fashion:

> There is, first, my great desire to bring into the lives of others the delights to be found in the study of Nature, which necessitates the using of an unscientific publication, and a title that shall attract, even though it may, in a measure, "ambush" my subject.

> I have never studied scientific ornithology. . . . Let those who will spend their days killing, dissecting and classifying; I choose rather to give my time to the study of life, and to doing my small best toward preserving the tribes of the air from the utter extinction with which they are threatened.

> And lastly, a confession: I should take pleasure in "sharing my discoveries" were I so happy as to make any; but to me everything is a discovery; each bird, on first sight, is a new creation; his manners and habits are a revelation, as fresh and as interesting to me as though they had never been observed before. How am I to tell what is an old story and what a new one?

> Study these things who will. I study the beautiful, the living, the individual bird, and to my scientific confreres I leave his skin, his bones, and his place in the Temple of Fame.

Although she deferred to the scientists with characteristic ladylike modesty, Mrs. Miller's place — and Florence's — in that temple was more assured with each new book they published.

5

Birds and Broncos, 1893–1894

ALTHOUGH THE SUMMER DOSE of western air in Utah had helped Florence, the "great shadow" on her health had not yet lifted entirely. She had first gone west five years earlier, to the coast of California to breathe the beneficial air. Now, after spending the summer of 1893 in Utah, she headed farther west again to spend the winter in California.

Train travel was very elegant in those days. Florence was more interested in writing about birds than about trains, but the intrepid Englishwoman Isabella Bird had described train travel in a letter to her sister while crossing the American continent a few years before. Her berth was "a luxurious bed three and a half feet wide, with a hair mattress on springs, fine linen sheets, and costly California blankets. . . . Four silver lamps hanging from the roof, and burning low, gave a dreamy light. On each side of the center passage, rich rep curtains, green and crimson, striped with gold, hung from silver bars running near the roof, and trailed on the soft Axminster carpet . . . Silence and freedom from jolting were secured by double doors and windows, costly and ingenious arrangements of springs and cushions, and a speed limited to 18 miles per hour."[1] Florence felt right at home on the train; it was like Homewood on wheels.

Florence did put a brief note in her journal the day the train broke a coupling at Gila Bend, Arizona, when she had the opportunity to talk with the occupants of a passing emigrant wagon while waiting for the train to resume its journey. The small family included a baby born along the way. Florence was amazed at how they enjoyed their gypsy life. "When we get tired we rest a right smart while," they told her. She found it a revelation that such a life could be pleasure instead of hardship.

As always, Florence made the most of the opportunity to travel. She wrote her Smith College class letter that fall from Stanford University

On her way to Twin Oaks for a visit in 1893, Florence spent a term at the new Stanford University in northern California. Her cousin Helen attended there in 1896 and saved this photograph. (From the collection of Mr. and Mrs. Sheldon Gustavus Merriam.)

in California. "This seems a strange place for a Smith girl to hail from, but I have been given a prescription of 'climate'; and find its effect most tonic, taken in University. The work here would delight you. I am especially interested in a strong course of Dr. [David Starr] Jordan's on Evolution . . . and one by Dr. [Amos] Warner on Social Pathology or 'Philanthropology'—a course with field work—visiting of prisons, almshouses and charitable institutions. The breadth, optimism and earnest humanitarianism that pervade the place are very inspiring."

Dr. Warner was a pioneer in analyzing the causes of poverty. As a professor of applied economics, he is remembered as approaching everything with the shrewd regard of the investigator, who took his impressionable students on field trips so they could see and judge for themselves. He once remarked, "Others may agitate and preach; I have concluded I can do the most good by investigating these things and

Botanist Alice Eastwood had the same determined look as her friend Florence. (From the Archives of the California Academy of Sciences.)

just telling the whole truth."[2] Florence took his philosophy to heart.

Since health was still her first object, Florence bought a horse while she was at Stanford and spent much of her time "outdoors among the birds, on foot and on horseback," she wrote to reassure Hart. She took a short trip to the mountains with a biology class and Dr. and Mrs.

Barton W. Evermann, who must have been struck by her resemblance to another of their young friends, Alice Eastwood.

Botanist Alice Eastwood had moved to San Francisco the year before, and she and Florence became lifelong friends. Although neither recorded it, they may first have met during this period when both were so actively learning about the flora and fauna of California. The description of Alice Eastwood as "a blithe spirit that is ageless, living in a world of discovery that is ever new" applies equally well to Florence. The lives of both women also taught that "men have sought in vain the fountain of perpetual youth; what they needed instead was the fountain of perpetual adventure." They drank together from another fountain as well. "She set truth and the search for truth as the lodestar of her life, and as teacher and scientist she remained faithful to that course in all the years that followed. In her pursuit of truth, Alice Eastwood strove to cultivate the essential, to weed out the unessential, so that the garden of her life would be open and uncluttered."[3]

Florence spent the winter term weeding out the unessential in her own garden. Soon the stimulus of professional criticism that she received on her writing led her to her next adventure. As soon as the flowers began to bloom on the hillsides, she shipped her horse by water and then traveled south by train to the drier air at her Uncle Gustavus's ranch in Twin Oaks. His new wife, delighted by the opportunity for a change of scene, left him in Florence's care while she visited in Los Angeles. Florence predicted to Hart a good time except "alas for the cookin'!"

She had arranged to stay until August to have a longer look at the birds. By 1894 her uncle's family were oldtimers. When the San Diego newspaper published an article about the town, her family's visit, as well as her brother's successful career, showed their influence. "The Merriam family, know[n] from the Atlantic to the Pacific, are part of them located in the San Marcos valley. Major G. F. Merriam lives at the head of the Twin Oaks valley . . . has a large vineyard, an orchard, and raises all kinds of fruits; manufactures wines, brandies and raisins, and has a large apiary, which produces a great amount of honey. His house is situated under the live oak trees in a very attractive and romantic spot."[4]

Florence also found Twin Oaks very attractive and described it even more romantically in her next book, which combined the adventures of her two trips there. Like her book on Utah, Florence wrote *A-Birding on a Bronco* for easterners, both to encourage them to come west and to describe for those who couldn't come a bit of the fresh western air — and its birds.

On the title page Florence addressed her readers, most of whom

Downtown San Diego in 1876, shortly after Gustavus Merriam settled to the north. (San Diego Historical Society—Ticor Collection.)

were more comfortable on eastern sofas than on horseback in California and who still knew more about Shakespeare than they did about birds: "I do invite you . . . to my house . . . after, we'll a-birding together.— Shakespeare"[5]

She bragged a little about her horse, whose Mexican bridle of braided rawhide was given to her when she left the ranch. "It now hangs behind my study door, a proud trophy of my western life, and one that is looked upon with mingled admiration and horror by eastern horsemen." Florence and her horse were the best of friends, especially after she discovered that local birds were accustomed to seeing grazing horses and paid less attention to her on horseback than on foot. As for her horse, "He liked to watch birds in the high alfalfa under the sycamores, but when it came to standing still where the hot sun beat down through the brush and there was nothing to eat, his interest in ornithology flagged perceptibly."[6]

One of her biggest steps forward at Twin Oaks was to dare to ride astride. Eastern ladies simply didn't do that in the early 1890s. But Isabella Bird had, and bloomer costumes were becoming fashionable for bicycling, and in the West it was the only practical way to ride horseback over the rough terrain.

Her birding routine at Twin Oaks included gathering her opera glass, notebook, and Ridgway's *Manual of North American Birds.* "Every morning, right after breakfast, my horse was brought to the door and I set out to make the rounds of the valley. I rode till dinner time . . . After dinner I would take my camp-stool and stroll through the oaks at the head of the valley, for a quiet study of the nearer nests. Then once more my horse would be brought up for me to take a run before sunset; and at night I would identify my new birds and write up the notes of the day. What more could observer crave? The world was mine. I never spent a happier spring."[7]

She painted word pictures for her eastern audience, telling how she liked to start out "in the freshness of the morning, when the fog was breaking up into buff clouds over the mountains and drawing off in veils over the peaks. The brush we passed through was full of glistening spiders' webs, and in the open the grass was overlaid with disks of cobweb, flashing rainbow colors in the sun."[8]

Thoughts of her childhood at Homewood flashed through her mind as she dismounted and settled herself against a haycock one day. "It was a beautiful quiet morning. The night fog had melted back and the mountains stood out in relief against a sky of pure deep blue. The line of sycamores opposite us were green and still against the blue, the morning sun lighting their white trunks and framework. The songs of birds filled the air, and the straw-colored field dotted with haycocks lay sunning under the quiet sky. In the east we are accustomed to speak of 'the peace of evening,' but in southern California in spring there is a peculiar interval of warmth and rest, a languorous pause in the growth of the morning, between the disappearance of the night fog and the coming of the cool trade wind, when the southern sun shines full into the little valleys and the peace of the morning is so deep and serene that the labor of the day seems done. Nature appears to be slumbering. She is aroused slowly and gently by the soft breaths that come in from the Pacific. On this day I watched the awakening."[9]

At Twin Oaks, Florence continued her lifelong habit of sitting for hours observing the activities of the birds. She is at her best in describing these, and in a short paragraph brings her reader to the spot. "When the young hatched . . . Mother wren at least was kept busy looking for spiders, and later, when both were working together, if not hunting among the green treetops, the pretty little brown birds often flew to

A composite photograph of the Twin Oaks valley in 1889 shows the Merriam home-stead at the lower left and beehives at the lower right near the honey house. The

the ground and ran about under the weeds to search for insects. Once when the mother bird had flown up with her bill full, she suddenly stopped at the twig in front of the nest, looking down, her tail over her back wren fashion, the sun on her brown sides, and her bill bristling with spiders' legs . . . It is no bagatelle to keep half a dozen gaping mouths full of spiders, as any mother bird can tell."[10]

Then there was the grosbeak, who reminded Florence of an old friend. "The black-headed grosbeak has not the spirituality of the hermit thrush, and his ordinary song is not so remarkable, but his love song excels that of any bird I have ever heard in finish, rich melody, and music. As I listened, my surroundings harmonized so perfectly with the wonderful song echoing through the great trees that the old oak garden seemed an enchanted bower."[11]

"dim mountains far away" noted on the back of the print are now known as the Merriam Mountains. (From the collection of Mr. and Mrs. Sheldon Gustavus Merriam.)

Florence also used her studies to educate the local children. Once she found an old bushtit nest on the ground. "On taking it home and pulling it to pieces, I found that the wall was from half an inch to an inch thick, made of fine gray moss and oak blossoms. There was a thick wadding of feathers inside. I counted *three hundred*, and there were a great many more! The amount of hard labor this stood for amazed me. No wonder the nest pulled down, with a whole featherbed inside! Why had they put it in? I asked some children, and one said, 'To keep the eggs warm, I guess'; while the other suggested, 'So the eggs wouldn't break.'"[12]

In the warm spring air the hummingbirds were especially active, even coming into the house if the door was left open. Wild flowers were abundant around the ranch, and, as in Utah, Florence especially en-

The notation on the back of this photograph indicates that her cousin Edwin is "feeding young woodpeckers for Florence's book." She was writing A-Birding on a Bronco *at Twin Oaks in 1893. (From the collection of Mr. and Mrs. Sheldon Gustavus Merriam.)*

Gustavus Merriam's family at the homestead on the occasion of the visit of his brother Clinton and his family. Florence is seated on Billy, the "bronco" she used to ride along the valley studying the birds. (From the collection of Mr. and Mrs. Sheldon Gustavus Merriam.)

joyed riding her horse through the mustard that reached over his head. This was the country that Helen Hunt Jackson had written about in *Ramona*, and Florence felt even closer to the book's young heroine, who had walked through the tall mustard just a few miles away.

Another of the birds Florence most enjoyed meeting in California was the phainopepla. For those who don't know it, its name alone is enough to arouse curiosity, as Florence also recognized. "We may say that we care naught for the world and its ways, but most of us are more or less tricked by the high-sounding titles of the mighty. Even plain-thinking observers come under the same curse of Adam, and, like the snobs who turn scornfully from Mr. Jones to hang upon the words of Lord Higginbottom, will pass by a plain brown chippie to study with enthusiasm the ways of a phainopepla!"[13] She had only a few sightings on her earlier trip to California, but she had determined to study the phainopepla more thoroughly when she returned. Her friend Olive Thorne Miller urged her on, adding that she felt like making a journey to California just to see that one bird.

Feathers for women's hats were still much on Florence's mind. Although she had heard a great deal about egrets, she had only seen them as hat decorations until "One day I had a genuine excitement in seeing a snow-white egret perched on a bush by the water. I rode home full of the beautiful sight, but alas, my story was the signal for the ranchman's son to seize his gun and rush after the bird. Fortunately he did not find him, although he did shoot a green heron; but it was probably a short reprieve for the poor hunted creature."[14] Her message was clear—and aimed right at the eastern women who would read her book and perhaps think twice about wearing feathers on their hats.

Florence had the virtue of patience in large measure, and she reassured readers of its benefits in watching birds. When an acorn woodpecker kept her waiting for its return to the nest, she commented, "Patient waiting is no loss, observers must remember if they would be consoled for their lost hours."[15] But she was tweaked later by Emerson's poetic question, "Hast thou named all the birds without a gun?" and in trying to identify one bird showed a streak of impatience that she rarely exhibited. "You can identify perhaps 90 per cent. of the birds you see, with an opera-glass and—patience; but when it comes to the other 10 per cent., . . . you are involved in perplexities that torment your mind and make you meditate murder; for it is impossible to 'Name *all* the birds without a gun.' On bringing my riddle to the wise men, they shook their heads and asked why I did not shoot my bird and find out who he was . . . but after knowing the little family in their home it would have been like raising my hand against familiar friends. Could I take their lives to gratify my curiosity about a name?"[16] Her curiosity was later assuaged by an authority on nests, who decided that the bird had probably been a Hutton's vireo, a plain little bird difficult to spot, much less to identify, even with today's sophisticated binoculars.

Florence considered herself an "ornithological landlady" at Twin Oaks and spent each morning getting acquainted. "The queerest of all my tenants was an old mother barn owl who lived in the black charred chimney of one of the sycamores. I found a white feather on the black wood one day in riding by, and pulled [my horse] up by the tree, broke off a twig and rapped on the door. She came blundering out and flew to a limb over our heads—such a queer old crone, with her hooked nose and her weazened face surrounded by a circlet of dark feathers. The light blinded her, and with her big round eyes wide open she leaned down staring to make out who we were. Then shaking her head reproachfully, she swayed solemnly from side to side. As the wind blew against her ragged feathers she drew her wings over her breast like a cloak, making herself look like a poverty-stricken wiseacre. Finding that we did not offer to go, the poor old crone took to her wings; but as she passed down the line of sycamores she roused the blackbird clan, and a pair of angry orioles flew out and attacked her. My conscience smote me for driving her out among her enemies, but on our return to the sycamores all was quiet again, and a lizard was sunning himself on the edge of the old owl's chimney."[17]

Florence found California the place of all places to study hummingbirds. Burroughs had written that "the woods hold no such other gem as the nest of the hummingbird. The finding of one is an event to date from."[18] Florence was especially interested in how they built their nests and carefully described the ones she found. One "was saddled on a twig and glued to a glossy dark green oak leaf. Like the other nest, it was made of a spongy yellow substance, probably down from the underside of sycamore leaves; and like it, also, the outside was coated with lichen and wound with cobweb." She watched the female. "The peculiar feature of her work was her quivering motion in moulding. When her material was placed she moulded her nest like a potter, twirling around against the sides, sometimes pressing so hard she ruffled up the feathers of her breast. She shaped her cup as if it were a piece of clay. To round the outside, she would sit on the rim and lean over, smoothing the sides with her bill, often with the same peculiar tremulous motion. . . . She made nest-making seem very pleasant work."[19]

If the people of southern California were not yet tame, the land was even less so. Rattlesnakes were common, and wildlife still freely roamed the hills. In fact, local children on the way to the major's school occasionally chased off a mountain lion with rocks;[20] and not many years before, her cousin Helen at the age of fourteen had killed a wildcat on a neighbor's ranch. That incident brought comment in the San Diego newspaper: "Good for Miss Helen! It won't do for any timid youth to give that young lady any sass!"[21]

But in the five years between her visits, Florence found many changes in the land. Progress was already coming to southern California. One evidence was her remembrance of a shrike's nest. He "had pitched his tent on the farthest outpost of my ranch," but the place had now been "converted into a well kept prune orchard." And she noted that her uncle had built his schoolhouse across the road near an abandoned adobe where some phoebes had nested. Although they "perched on its gables, on the hitching posts in front of it, and on my prune-tree . . . they could not find what they wanted and flew off to build elsewhere."[22]

On this second visit Florence stayed at La Mesita, the ranch house that her uncle had built for her father, decorating her attic study with a wagonload of "pale green aromatic boughs" from their nearby eucalyptus grove. For Florence the grove was a magic place of healing. In it she had found "the highest hummingbird's nest I had ever seen. It was attached to a red leaf — to mark the spot, perhaps — one often wonders how a bird can come back twice to the same leaf in a forest. How one little home does make a place habitable! From a bare silent woods it becomes a dwelling-place. Everything seemed to center around this little nest, then the only one in the grove; the tiny pinch of down became the most important thing in the woods. It was the castle which the trees surrounded."[23]

"Often, while watching the nest, my thoughts wandered away to the grove itself. The brown earth between the rows was barred by alternate lines of sunlight and shadow, and the vista of each avenue ended in blue sky. Sometimes cool ocean breezes would penetrate the forest. The rows of trees, with their gently swaying, interlacing branches, cast moving shadows over the sun-touched leafy floor, giving a white light to the grove; for the undersides of the young eucalyptus leaves are like snow. From the stiff, sickle-shaped upper leaves the sun glanced, dazzling the eyes. Mourning doves cooed, and the sweet notes of yellowbirds filled the sunny grove with suggestions of happiness. A yellow butterfly wandered down the blue aisles. Such a secure retreat! I returned to it again and again, coming in out of the hot yellow world and closing behind me the doors of my 'rest-house,' for the little wood had come to seem like a cool wayside chapel, a place of peace."[24]

By late July she was ready for the "final dose of climate" in Arizona, she wrote her Smith College friends. Hart had recommended the San Francisco Mountains near Flagstaff, where he had done field work. To him it was one of the most intriguing areas of the country, with seven life zones in one isolated mountain range.[25] Here Florence found the beneficial dry heat she had missed in the coastal climate at Twin Oaks. She wrote Hart that the air was like velvet and that she hoped some birds were still nesting on the mountain. With the added attractions of the Grand Canyon and cliff dwellers, she could hardly contain herself. "What a contrast to that treeless desolate California!" Then the final delight: Hart wrote that he was coming west and could see her there. "It's a great thing to have a brother to look after you in this world!" If her cough didn't go away, she planned to spend the winter in Phoenix or possibly Albuquerque. "I'd like to see the New Mexico country and life." But she left the final decision to Hart, after he had arrived and seen her progress. The trip to New Mexico didn't happen that year, but Hart remembered her wish, and it wasn't many years before he gave her the opportunity to fulfill it.

Near Flagstaff she bought another horse and settled into a log house "with a pair of the lovely Mountain Bluebirds raising a brood over my window." Flagstaff is 7,000 feet high, and Florence reported to Hart that she thought she had seen a Clark's nutcracker and a hepatic tanager. She was still the dutiful field helper reporting new species. When he arrived, they went by wagon to the Grand Canyon, sharing the "spiritual unity of the universe" that her first view elicited, where one is "humbled before such handiworks of nature," she noted in her journal. She wrote an article about Arizona which Hart edited, adding definitions for western terms that she had not supplied. He warned her in western lingo, "For heaven's sake don't publish all the infernal lies you've been stuffed with" about western mythology. She never published the article.

In northern Arizona, she found the soul-satisfying woods that she had missed — without realizing it — since leaving Homewood. "What a noble thing a great tree is! . . . It and the mountain give a challenge to our lives." She accepted the challenge then and there, and spent her life meeting it.

But Flagstaff gets cold and snowy early, so by fall she returned east "to get in touch with intellectual life again." From Washington, D.C., she wrote to her Smith College class full of enthusiasm and plans. "When your friends start for California for 'lungs' you can send them to the pine forests of Arizona instead. The climate is wonderful. I have come back from it so well that I expect to spend the winter here and to give courses of 'bird talks,' to boot."

After her second trip west, Florence had moved to Washington to live with her brother and his wife and their two young daughters. Her father had remarried, and so she found a new home with this growing young family instead. They had a big house and help "by the day," so Florence had the third-story room and bath to herself.[26] Besides the opportunity to be near Hart and his work, she was also stimulated by other scientific activity in Washington, such as the recently established Women's National Science Club, the largest organization of its kind.[27] Developed from an earlier discussion group, by 1894 the club, including Florence, was working hard to get women to start branches across the country. At its height it had more than two hundred members nationwide. They met annually in Washington to read papers that they then published, one of the very few outlets women in science had to report their studies at that time.

Florence's halcyon summer had ended, the great shadow had surely passed (and was never heard of again), and a new life in the scientific whirl of her brother's home in Washington was opening into the future. In California she had written, "the world is mine." She had now studied birds on both the east and west coasts. Could the rest of the continent be far behind?

Nesting Time, 1893–1899

Florence found herself in both the scientific and the social whirl of Washington, D.C., during the 1890s, but that did not keep her from thinking and writing about birds. If anything, it encouraged her as she watched with horror the growing fashion parade of ladies wearing "murderous millinery," as author William Henry Hudson described it in the *London Times*. He quoted Professor Newton, "feathers on the outside of any biped but a bird, naturally suggests the association of tar." Hudson was worried especially about the hummingbird, which he believed "exceeded all creatures in loveliness. Not dead in the hand . . . nor a dead humming-bird worn in a lady's hat. . . . For it is the art of savages . . . to decorate themselves with . . . feathers."[1] Florence nodded in agreement, remembering the lovely tiny jewels she had watched drinking nectar from the wild flowers around Twin Oaks.

More women, especially in fashion-conscious Washington, were reading the new ladies' magazines that encouraged them to think more about fashion and feathers. What was a lady to do? Although Washington women were supposed to be seen more than heard, Florence knew what she had to do: She continued to write and to educate women about live birds.[2]

Her friend John Burroughs, with his flowing white beard, had become increasingly popular in the decade since he had visited her group at Smith College. Besides other bird books, he had just written an introduction for a new edition of Gilbert White's *Natural History*, first published for the "famous nature loving parson" in 1789, before Florence's great-grandfather had homesteaded in Locust Grove. White's book had also been a part of Florence's childhood, for a copy was in the library of her grandparents' home. Burroughs's words about White fired Florence to expand her own writing. "It requires no great talent to go out in the fields or woods and describe in graceful sentences what one sees there . . . but to give the atmosphere of these things . . . and to

Florence's mentor, nature writer John Burroughs, shown at Slabsides, the retreat he built on the Hudson River. The photo was taken by flashlight by Frank Chapman, noted naturalist later with the American Museum of Natural History. Florence introduced the two men. The photograph appeared in the first issue of Bird-Lore magazine in February, 1899. (Courtesy of the Natural History Museum of Los Angeles County, Section of Birds and Mammals.)

put the reader into sympathetic communication with them, that is another matter. . . . The style of the born writer is like an open fire: we are in direct communication with his mind."[3]

Burroughs visited Washington and dined with Theodore Roosevelt, not yet president but working his way up in Capitol politics. While there, Burroughs continued one of his favorite pastimes, leading young ladies through the fields on nature walks, this time the students of the local normal school, to prepare them to teach children about live birds.

Florence wrote up her notes on the phainopepla for *Auk*, expanding her comments from *A-Birding on a Bronco*. For the scientific audience of the journal, however, she included a chart of observation times for the male and female at the nest, more detailed than any of her later writings. She even footnoted one entry, "I was absent from 9:50 to 10 o'clock." None of the nests she observed had been successful. In her conclusion, Dr. David Starr Jordan's pupil from Stanford used a principle of evolution and indeed predicted what has happened since. "As there was a schoolhouse near the nesting ground, the birds should have paid better heed to the laws of evolution. Supposing that the ancestors of these birds came from deserts unfrequented by small boys, it would be interesting to know if civilization will eventually modify the habits of the Twin Oaks' Phainopeplas."⁴

By fall, *A-Birding on a Bronco* was at the publisher's, complete with "spirited drawings of birds and birds' nests," as they were described in one review. This was the first book illustrated by Louis Agassiz Fuertes, the upcoming young bird artist she had befriended, who was then a junior in college.⁵ He was already at work on drawings for *Citizen Bird*, a children's bird book by Elliott Coues, the most renowned ornithologist since Audubon, and by Mabel Osgood Wright, another of the four women later considered most important to nineteenth-century bird literature. In reviewing *Citizen Bird* for *Auk*, Frank Chapman might also have been describing Florence's book as he characterized Fuertes' beautiful drawings as "portraits of the leading characters in a fascinating story."⁶

Of all the birds Fuertes was to paint in his lifetime, he rarely depicted violence, preferring to focus instead on the harmony and balance in the world around him, a principle that harmonized well with Florence's approach to birds. He later provided many illustrations for government publications at reduced rates because he felt strongly about protecting birds, especially the much-maligned birds of prey.⁷ The same motives prompted Florence to strive to keep the prices of her books low so more people could afford to use them.

Forest and Stream may have given up on the Audubon Society it had so ambitiously tried to create, but Florence still saw the sportsmen's magazine as a way to reach the public with her writing, to the horror of at least one purist of her acquaintance who protested because the magazine "uses rod and gun." Florence sent the editors a series entitled "How Birds Affect the Farm and Garden." The title is a good layperson's synonym for the then popular scientific term "economic ornithology," which was still her brother's charge as head of the U.S. Biological Survey. *Auk* called her series "a further excellent contribution to the literature of economic ornithology" that describes the losses caused by insects and the "usefulness of birds in holding the insect pests in check."⁸

Hart had a talent for story telling, and at home Florence laughed

*Louis Agassiz Fuertes, whom many consider an even better bird artist than Audu-
bon, shown here leading a bird walk in Ithaca, New York. The first book he illustrated was for Florence. (Reprinted from Peck's* A Celebration of Birds. *From the
Department of Manuscripts and University Archives, Cornell University Library.)*

with him and Elizabeth over many tales of those early days at the survey. One night he described the panic at the Washington post office
when a box arrived from Vernon Bailey in the field. The box, contain-
ing live snakes, had broken open. Hart dictated a letter to his field
naturalist, which he read after dinner to his wife and to Florence. "You
know that our relations with the Post-Office Department are not too
satisfactory or pleasant at the present time, and that incidents of this
character do not exactly tend to smooth over the irritation remaining
from former difficulties. . . . The advantage to this Division of receiving live snakes is not apparent to me and is not likely in any event to
compensate for the disadvantage of losing favor with our officials [and]
those of the Post-Office Department."[9]

Two days later Hart wrote to Vernon again. "This morning we received notice from the Post-Office Department that another live reptile
had escaped from the mails addressed to this Division. This time it
proved to be a Box Turtle instead of a Rattlesnake, for which we are
devoutly thankful, although we regret much that the incident has oc-

curred. In sending live turtles by mail they should be wrapped firmly
. . . in a tight, compact package which cannot by any possibility be
damaged, unless the turtle himself is smashed, which would require
a railway accident."[10]

Bailey had been collecting for Hart for ten years and been a paid
employee for almost as long. More than that, he was a close friend
who stayed at the Merriam home on occasion when he was in Washington and not in the field trapping turtles and snakes. But even a right-
hand man can make mistakes. Bailey was equally known for his quick
wit, but he always kept himself secondary to Hart. Whatever response
he made to Hart's letters is not recorded.

Florence might have written a book about these adventures, but she
left their telling to her brother. Instead, she kept her educational priority in mind and started a bird book for beginners so that they could
know the birds without shooting them.

Birds were still being shot, in even greater numbers than when Florence had started the Smith College Audubon Society and still for the
same reasons, primarily the profit to be made from selling them to
milliners. Profit, in fact, had become the key word. Professional hunters in growing numbers and with efficient techniques were making the
slaughter of birds even more complete. Local people like the Seminole
Indians in Florida had gone about it in traditional ways, but the new
breed of plume hunter was well organized and could systematically ex-
terminate a rookery in a day or two. A survey by the New York Zoological Society reported that birds across the country had declined by
almost *half* in the previous fifteen years, with the plume business a
major factor in their destruction.[11] Few of the fashionable ladies sport-
ing feathers on their bonnets knew — or cared — where they came from;
but to people like Florence, *live* birds were more important than fashion.

In the Capitol, unsuccessful efforts had been made to pass a bird
protection bill. Florence chose to work through channels she knew better than the halls of Congress. Like John Burroughs, she knew where
her place was and where she could be most effective. Burroughs's biographer noted that "what he might have done in a militant way for the
birds, was but a drop in the bucket to what he did do, in his own way,
for more than fifty years."[12]

So Florence went to work with the AOU Committee on the Protection of North American Birds. Olive Thorne Miller was another of its
distinguished members. Its formation was the first direct action taken
by ornithologists to combat the millinery trade in birds.[13] The cause
had appeared hopeless to some until the Audubon Society was reborn,
first in Massachusetts with William Brewster as president, and then

in a dozen other states in the next year. Florence was in the forefront of this resurgence of interest, bolstered by her newfound health and energy after summers in the West. She was especially attracted to the society's goal of educating school children as the true solution to the bird destruction problem.

Although Florence did not attend the next annual meeting of the AOU that fall, she sent a letter in which she "very forcibly expressed her sentiments on this subject," the chairman announced in reading it. Florence urged the AOU members to introduce bird study into the schools by teaching the teachers. "Field work, of course, should be the basis in every possible case," she concluded.[14]

Florence took up her pen to do her part to make this bird work possible. She wrote articles for children's magazines and several for the *Observer*, including a tribute to her friend Mrs. Miller. She also compiled her updated field notes and other magazine articles into *Birds of Village and Field*, "a bird book for beginners." With tongue firmly in her cheek, she wrote her Smith College classmates, "for variety I have been writing a bird book."

In the preface to her new book, Florence encouraged her readers by reviewing the advantages of bird study and reminding them that it is not a question of finding birds but of knowing their names once found — in other words, becoming friends with them. She also urged them to go out into the fields so they could see "the songsters in their homes" and go on to study birds more deeply.

The introduction to *Birds of Village and Field* is a short course in bird study:

> How to find a bird's name.— . . . Four things only are necessary — a scrupulous conscience, unlimited patience, a notebook, and an opera-glass. The notebook enables one to put down the points which the opera-glass has brought within sight, and by means of which the bird may be found in the key; patience leads to trained ears and eyes, and conscience prevents hasty conclusions and doubtful records. . . .

> Where to find birds.— Shrubby village door-yards, the trees of village streets and orchards, roadside fences, overgrown pastures, and the borders of brooks and rivers are among the best places . . .

> How to watch birds.— In looking for birds be careful not to frighten them away. As shyer birds are almost sure to fly before you in any case, the best way is to go quietly to a good spot and sit down and wait for them to return . . .

> How birds affect village trees, gardens, and farms.— Village improvement societies are doing a great deal to better and beautify our towns; but

in their attempts to preserve the trees against the plagues of insects that in late years have descended upon them, they sometimes seem to be baffled by the magnitude of their task. Their best allies in this work have hardly been recognized . . . The relation of birds to insects is only just becoming known.

For the observer who followed all of her suggestions, Florence included migration blanks from the Biological Survey to show how to set up a notebook. In today's scientific world such information seems commonplace, but in 1898 Florence entered new territory by suggesting careful observations, because at that time few birds had ever been studied exhaustively in the field.

When *Birds of Village and Field* was published, Florence received reviews in both *Auk* and in a new birding journal, the *Osprey* (April 1898), which praised her efforts — and didn't fail to mention her family connections. "On picking up this book one at once is aware of a very original little work. In it economic ornithology enters largely. Miss Merriam is a favored person in this field being a sister of Dr. C. Hart Merriam . . . Miss Merriam has given the new student of birds a very nice little book, and one which the ornithologist will lay down with the satisfaction of time well spent."

The teaching of botany had gotten a head start on birds. To help introduce bird study into schools, Florence wrote "How Our Birds Protect Our Trees" as part of the Arbor Day Annual of the New York Department of Public Instruction. Again, we take the information so much for granted today that introducing teachers to bird study with such basics seems inconceivable. "Trees are like great hotels, they are so alive with their busy little insect people . . . but fortunately there are not only hungry insects, but hungry birds, and the birds, knowing full well that the trees are among the best bird restaurants, flock to them eagerly."[15]

Continuing her educational efforts, Florence had helped to found the Audubon Society of the District of Columbia in 1897 and started its famous bird classes the following year.[16] One of its first projects was to encourage Mrs. George Colton Maynard to publish a book, *Birds of Washington*. No question about who was really behind it; in the preface Mrs. Maynard states, "Miss Florence A. Merriam has been the inspiration of the work from its inception."

Florence also wrote the introduction to the book, giving some familiar hints. "In these days we have not the excuse that it is necessary to shoot a bird to find out what it is. With museum collections and bird books to refer to, one has only to go to the field and watch the

Traveling west again for her health, Florence studied the birds at Cloud Cap Inn on Mount Hood in Oregon. Still standing, the inn is now used as an emergency shelter by mountain climbers. (From the collection of the Oregon Historical Society, Negative ORHI 58091.)

birds." Expanding her horizon and speaking from her own experience, Florence exhorted her readers, "Year by year as one's field experiences accumulate, the pleasures of bird study deepen. Not only does the acquaintance of one year become the friend of the next, but drawn more to the woods and fields by the delight of our new interest in the birds themselves, all unwittingly we come closer and closer to nature and are blessed by her healing touch." To her special delight, the book was introduced as a textbook in the schools.[17]

The following summer Florence finally had her first opportunity to take part in one of Hart's expeditions and served as a field assistant to study the flora and fauna of Mount Shasta, California. Hart was still expanding his theory of the distribution of wildlife into life zones. Another member of that party was Vernon Bailey, by then chief field naturalist for the survey. Their lives were becoming more intertwined.

The official group returned east after exploring Mount Shasta. Florence wanted to go south to Twin Oaks, but Hart felt that the September heat would undo the good the mountains had done her health. He advised her to go north to his favorite place, Cloud Cap Inn on Mount Hood in Oregon, and then to return east by train from Portland. She agreed. Although Florence didn't attend the AOU annual meeting that November, her paper on the Clark's nutcrackers and Oregon jays that she watched at the inn was read and then published in *Bird-Lore*.

"Cloud Cap Inn, the loghouse hotel fastened down with cables high on the north side of Mount Hood, is too near timber-line to claim a great variety of feathered guests, but . . . You could sit in the front doorway and when not absorbed in looking off on the three wonderful snow peaks — St. Helens, Rainier, and Adams — rising above the Cascade range, could watch Oregon Juncos, Steller's Jays, Oregon Jays, and Nutcrackers coming down to drink at the hydrant twenty feet away; while the Ruby Kinglet and White-crowned Sparrow, together with Townsend's Solitaire and other interesting westerners, moved about in the branches of the low timber-line pines; and Lewis' Woodpeckers, with their long, powerful flights, crossed over the forested canyons below. Crossbills had stayed around the house sociably for three weeks together, Mrs. Langille, the noble old mother of the mountaineers, told me. She said they would fly against the logs of the house and call till she went out to feed them."[18]

At the AOU meeting where this paper was read, Louis Agassiz Fuertes showed another talent, by special request: imitating the songs of birds. It was a trick he had learned in order to call the birds closer so that he could draw them. One of his favorites, which drew Florence's attention later, was described by Frank Chapman. "The reverent spirit with which an audience listened to his rendering of the song of the Hermit Thrush was a tribute alike to the bird and to its imitator."[19]

The Committee on Bird Protection also reported at the AOU meeting, reading some additional fervent comments by its absent member, Miss Merriam.[20] "The protection we give birds during the nesting season in the North is not wholly satisfactory if they are shot on migrating South, and, as is well known, many of our most valuable insectivorous birds are used for food in the South, and as soon as they begin migrating are subjected to a persistent fusillade. During one week in the spring of 1897, 2600 Robins, shot in North Carolina, were exposed for sale in one market stall in Washington."

She went on to tell what she had done about it. "Some valuable hints were given me last winter by the bad boys of a Summerville, S.C.,

school. . . . Believing that the only way to prevent killing is to create
an interest in the live bird, I preached merely by telling tales of my
bird friends, drawing out the boys to tell in turn what they knew. . . .
it was easy to stimulate their interest in the habits of the birds by picturing the delights of observing. This plan quickly bore fruit. A Chickadee was building near the house of one of the boys and one day the
child came to me full of enthusiasm — he had spent half a day watching
it. Graphically he explained the way it had worked . . . I felt the child
had given me the answer to the bad boy problem. *Prove to him that
the live bird is more interesting than the dead one,* or rather enable
him to prove it to himself."

At Summerville she also met an old friend and reported enjoying
the company of this hermit thrush who responded when she whistled
its song. "I thought of its wonderful summer song in the old home
woods and was thankful that it should keep hidden under the thickets
and it might perhaps escape the guns and get home at last."

Another way to educate the public was being born at this time. Although there were now seventeen state Audubon societies, the movement had no single voice. Seeing that need was ornithologist Frank
Chapman of the American Museum of Natural History, another devotee
of John Burroughs. Florence had first introduced the two men at Slabsides, the retreat that Burroughs had built for himself. As Florence and
Chapman walked in the woods and enjoyed the company of people
like Burroughs, her relatives wondered if something might develop between them, but nothing did.[21]

Chapman singlehandedly raised the money to create *Bird-Lore* as
a popular journal of ornithology. It was perhaps the most influential
act of his life, according to one conservationist, who also called Chapman the greatest popularizer of ornithology since Audubon. As a writer,
Chapman had recently published a *Handbook of Birds of the Eastern
United States,* as well as *Bird-Life,* a book for beginners with illustrations by Ernest Thompson Seton. In *Bird-Lore* (later named *Audubon
Magazine* and then just *Audubon*), Chapman saw a way to meet the
rising need for a journal "which should be addressed to observers rather
than to collectors of birds, or, in short, to those who study 'birds through
an opera-glass.'" Florence's book title had become a household word
in ornithology. In keeping with his enthusiasm and high standards,
Chapman announced in his first editorial that "with one or two exceptions, every prominent American writer on birds in nature has promised to contribute to *Bird-Lore* during the coming year."[22] Florence was
one of them. That first issue started with an article by John Burroughs
and a flashlight photograph Chapman took of him at Slabsides. For

young observers there was an article entitled "Our Doorstep Sparrow" by Florence, illustrated with a photograph of a little girl holding her doll in one hand and feeding a chipping sparrow in the other.[23]

While the presses were rolling with Chapman's first issue of *Bird-Lore* and Florence was still living at her brother's home in Washington, Hart received a visit that was to change his life. E. H. Harriman was a financier and railroad magnate, C. Hart Merriam a government scientist. Their paths had never crossed before, but each quickly found out about the other when Harriman proposed that Hart organize for him a group of scientists for an expedition to Alaska, all expenses paid, to include an eminent representative from each branch of natural history. Hart had never heard of such an offer and was convinced that the visitor in his office was a bit deranged, but Harriman had been given Merriam's name as the best person to do the job and he meant to succeed.[24] He asked Hart if he could bring his wife and daughter to his house that evening to discuss the venture further, and Hart agreed.

One can imagine that on such a social occasion Elizabeth Merriam and Florence would entertain the ladies in the parlor on the first floor of the large three-story brick house, while the two men discussed their business in Hart's upstairs study, replete with his mammal and artifact collections.[25] Florence's curiosity must have been piqued at the interchange. Hart's curiosity certainly was, and he agreed to meet Harriman again the next night with two of the men he proposed as participants.

The expedition was the most important one Hart ever headed, and the people he gathered for it are a blue book of foremost scientists and naturalists of the time, including many names familiar to Florence: John Burroughs, John Muir, Louis Agassiz Fuertes — on his first extended scientific expedition — and George Bird Grinnell. David Starr Jordan declined since he had been into that area twice previously.[26] Although Harriman's wife went along, no women scientists were included and apparently Florence was not invited. She had never learned to swim and was not comfortable on water, which may have influenced the decision.

A special train took the group west for the rendezvous with their waiting ship. Harriman and the Union Pacific Railroad president conferred on business matters in their "plush office on rails," while the scientists spent the week observing the terrain through the train windows. For some it was the first view of the West; for others like Hart, it was familiar country, and he entertained his companions with tales of his explorations in the Rockies. In their book about the expedition, William Goetzmann and Kay Sloan described the trip. "The train passed

mountain ranges which Merriam had personally named in his government surveys years before . . . Louis Fuertes was amazed at the rich
experience and travel claimed by his prestigious older companions. For
both the young bird artist and his new friend John Burroughs, the trip
through the west was a first-time journey into strange country, and the
two often sat together on the train, marveling at the vast stretches of
wilderness and pointing out birds to each other . . . By the end of the
expedition, Fuertes was affectionately referring to the old naturalist as
'Uncle John.'" Burroughs had made another convert.[27]

While her brother and many of their friends were off exploring Alaska
with the Harrimans, Florence stayed busy in Washington with her Audubon work. She gave "several valuable talks," the secretary reported in
Bird-Lore, including one to an audience of two hundred women at the
Washington Club, which not only created great enthusiasm but also
brought the society some new members.[28] No doubt the local milliners
also had a rush of business afterward on hats to be retrimmed without
feathers.

Florence also led bird walks that summer. While she was in New York
City, one walk brought out sixteen people — at 5:00 A.M.! — including
a blind woman with a horse and buggy and a man who came "on his
wheel."

Florence also took up bicycle riding and wrote to Collie, "We are
all flourishing this spring, thanks to the wheel. You'll never moult your
gray hairs and frisk with the lambkins till you sally forth on one. They're
great." After learning to wear divided skirts for horseback riding in
California, Florence was more comfortable in riding than the wife of
one senator, who noted in her diary, "Everyone rides now. James and
I have beautiful wheels, and I hope I shall learn to enjoy it, but the
divided skirt, for all its modesty, is so hideous and uncomfortable I
feel as if I were in a bag."[29]

Besides cycling, Florence had another interest that spring: the chief
field naturalist for the Biological Survey. They bicycled together through
the Washington parks, and along with the bird species she recorded
in her journal "a warm soft day when the flowers could reach up to
the earth. We found a sleepy little spring beauty getting ready for her
days of bloom." She spoke to Vernon of her enjoyment of rustling leaves
underfoot, but he replied that "it touched him differently, as all his life
he had been trying to go softly in the woods. As a boy he trained himself to go barefooted even over thorns to be able to go noiseless through
the woods."[30]

What could a government scientist like Vernon Bailey offer to Miss
Merriam? His modest pay was then little more than one hundred dol-

lars a month, but a house could be rented for about three hundred dollars a year.[31] They shared the most important priority — love of nature, and the enthusiasm and need to share that love with others. She knew all about the kind of life he led. She had watched her brother all her life and had known Vernon for years as he and Hart traveled and worked together on their mammal studies. And she had laughed with Hart about Vernon's sending live snakes that escaped in the Washington post office.

What could she offer to Mr. Bailey? She loved the scientific community in Washington that she had helped her sister-in-law to entertain over the past few years. She loved the West with an enthusiasm equal to his own. And she was eager to discover more of it with him. Her grandniece put it simply, "Vernon was perfect for her, a very simple gentleman. She fussed over details he wouldn't have. Vernon was very outgoing and everyone adored him. Auntie Florence basked in his glory."[32]

On December 16, 1899, Florence Augusta Merriam and Vernon Orlando Bailey were married. To play the wedding march at the ceremony she invited Mrs. Maynard, author of *Birds of Washington*, because she had a Hart ancestor.[33] Since Hart was her mother's maiden name, they were therefore distant relatives. At the age of thirty-six, the maiden aunt of the family announced to her Smith College friends that she had moved with her new husband to The Portner at the corner of U and 15th streets.

The year, and the century, ended with a burst of enthusiasm. Pioneered by Thoreau and Burroughs, nature writing had become an accepted part of American literature, and 70,000 bird books alone had been sold in the past six years.

At the time, nature was considered "the spiritual force which refreshed the inner man seeking the peace and quiet of the country 'beyond the trolley lines' without relinquishing the amenities of life," as one historian of urban life defined it.[34] Writers of the time didn't just talk about nature; they invited readers to experience it. Most were not scientific writers, but people who wanted to share with others the joy they knew in the outdoors. One who compiled some of their experiences himself stayed unidentified, but his preface speaks to this point. "We went, because they got no farther than the back-pasture fence. It was not to the woods they took us, but to nature; not a-hunting after new species in the name of science, but for new inspirations, new estimates of life, new health for mind and spirit."[35]

John Burroughs had also seen the dangers of staying too much in the city. "The city rapidly uses men up . . . A fresh stream of humanity is always setting from the country into the city; a stream not so fresh flows back again into the country . . . A nation always begins to rot first in its great cities, is indeed perhaps always rotting there, and is saved only by the antiseptic virtues of fresh supplies of country blood."[36] It was this fresh blood that Florence carried to the city readers.

Birds were important to this rural restoration because they recalled a pristine past and were part of the book of nature that so many of Florence's friends had also studied. For the biologists and earth scientists, birds were a part of the growing perception that human activities reverberate throughout all realms of nature, as author Robin Doughty so eloquently describes. Interest in humanity's relationship to the grand scheme of nature was shifting to the observation of nature. Today we are coming full circle once again to an interest in the larger scheme of which we are all so evidently a part.

By 1900 Florence was one of the major standard-bearers for women as writers and as career professionals as well. As the twentieth century advanced, naturalists like her would give way to the scientific specialists. As the century turned, however, creeping urbanization surrounded people, and they sought relief in the simple pleasures of nature. What more fitting symbol of nature is there than the bird? Bird study, bird books, organizations to protect birds were all on the move, and Florence Merriam Bailey was right there moving with them in the scientific and social whirl of Washington.

Meeting Spring Halfway, 1900–1901

Florence and Vernon Bailey walked into the new century together. They talked about the past and the struggles they had each had in trying to protect birds. And they talked about the future, of heading into the American Southwest for a summer of field study together.

The Biological Survey sent Vernon into the field to help farmers resolve problems with small mammals. The survey gave him a specific itinerary, and Florence went with him whenever she could to study the birds. This helped his work and at the same time provided her with additional field notes from which to write articles and perhaps a book or two. It was the springtime of their marriage, and soon, when the crocuses bloomed on the White House lawn nearby, spring would hasten their planning for the coming summer.

Meanwhile, Florence wrote an article for *St. Nicholas*, a popular children's magazine, about the spring bird migration. She was in good company. The same issue also featured articles by Theodore Roosevelt and by Mary Austin, who was later to share another public notice with her in their mutually beloved New Mexico.

In her article, Florence encouraged young people to watch for the return of familiar birds and especially to see what new birds came through, urging them to keep lists to compare the changes year by year. This was simply another way she could involve young people in bird study. There was still much to be done to protect wildlife before more species went the way of the buffalo and possibly the passenger pigeon and the egret.

Even before the century turned, milliners could see the handwriting of federal legislation on the walls of their workrooms. Those who hunted plumes for the market could also see that their turn was quickly coming and so they hunted even more, but many who hunted for sport worked to protect wildlife in response to their alarm at the decline in game. Most women were still not aware of the problems caused by their wearing feathers on their hats, and the fashion was still to be in full plumage. Besides, there were only two or three hairdressers in all of New York City before 1900, and big hats helped to hide long hair.[1] Moreover, since women couldn't vote, they had little reason to pay attention to the arguments in Congress.

Florence was still horrified at the hats she saw in the streets and parlors of Washington. She was in full sympathy with the editorial she read in the *Osprey* (April, 1900) lamenting that feathered hats were so common that no one noticed them and that women continued to bow to the "barbaric taste" of some milliners. Although some took a moderate stance that a few feathers from a few birds were acceptable to wear, others like Florence's fellow writer Mabel Osgood Wright thought that Audubon members should "join the total abstainers" because to wear feathers at all gave credence to the idea that it was good to do so, and many women didn't differentiate among the birds used.[2] Mrs. Wright recommended that ladies show their interest in birds by adopting the Audubon hat with ribbons or lace for trim and no feathers.

But legislative help for the birds was on the way. One bill finally passed Congress. It wasn't the whole answer — what law is? — but it dealt with interstate shipping of birds that had been killed in violation of state laws. Sales dropped significantly, particularly for seabird plumage, which only the year before had amounted to some two million birds. Nor was the traffic in birds all on the East Coast. If a white pelican skin from California brought one dollar in New York, imagine how many grebes — a small fraction of the size of a pelican — were shot by the hunter who reported making five hundred dollars a day![3] Encouraged by his new bride, Vernon used his influence in writing "Where the Grebe Skins Come From" for that thriving journal of popular ornithology, *Bird-Lore* (February, 1900).

Meanwhile, Florence's father lay gravely ill at his son Hart's home in Washington, true to his reputation for "punctilious honesty" to the end. Upon entering his room, Florence later recalled, she "was terrified to find him sitting up at a table bending low over his checkbook laboriously drawing a check — of a few dollars to pay a local grocery bill. In these days, when some of the best stores fail because their rich patrons do not pay their bills, it is good to remember."[4]

He died in February. The task of selling Homewood fell to Florence and Collie, helping their father's second wife. The sale circular described the property in believable words that bring back pictures of a different way of life, a different time, and a different style of advertising real estate.

HOMEWOOD
The Country Residence of the Late Hon. C. L. Merriam
Is To Be Sold

Located on the New York Central Railroad, between New York and the Thousand Islands, it is about an hour north of Utica, six hours from New York, three from Syracuse, and seven from Buffalo. The railroad station, Port Leyden, is a two and a half mile drive from Homewood; the post-office, Locust Grove, is one mile distant. The estate comprises a hundred acres of land, half in orchard, pasture, and meadow, and half in well preserved forest, through which wind bridle paths and extensive carriage drives.

The place is set back a quarter of a mile from the highway and is reached by two driveways, one following a picturesque ravine, the other leading through the woods to the house. The cut above shows the residence as it stands in the edge of the forest on the heights looking off over the Black River Valley to the blue hills of the Adirondacks. From the wide verandas one looks out on one side upon the lawns and gardens with their ornamental shrubs and low-branching Norway spruces, on the other through vistas that pierce the woods to the range of hills that faces the Adirondacks.

The house contains eleven living rooms, and a commodious billiard room, besides storage and servants' rooms, kitchen, laundry, bath, and basement, and is heated by a coal furnace and three fireplaces. Among a dozen other buildings on the place are a cottage for the farmer or coachman, a well-built horse and carriage barn, a large cow and hay barn, a workshop, tool, and storage house, ice house, woodsheds, and a building used formerly as museum, office, and studio. The buildings were put up without regard to expense and alone cost many times the sum for which the whole estate will now be sold.[5]

Before it could be sold, Homewood burned to the ground. It was truly only a memory. The original Merriam farm, Locust Grove, still remains. It's now called Homewood Farm, and not many years ago a sign hung outside advertising tourist rooms, a return to the purpose it had served a hundred years before, when Florence's grandfather kept an inn on the property.

Family affairs settled, Florence watched the cherry blossoms brighten Washington and redoubled her efforts to help the birds. She contributed an article to *Bird-Lore* on "How to Conduct Field Classes," based on her own experience beginning at Smith College. She reiterated the need for good field data, but one wonders if Hart reviewed *this* manuscript, for she twitted those who place importance on Latin names. "In learning the Latin names, let us not forget the live bird. The advance of ornithology, as well as our own good, demands this, for while the

Latin names are already set down in the books, the knowledge of the life histories of even our common birds is painfully meager." She urged field leaders to let their students watch a brightly colored bird like the scarlet tanager instead of a flock of warblers, and if possible to pay repeat visits to a young family of birds to see the various tasks of their life. "I remember with delight of a class of Miss Porter's girls at Farmington over the discovery of a Kingfisher's nest in the river bank."[6] There was that kingfisher again. Did she remember the ones her schoolmate had admired on the city lady's hat? Perhaps so, for she was still trying to repay their deaths by teaching about live birds.

A few months later, Olive Thorne Miller published an article entitled "The Study of Birds—Another Way." While crediting field classes like those Florence had described, she explained her own larger view of bird study: "to lead the student to Nature herself; to acquaint him with the delights to be found in woods and fields, and the benefit to mind and heart, as well as to body, of close friendship with the great Mother. This can be accomplished only by each person alone."[7]

Between the appearance of the two articles, Florence and Vernon were happily immersed in a full summer of field work. From April to September they traveled, first by train to Texas where they studied the wildlife to the Mexican border and then into the Territory of New Mexico. In writing Hart, she recalled her earlier trips west. "How thankful I am not to be coming back to it alone! But all the years of loneliness and wandering, which have been brought back so vividly by the misery of the poor 'lungers' alone on the train, seem now a part of another existence, for all the pain and weariness of my life have gone, and it is filled with peace and happiness. It seems almost wicked to be so happy when the world is so full of sorrow."

After New Mexico they went on to California for more field work as well as a visit to Twin Oaks, where she introduced her new husband to her Uncle Gustavus and his family. They stayed at La Mesita, the home that her father had built, and posed for photographs outside the front door. Large trees had already grown up around the house she had decorated with eucalyptus branches just a few years before.

Florence described this summer of adventure tersely in the next annual letter to her Smith College classmates. "My husband and I spent three months in Texas doing Biological Survey field work, and made an intensely interesting wagon trip across the prairies to the Mexican line. Then we crossed over to California and spent three months more with a pack outfit in the high Sierra. The western girls know what that means, and the eastern will if they read Mrs. Ernest Seton-Thompson's

On their honeymoon summer (1900) of studying western birds and mammals, Florence and Vernon Bailey stayed at La Mesita. (From the collection of Mr. and Mrs. Sheldon Gustavus Merriam.)

Woman Tenderfoot in the Rockies. It was a glorious summer, rich in experiences and interests."

Grace Seton-Thompson's book, to which she referred, had just been published. In it she told that the year after they were married, her naturalist husband had announced that "the mountain madness was again working in his blood, and that he must go west and take up the trail for his holiday." Being a dutiful wife, she went along, explaining the situation in her foreword to the book: "Of course, plenty of women have handled guns and gone to the Rocky Mountains on hunting trips — they were not among my friends. However, my imagination was good, and the outfit I got together for my first trip appalled that good man, my husband, while the number of things I had to learn appalled me."

Her reason for writing unabashedly about her adventure had a more direct lure for the sofa-sitting eastern woman whom Florence had also addressed. "The events related really happened . . . and this is why, being a woman, I wanted to tell about them, in the hope that some going-to-Europe-in-the-summer-woman may be tempted to go west instead." She described what she took to make herself comfortable. For sleeping: a piece of waterproof brown canvas, one rubber air bed, and a sleeping bag. Florence later devised a sleeping bag by dipping sheets in beeswax, then painting them green so they wouldn't show the dirt. Instead of using an air bed, she learned from Vernon how to dig a hip hole underneath, to keep her back straight while she slept.[8]

Mrs. Seton-Thompson had other suggestions for roughing it in comfort. Since no costume was available yet for riding horseback astride, she had designed one, and she provided a detailed drawing for her readers to take to their dressmakers to copy. "Then you will want a lamb's wool night wrapper, a neutral grey or brown in color, a set of heavy night flannels, some heavy woollen stockings and a woollen tam o'shanter large enough to pull down over the ears. A hot-water bag, also, takes up no room and is heavenly on a freezing night when the wind is howling through the trees and snow threatens. N.B.—See that your husband or brother has a similar outfit, or he will borrow yours." She also described the wilderness and assured her readers that "a summer in the Rockies would enable you to cheat time of at least two years, and you would come home and join me in the ranks of converts from the usual summer sort of thing." Mrs. Seton-Thompson's party arrived by train in Idaho and then started on horseback for Jackson Hole, Wyoming, "miles over gradually rising hills, with the huge mass of the Tetons looming ever nearer, and the next day we climbed the Teton Pass. There is nothing extraordinary about climbing the Teton Pass—to tell about. We just went up, and then we went down. It took six horses half a day to draw us up the last mile—some twenty thousand seconds of conviction on my part (unexpressed, of course . . .) that the next second would find us dashed to everlasting splinters. And it took ten minutes to get us down! Of the two, I preferred going up."[9]

"Around us," Mrs. Seton-Thompson continued, "sighed the mighty pines of the limitless forest. Hundreds of miles away, beyond the barrier of nature, were human hives weary of the noise and strife of their own making."[10] No wonder Florence wanted her college friends to read Grace Seton-Thompson's book. Had she herself written a descriptive adventure tale, it would have sounded very similar. But she would rather write about birds and leave the travel description to others.

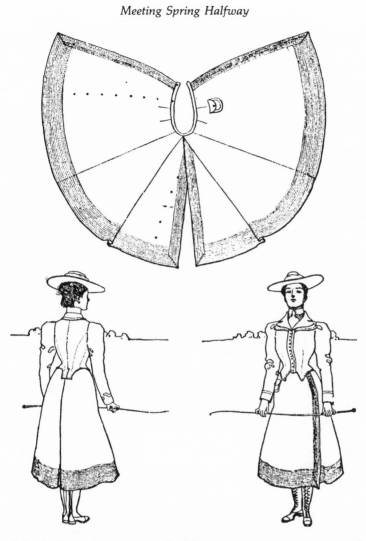

One of the challenges for women in the West was an appropriate costume for riding horseback. In her book, A Woman Tenderfoot, Grace Seton-Thompson described her solution in detail so readers could show the design to their dressmakers. (This item is reproduced by permission of The Huntington Library, San Marino, California.)

Florence's major writing about that summer's adventures went into a serialized article in *Condor* some years later, perhaps triggered by the response to her earlier shorter accounts. "Meeting Spring Half Way," abridged below, was one of her most popular magazine articles.

"'Texarkana,' the porter announced to a curtained aisle on that April morning. Texarkana! We raised the shades to find that in the night winter had been left behind, spring had come in Texas, spring with its birds and flowers and green things growing. 'The trees are all green!' a boyish northern voice exclaimed with fervor born of snowbanks passed in the Alleghenies. And so they were, all green, not with the dark heavy green of summer's fulfillment but with the delicate green of the first blush of spring promise; a green that is almost white with the young hickory leaves, a tender pink with the oaks, making the woodland pools reflect a veritable fairyland forest. Blooming apple and peach trees gathered butterflies, leaf-crowned oak tassels swayed in the wind, and as the train passed through a stand of pine we breathed the velvety air of sulphuring pineries — nature was full of rich promise.

"Through the open windows came the spring songs of Tomtits, Cardinals, and Mockingbirds, and as if to furnish appropriate setting, there passed in rapid succession cotton fields with last year's bolls hanging, darky shanties flanked by outside chimneys, groups of pickaninnies, colored women in sunbonnets driving mule plows, and oak woods in which small brown pigs rooted for acorns. The handsome red horse-chestnut blooming in the woods recalled Audubon's famous painting of the Carolina Wren.

"[On] Corpus Christi Bay, where we stopped for a little work, the prairie cover was a mixture of mesquite, cactus, and wind-compacted chaparral. The flora was Mexican, strange thorny bushes being interspersed with brilliant flower masses. The fences were made by pitchforks with cactus pads, the pads laid along a line on the ground rooting and branching till they grow to high impenetrable fence walls that in their season become beautiful with large yellow tuni flowers. When spring comes on the prairies of Texas, even the fences burst into bloom.

"The song that dominated part of the brushy prairie was a new one to my ear and became the song of songs to me. The Cassin Sparrow! It was on an ordinary sunny Texas morning that I walked out into ordinary chaparral prairie in an every day mood, all ignorant of the existence of *Peucaea cassini*, when lo! from the grown bushes in front of me up sprang a little winged creature, a 'blithe spirit,' an embodiment of the deepest joy of life, and with head raised and wings outspread, from a well spring undefiled poured out a song that held both the gladness of the blooming prairies and all the joy and hope of his mate on the nest.

"The shore line from Corpus Christi Bay south afforded many novel sights. A line of pasture fence posts that extended thirty or forty rods out into the shallow water of the bay, were favorite perches of a variety of water birds. Three Cormorants, a Great Blue Heron, and two Brown Pelicans made up the row one day, the Pelicans making droll figures like china toys with heads erect and chins drawn in. Formerly, we were told, a thousand Pelicans nested on a small island twelve miles from Corpus Christi, but the colony had been entirely broken up.

"We began our 360-mile drive from Corpus Christi to the Mexican boundary and return on April 24, 1900, and that day made 22 miles to Petranilla Creek. One section of prairie had miles of pink evening primroses stretching as far as the eye could see. In the mesquite orchards the beautiful trees suggested the pepper trees of California. Though not yet decorated with their delicate tasselated yellow blooms, two trees that we saw bore brilliant blossoms — scarlet-breasted Vermilion Flycatchers!

"Jack rabbits were the only animals seen on the open prairie but on the clay banks of Petranilla Creek when we made camp, tracks of coon, wild cat, and coyote, besides the excitingly strange tracks of armadillo — curious round, stumpy nail prints — suggested many stories. Big armadillo burrows were also found on our trip, slanting under cactus roots, and under tufts of marsh grass. How ardently I wished for a sight of the ancient armored beasts!

"Our second night's camp was on King's Ranch, one of the largest cattle ranches of Texas, where we met the Brownsville and Alice stage road and turned south across the rich stock range. The cattle king was at that time a cattle queen who spent her winters in New York, leaving her superintendent in charge. At his advice we camped at Santa Gertrude, as two windmills and their water tanks were called. A vivid green circle enclosed by mesquites branching to the ground with abundant water made indeed a camping place to commemorate a saint. Quail, a pair of Cardinals, and a pair of Thrashers carrying food showed their appreciation of the tanks, which were evidently well known in the region. As we had been warned regarding fellow travelers near the Mexican border, when a party of dusky faced men rode in and proceeded to camp on the opposite side of our enclosure, I made sure that our firearms were fully in evidence and valorously determined to protect the camp from midnight Mexican daggers! Terrors of the night! The first Mexican to cross our camp ground, well after sunrise, was a mild mannered lad with a piece of drawn work to exchange for coffee and sugar for his breakfast! Nevertheless, on leaving the windmills we had to abandon the Alice and Brownsville stage road we had been enjoying as, beyond that point, the stage drivers locked the gates behind them to prevent horse thieves crossing private pastures.

"Before sundown we passed our next landmark, Santa Rosa Ranch — the names marking the road between Corpus Christi and Browns-ville are those of ranches, windmills, or motts ["the local name for a small grove on the open prairie," she defines elsewhere] — and after driv-ing up to the [wagon] hubs through freshet lakes we camped for the night between two runs, much to the dissatisfaction of the old Texas camp man who said that he had been caught that way in winter, camp-ing beside a dry wash and having to stand up to his knees in water half the night! The only excitements of the night, however, proved to be the passing of birds in the darkness, the fine chip of small migrants, the squawk of Black-crowned Night Herons, and low over us the thrill-ing swishing of heavy wings, probably those of Wild Turkeys.

"[Another day] At last the low line of trees we had been wearily traveling toward for hours was reached and proved a veritable oasis in the sand belt. An oak mott, San Ignatia by name, raised only a few feet above the general level but made up of large old live oaks that dispensed cool shade through the hot hours and offered shelter to birds from all the region round about. When the aviary had settled down for the night a rattlesnake, discovered too near our tent, had to be shot, and at the report of the gun an amazingly large flock of Scissor-tails burst out of the tree, proving what the oak mott meant on the treeless prairie.

"The stars came out so temptingly that we carried our sleeping bags out under them on the open prairie. To sleep under the stars on the open, level prairie — the dream of years was to be realized at last! As if from a raft on the ocean the entire circle of your horizon is star-filled sky! As night closes in around you, you seem to be alone with the stars. Mortal no longer, you become a point in the universe. All human cares, all the littleness of human life drops from you, the great universe lies close around you.

"After our long journey through country whose occasional houses were Mexican hackells [jacals, a type of mud-and-stick construction], when approaching Brownsville we looked twice at an unfamiliar ap-pearing building and then exclaimed, 'Why, that house has boards on it!' so quickly had our eyes accepted Mexican standards.

"From Brownsville we ferried across the Rio Grande to Matamoras, the river, which was rising rapidly, swirling around cutting its banks at such a rate that it was plain to see how it had cut its way down from Rio Coloral. On both sides of the river the chief crops were then cotton, corn, and sugar cane, but oranges, lemons, bananas, and guavas were also seen growing. Both Brownsville and Matamoras were formerly towns of great wealth, Matamoras having been the distributing center during the Mexican war; but externally the flat-roofed, one story adobes with their softly tinted walls and blinds were merely characteristic Mexican dwellings. The iron gratings for doors and windows may have hinted at vaults and safes of days of opulence but they also bespoke the southern climate where doors and windows must needs be open at night. The plaza and market place were characteristic and the picturesque old cathedral whose chimes could not be rung without the payment of a tax had bullet holes left from war times.

"With all this foreign setting it was a surprise to find an enthusiastic botanist, a woman connected with the Presbyterian mission, actually teaching botany to the Spanish Senoritas. Would that some one could have taught them the birds!

[Campsites were named for the Baileys' adventures.] "There was also one Rattlesnake Camp, though two earned the name, and the shooting of a third rattler coiled in a trail almost led to serious consequences. The shot roused a band of range cattle, the most dangerous animals one encounters in the west, and with their keen hunting instinct they took after the hunter, who only escaped them by dodging into the chaparral as they came charging furiously along, heads and tails up. A Texas long horn at one ranch that we passed had a spread of horn measuring about five feet, for the old Spanish stock which has nearly run out has gone to horns, in southern Texas.

"While the bulk of migration had passed, on May 6, two Whooping Cranes were seen going through their maneuvers in the sky.

"The prairie flowers as we went north also underwent a remarkable change. Although we made the whole trip of about 360 miles in 17 days, not only had the great waves of migration passed north but in places the prairie carpet had changed completely during the interval. An entire set of social plants had gone out of bloom and been replaced by others.

"But one gets to expect big things of the prairie — waves of flowers, passing throngs of birds, overhead the starry host of heaven, and round about the encompassing clouds. One moonlight night we camped among huisache trees and slept on a bed of daisies, and after the moon set the sky grew fuller and fuller of stars till one could but marvel at their myriad host. Silent night! What infinite peace Nature offers her children!"

8

A Bird in the Handbook, 1900–1902

As FLORENCE SAT at her desk in Washington, looking out the upstairs window at the snow blowing in from the north, she was reminded of the flock of white pelicans she had watched maneuvering in the north wind in Texas last summer. She reminisced with Vernon about crossing those plains whitened by daisies and by the Indian wheat "whose miniature grain the pocket mice carry home in their pouches."

Vernon had fallen in love with the desert country of the Southwest early in his career with the Biological Survey, when he first explored Death Valley in late 1890. Hart had joined him there the next spring. "With my old camp wagon, a fresh team of mules, our two saddle horses, and a good camp man, Dr. Merriam and I made a rapid reconnaissance . . . In a month and a half we covered on horseback 960 miles [measured by the odometer on the wagon wheel], collected 240 mammals and a considerable number of birds, reptiles, and plants; and, most important, noted every change of life zone limits on every slope traversed."[1]

One episode Vernon recounted was Hart's first encounter with a sidewinder. He jumped off his horse to shoot it, and as he reloaded his gun before picking up the snake, "I told him to look out, he was standing on another one. He looked down and gave one jump, then turned and shot that one, so we got two good specimens while he was off his horse."[2] Hart may also have remembered that when he later wrote to Vernon to stop sending him live snakes through the U.S. mails.

Fifty years later, when asked if he would like to see Death Valley the modern way—by air, Vernon demurred. "Such a trip does not appeal to me. When I go back I want to travel over the Valley floor so that I may see all the things that live there and recognize old friends in plants and animals. I hope to return once more to the Valley on a camping expedition and, just as I did fifty years ago, make my bed at night on the good, warm earth."[3] Vernon preferred to sleep on the ground whenever he camped out, until the day he died, but Florence came to prefer a few creature comforts when camping in her later years.

By 1900 Florence had already explored a bit of the Southwest herself in Utah and Arizona, before she had married Vernon. And the area around Twin Oaks that she explored on her "bronco" had more in common in many ways with the Southwest than with coastal California. So it is small wonder that both Florence and Vernon enjoyed his new assignment to study in depth first the state of Texas and then the Territory of New Mexico. They looked forward to the next summer even while the snow was falling in Washington. They spent several seasons of detailed field work in the Southwest, expanding on the small amount of that country they had covered during their honeymoon summer of 1900. It was a systematic coverage of the country typical of Hart's meticulous itineraries for his field staff.[4]

While Florence stayed in Washington during the early part of the field season of 1901, Louis Agassiz Fuertes joined Vernon in Texas to supply drawings for his survey. Fuertes found this experience quite a contrast to the Harriman expedition with all its luxuries. Life in the field was very simple for the Baileys. They trusted the animals and slept soundly without watchfires. "Too much trouble and unnecessary," Vernon dismissed them, to which Florence added that they were "for tenderfeet."[5] As Fuertes described it, Vernon's outfit consisted of "a few horses and mules, a chuck wagon, and one man to cook and do camp chores. [Vernon] liked to travel light and live hard; their rations were as simple as they could well be—and all the coffee was burnt the first day out." Before the summer was over, Vernon and the young artist were lifelong friends. As Vernon expressed it, "There is no place like camp to get acquainted with and appreciate the sterling qualities of a real man."[6]

The object of the trip for Fuertes was the Chisos Mountains at the big bend of the Rio Grande, now in the center of Big Bend National Park.[7] The park was just being established at the time of Vernon's death many years later, and one of the major landmarks was named Vernon Bailey Peak in his memory and in recognition of the pioneering biological survey work he had done there.

At the end of the summer of 1901 Vernon and Fuertes surveyed the Carlsbad Cavern area, providing information on the birds later used to support the preservation of the cavern as a national monument.[8] Florence joined them there and conferred with Fuertes on drawings for the new book she was writing. The Baileys welcomed Fuertes like the son they never had. In spite of the lack of luxuries, which he had never really experienced anyway except on that expedition to Alaska, Fuertes shared their approach to simple living in camp. Frank Chapman described him as "an experienced woodsman, a good packer, a capital cook, a master hand with tools, who could mend anything, and in adversity and sickness no mother could have been more tender."[9]

After leaving the Southwest, where Fuertes stayed on to visit friends, the Baileys went farther west. At Lake Tahoe they were joined by Hart and John Muir, who spent evenings around the campfire repeating his story of Stickeen and many of the experiences they would later read in his book, *Boyhood and Youth*. He also traced for them the glacier's course as they made their way down into the Yosemite Valley he knew so well.

By the time they had finished their first summer alone together in the field, there was no doubt that Florence and Vernon sparked in one another the creative talent each had. They usually maintained separate writing projects, although later they did collaborate on two books. Their interests, while overlapping, took separate avenues: Vernon mainly studied mammals, and Florence kept to her birds. But they often wrote together, and later they arranged their rolltop desks back to back in the study of their Washington home, which they built that winter.

Also while they were back in Washington, Florence began a new approach to education, introducing bird study into the popular Chautauqua course. At the first conference of state Audubon societies held in November, one of the speakers was Frank Chapman, whose editorship of *Bird-Lore* had done so much to foster the Audubon growth.[10] To illustrate "What We Can Do for Our Members," he cited the remarkable success of Florence's Chautauqua work, urging the Audubon societies to use their organization to form such classes locally. Conversely, Florence urged those in the Chautauqua Literary and Scientific Circles to study Audubon material to supplement their field work.[11]

More help for the birds was on the way. In 1901 a friend of Hart's since boyhood, as well as of Vernon and John Burroughs, took office as president of the United States. Theodore Roosevelt was committed by personal philosophy and actions to saving what he could of wild America. Hart and his family were invited to many presidential social events, and Theodore Jr. joined Vernon in some field work for the survey. Vernon and young Ted had bicycled together outside of Washington, where Vernon taught the boy how to trap wild animals and then to prepare them as specimens.[12]

On the local level, the District of Columbia Audubon Society began field meetings for the public, instead of only for teachers, with Florence as the prime mover. Nationally, with Hart as its president, the AOU took the bold step of including women as members rather than just associates. Florence, as well as Olive Thorne Miller and Mabel Osgood Wright, was raised to that status as a result of her numerous writings.[13] If Florence's recognition was in any way due to her brother, there was never a hint in her lifetime that she resented that situation, as much as feminist ideas today might suggest it. Instead, she continued to admire Hart and to remain always his close ally. When she was listed in *Who's Who in America* in 1900, she was identified as an author, with the rather curious notation — by today's standards but not by hers — "the sister of C. Hart Merriam." Perhaps in deference to him, or to her husband, she was not even listed as "interested in ornithology" until after their deaths many years later.

Florence was more interested in pursuing her study than in being recognized for it. She had her own priorities to accomplish. She didn't even take time to write up her Southwest field notes for journal publication because she was involved in her first major writing project, a *Handbook of Birds of the Western United States*. Although publication was still a year away and she had another summer of field work ahead of her in the Southwest, the sheer effort of compiling all of the data took many snowy winter days in the Baileys' Washington apartment. She also spent many months studying skins in the "cramped but delightful old bird gallery of the Smithsonian, receiving generous help from Mr. Ridgway." Like her brother, Robert Ridgway was an early protégé of Spencer Baird at the Smithsonian.[14]

Hart encouraged her in this project, as he did in all her writing, but this one was especially important to him. He knew that the men under him in the Biological Survey were too busy doing field work — at his own untiring pace — to write such a book. He also knew that no one had the experience with birds in the field that his own sister had. She had already spent four summers in the West, three specifically to study birds and one of those under his personal direction. Frank Chapman's *Handbook of Birds of the Eastern United States*, published in 1895, was already a standard text and a complement to it was sorely needed.

Florence's desk became increasingly full of information that Hart and Vernon supplied from the Biological Survey, including illustrations of birds. She drew on every resource known, few as they were, and quoted freely from the magazine articles and meager lists that had been prepared. But as she herself had written, very little was known about live birds, and her own field notes were her most important resource. The list of references she cited in the introduction forms an impressive collection even by today's more sophisticated standards of scientific research. This handbook was no small task. When complete, it contained almost six hundred pages and as many illustrations.

Florence once again had the benefit of drawings by Fuertes, some newly completed for this work and some repeated from her earlier books. She also drew on other artists and publications, primarily from the Smithsonian Institution and from the Biological Survey. Hart provided an article on life zones. Although he had solidified his theory only a few years before, it had been quickly adopted and by then was generally accepted. Her husband contributed an article on collecting and preparing birds, nests, and eggs in support of *scientific* collecting that would add information about birds.

In essence, Florence combined the best scientific knowledge and the best field experience of the time into one field guide. Later guides have left out most of the field experience information and relegated that to other texts. Birders have been the losers, because prose descriptions help to bring the birds alive when you're viewing them in the field. For example, she described the hermit thrush's nest "in bushes or low trees, 3 to 10 feet from the ground; partly made with moss." Then she told of its food: "Flies, ants, weevils, and other insects and berries. As you travel through the spire-pointed fir forests of the western mountains, you know the thrush as a voice, a bell-like sublimated voice, which, like the tolling of the Angelus, arrests toil and earthly thought. Its phrases can be expressed in the words Mr. Burroughs has given to the eastern hermit, '*Oh, spheral, spheral! oh, holy, holy!*' and the first strain arouses emotions which the regularly falling cadences carry to a perfect close. The fine spirituality of the song, its serene uplifting quality, make it fittingly associated with nature's most exalted moods, and it is generally heard in the solemn stillness of sunrise, when the dark fir forest is tipped with gold, or in the hush of sunset, when the western sky is aglow and the deep voice rises from its chantry in slow, soul-stirring cadences, *high-up-high-up, look-up, look-up.*"[15]

Today's field guides have traded prose that appealed to the ear for the more visual color maps of distribution and for color renditions of the species. Information on nesting and food is sparse if given at all. But then, the pace of birding — and life — has changed considerably, or we like to think it has. Birders today rarely sit quietly for several hours to observe nests or even stand still long enough to read a page of prose, and so they no longer usually carry large handbooks when they go "a-birding."

Florence's book was hailed by the press and widely reviewed. It remained a standard manual for nearly half a century, serving both amateur and professional bird students.[16] Reviewing it in *Bird-Lore*, Frank Chapman called it "the most complete text-book of regional or-

nithology which has ever been published." That was high commendation indeed, since Chapman himself had authored another major regional
text. His words were a publisher's delight, and Houghton Mifflin lost
no time in appropriating them for an ad in a later issue.

In *Auk*, Dr. Allen extolled her *Handbook* as "thoroughly scientific
yet not unduly technical" and its author for her "rare opportunities for
personal observation of the birds in life." Walter Fisher added further
publicity for the book by featuring it first in the Editor's Book Shelf
of reviews in the *Condor*, where he commented that the *Handbook*
"will certainly exert a very wholesome influence on bird-study in the
west, no doubt stimulating to good work many who, heretofore for
lack of proper literature, have felt their enthusiasm scarcely equal to
the task of mastering our perplexing avifauna."

Within a year *Bird-Lore* editorialized, "We learn with much pleasure
that Mrs. Florence Merriam Bailey's 'Handbook of Birds of the Western United States' has already reached its second edition."[17] During its
publishing history, the book went through at least seventeen printings,
which included several revisions but never the major rewrite that Florence once envisioned. Modifications were limited mainly to updating
bird names as the AOU updated its own official terminology through
its Check-list.

It would be difficult to begin listing the authors who have quoted
or even acknowledged Florence's *Handbook*. Almost every book on
birds seemed to include it among the credits, including guides by that
most famous writer of bird books, Roger Tory Peterson. He had found
the early guides, like hers and Chapman's, too complicated and difficult to use, which led him to develop his successful compact field guides
thirty years later, referenced with due respect for his predecessors.

The *Handbook* also served in the wider context of natural history.
Dr. William Temple Hornaday of the New York Zoological Society
gratefully acknowledged his indebtedness to it, as well as to papers on
mammals by Hart and by Vernon, in his *American Natural History*.
Turnabout is always just compensation; his survey had helped to define
the real need to protect birds just a few years before.

The *Handbook* also helped to lead many naturalists to the Baileys'
doorstep. Among them was a young biologist, Olaus J. Murie, who
was to become one of the Biological Survey's most able assistants. Murie
later recalled, "My first knowledge of Mrs. Bailey was my purchase
of her Handbook of Birds of the Western United States, the blue-covered
edition of 1908. I have just taken this battered copy from the book-
shelf . . . throughout the book, following the necessary technical de-

scriptions, are the delightful informal accounts of the birds, accounts that help to make each bird something of flesh and blood, a living thing. . . . she did her best to bring the outdoors into its pages."[18]

Besides bringing the outdoors into her pages, with this book Florence showed once and for all that following birds into the woods was not the "eccentricity of conduct" for a woman that one early ornithologist had pronounced it.[19]

Enchanted Birdland, 1903–1906

NEW MEXICO has become known as the Land of Enchantment, but in 1903 it was thought of — if at all — primarily as the Land of Cowboys and Indians. Those were the days of the cattle barons and of the first romantic interest by artists and then scientists in the Pueblo Indians, who posed for their portraits and shared their cultures and their crafts. The Indians had had a long history of dealing with "white men," for the Spaniards had been there more than three hundred years, long before the Pilgrims landed at Plymouth. But the New Mexico mountains were still mysterious unknown territory to most Americans, penetrated mainly by fur traders, timbermen, and a few adventurers.

Vernon Bailey had a special challenge in 1903: to make a detailed biological survey of the Territory of New Mexico, part of which could provide enough scientific information to create a forest preserve in the mountains north of Taos. Theodore Roosevelt was eager to protect the vanishing wild parts of the country he presided over, and Hart was close enough to him to know that he needed a good technical basis on which to push through his protective legislation. So Hart turned naturally to his chief field man in the Biological Survey to provide it, a man who, happily, also loved the Southwest and enjoyed nothing better than spending the summer field season there.

With Florence's new *Handbook of Birds of the Western United States* now off the presses, she was free once again to join Vernon for the summer and to add to his survey by her own personal studies of the birds of New Mexico. She was the only woman naturalist known to be working in the territory during that period, and she and Vernon kept their field notes independently.[1] In fact, she always worked independently. As one naturalist put it, independent women didn't suffer in the West. She could be exactly who she was. Because her position was without precedent, she was an object of curiosity but not of scorn. When men or women keep to their own business, they are generally accepted, now

*Vernon Bailey photographed these Taos Indians on horseback while conducting
a survey, near their New Mexico pueblo, in order to protect the forest for the tribe.
(National Anthropological Archives, Smithsonian Institution Photo No. 1910-c-4.)*

as then. As she walked on one mountain trail, an old prospector came
up behind her. His only comment, noted in her journal, was on her
field glasses: "There's a lady carries her eyes in her fist." Perhaps that's
one reason why she always loved the West. To her it was a very real
place to be, where she had work to do and she did it. That was all,
and it was enough.

At the time of her visits, Florence envisioned writing magazine articles and using her field notes to update the *Handbook*. Circumstances
led her to a far greater task—a definitive book on the birds of New
Mexico, completed more than twenty years later but based primarily
on these early years of field study with Vernon.

Their earlier time in the territory had been limited to a short visit
to the flat plains of the southeastern portion, with one side trip into

the Sacramento Mountains at Cloudcroft. Ever since then, they had been "haunted by visions of New Mexico's noble coniferous forests."[2] The northern mountains were new to them both, and through the long Washington winter they looked forward to exploring that new enchanted land. The mountains there are more akin to Colorado's high Rockies, with 10,000-foot-plus peaks, largely inaccessible pine forests, and deep canyons. The high plateau below the mountains is furrowed with eroded arroyos, dry except in flash floods not uncommon after summer thunderstorms over mountains miles away.

During the spring in Washington, while Vernon prepared for the summer's work, Florence taught bird classes for the local Audubon Society. The schools were by then well equipped with collections of bird skins and books like Mrs. Maynard's *Birds of Washington* and had enough trained teachers to lead classes. So the society turned to helping the public with a six-session course that included talks on "distribution and classification, migration, economic and esthetic values, color, song, nests and eggs, and bird protection."[3] The outdoor meetings of the class were held at the Zoological Park so the students could examine the birds on exhibition. Florence was the only woman instructor for the fifteen enrollees. Two years later enrollment had doubled. By the end of the decade, with Florence in charge and separate classes for beginners and advanced students, it was over two hundred.

There was still grave need for education about birds. Hats had reached even more absurd proportions, sometimes 36 inches across. Elevator doors and telephone booths couldn't even accommodate them. Although tearooms placed their tables farther apart, a man seated behind a woman often swatted flies on the back of his neck only to find that the tickle came instead from the tip of a feather on her hat.[4]

Florence had just turned forty, and her writing was having an increasing effect on the bird world. She looked every inch the "earnest doer" in a portrait published in 1904. Attired in her tucked white wedding dress and long gloves, she hardly looked like a woman who had just returned from a summer in the high Rocky Mountains of Colorado and New Mexico. In publishing her photograph, the *Condor* also honored her career. "There are probably few writers who have exerted a more wholesome influence on the trend of popular ornithology than Mrs. Florence Merriam Bailey, whose 'Birds Through an Opera Glass' (1889) has been one of the most successful and effective books of its class. Mrs. Bailey has had the advantage of a wide and varied field experience throughout the West, as well as in the eastern states, and her 'A-Birding on a Bronco,' like all of her works, reflects an intimate acquaintance with the live bird."[5]

In this 1904 portrait Florence bears little resemblance to the rough-and-ready ad-venturer who studied the birds on western mountains. (From the collection of Florence Merriam Youngberg.)

Her beautifully tucked dresses and heirloom jewelry were left behind, though, and her keen powers of observation were soon brought actively into play when she and Vernon again boarded the train and headed west. Their itinerary in New Mexico would challenge the hardiest young mountaineer today, although at least one of those two forty-ish travelers was decidedly not in that category. As detailed later in her book on New Mexico birds:

> After collecting at Santa Rosa and vicinity from May 19 to June 9, 1903 . . . they started by wagon to the northeastward, collecting near Cuervo, June 9–14, camping near Montoya, June 14–20, and exploring to the top of the Staked Plains, 1,000 feet higher. Moving camp to a little north of Pajarito Creek on June 20, on June 22 they rode 12 miles northeast to the Canadian River, on June 23 proceeding north to the mouth of Cuervo Creek, then west to Cabra Springs, and thence north 15 miles, June 25, to the top of Mesa Yegua. They returned to Cabra Springs, June 28, west to Gallinas Springs, June 29, and by way of Casous and Anton Chico to La Cuesta, June 30, and on to Ribera, July 1 . . .
>
> The Baileys' work in the Pecos Mountains began at Ribera, July 1–3, from which point the Pecos River was followed up to a camp between Rowe and Pecos City, where a night's trapping was done, July 3–4. Then the ridge at Glorieta was crossed and Santa Fe reached July 5. Returning to Glorieta, they collected there July 7–12, and reaching the Pecos River at Pecos City followed the river up to its junction with the Rio Mora, where they collected at 8,000 feet, July 13–18. Camp was moved to one mile above Willis at 8,500 feet, and after collecting there until July 21, they exchanged their wagons for a pack outfit and made camp, July 21–August 7, at 11,000 feet, on the meadows near the head of Jack Creek. The next move was to the east base of Pecos Baldy near a lake at 11,600 feet, where collecting was done, August 7–17, covering the region between Pecos Baldy and the Truchas Peaks, a trip also being made by Bailey down the Rio Media on the Rio Grande slope, August 17. After returning to the wagons at Willis for two days, they collected at the fork of the Pecos and Mora Rivers three days at a camp two miles above El Macho, August 21–24, and spent two nights trapping at the old camp ground between Pecos and Rowe, after which they made camp at Ribera, August 26, near Bernal, August 27, and the next day on the edge of Las Vegas, [N.M.] where they collected until September 1. Proceeding north they left Las Vegas September 1 and passed Sapello September 3, Penasco Blanco, Mora, and La Cueva, September 5, and Guadalupita, September 6. They went up Coyote Creek to Black Lake, September 9, to the Moreno Valley at the west base of Agua Fria Mountain, September 10, and to the east side of Taos Pass, September 12–15, camping near Elizabethtown, September 15–20, when Bailey climbed Taos Mountain, September 17. On September 20 they turned back and crossed Taos Pass,

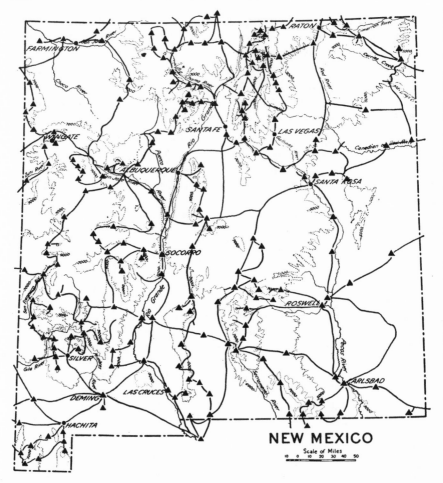

Vernon prepared this map for Florence's monumental Birds of New Mexico *to show the areas studied by Biological Survey parties.*

reaching Taos, September 21, camping and exploring six miles north of Taos on Lucero Creek until October 1. On September 25 they went up Hondo Canyon and to the west base of Wheeler Peak. Leaving Taos on October 1, they reached Santa Fe, October 2, by way of Tres Piedras.[6]

This full summer was followed by two more in much the same pattern. The thoroughness of the survey is easily seen on the map Vernon prepared. For a woman sent west for her health less than a decade before, the trip seems incredible. As Paul Oehser reminisced, "She was no 'woman tenderfoot,' and the wagon trips across the prairies and the pack-outfit travel in the western mountains, in those early days of the century, were not to be laughed off. Though not a robust woman, and as a girl threatened with tuberculosis, she developed a wonderful vitality, both physically and mentally. The rich experiences of the out-doors, especially in the great Southwest which she loved, the companionship of her husband, and the stimulation of the work they were accomplishing—these were the rewards of the arduous life she chose to pursue."[7]

Undaunted by the challenge, Florence went wherever Vernon's work took him, keeping up her field notes and writing from whatever seat she could manage in camp, in a tent, near a wagon, or on an available tree stump. She distilled these experiences into articles over the years for several of the ornithological magazines, abridged and woven together below.[8]

"Our appetites for big trees and mountains had grown into a veritable hunger. Now as we approacht Mesa del Agua de la Yegua, named apparently for some locally historic springs used for watering a band of mares its western fringe of trees lookt surprisingly high to us, and the more excited we got.

"At 7,000 feet, however, 400 feet below the top, to our great delight we at least reacht the edge of the Transition zone; at last, after endless treeless plains and orchards of juniper and nut pine we stood and lookt up the trunk of a yellow pine—a real tree! Here, leaving the horses in a beautiful grassy park, unsaddled and picketed so they could graze while we were gone, we climbed on up to the crown of the mesa. The barometer now registered 7,400 feet, and we were really in the pines. Bordering them was a fringe of oak brush and beyond that the plains stretcht away as far—farther than the eye could reach—to Kansas, as was said grandly with a sweep of the hand toward the horizon. As we wandered about under the tall trees it seemed as if pines had never smelled so sweet, nor the wind in them ever blown so musically.

"But what was that? Could it be? Yes! the glass revealed the pink glow on his breast and as he vaulted into the sky the form of the broad oval wings settled it—it was that handsome and most interesting bird, the Lewis woodpecker! Working and singing loudly among the tips of the pine branches were some warblers that to our delight proved to be the charming little gray and yellow Grace warblers.

"A flash of red led us thru the pines till we came to a beautiful clear pool. Was this the Agua from which the Yegua had come to drink, so giving the Mesa its name? If so, the mares had had a beautiful spring.

The red flash here materialized into a hepatic tanager — how I hugged myself — preening its feathers for a bath in the pool.

"When we were thinking that we had this most remote mesa top with its wildwood friends all to ourselves we were surprised by a fresh horse track, a shod track; and then something white thru the trees made us raise the field glass — a white rooster on the fence of an adobe! Of course, we might have expected it, for like all the rest of the country the mesa had been sheept. Even now, once disillusioned, we caught the suggestion of sheep bells in the air. On the way down, too, we found old sheep camps and a salt log. It brought the same surprise we felt everywhere in New Mexico, for while to us the country was new, in very fact this land of *poco tiempo* is an old, old land.

[Later in their journey] "Another grove of the beautiful cottonwoods near the Taos Pueblo, the Glorieta [arbor or bower] of the Indians, was perhaps the most notable that we saw. The old trees had seamed patriarchal trunks and their high-arching branches carried their finely cut leafage low to the ground. Many of the great trees had twin trunks, some stood alone, others in brotherly groups. An artist when visiting camp talked enthusiastically of the subtle tints of their bark and the effect of afternoon sunshine permeating their delicately foliaged green tops . . .[9]

"A teasing song that I did not recognize, one morning led me into the dense growth bordering the irrigation ditch of the Taos Indians. When whistled to, the invisible bird answered back promptly — or so it seemed — between songs moving about getting his breakfast. But where was he? When finally discovered, his dark gray head and breast were cut off so sharply from the yellow belly that went with the sunlit branch below, that the only wonder was that *tolmiei* had ever been separated from his background. For it was he, the lovely little MacGillivray warbler . . . A few days later under the cottonwood in a dense tangle of wild plum, wild rose, maple, and poison ivy, *tolmiei* was encountered in a still more attractive role. The absorbed musician was now the anxious guardian of the nest. He and his mate with food in their bills circled around the intruder chipping and switching their tails noncommittally. When they passed through a patch of sunlight the green on their backs warmed up prettily, and when the female went to a distance the white spots on her eyelids proved a good mark for an intimate friend to follow. And — there was the nest! Only about a foot above the ground in a small bush overgrown with clematis the pretty cup held four precious but undeniably plain nestlings with fuzzy heads and yellow bills.

"Our last mountain camp of the field season of 1906 was at 8500

Glorieta (meaning "bower or arbor") Canyon, near Taos Pueblo, New Mexico. The Baileys pitched their tent here in 1903 for a few days of field work. To Florence's delight, the canyon was "full of birds" and "big yellow butterflies fluttered through the delicate foliage of the grove." This photograph accompanied her article in the Condor, July, 1912. (Courtesy of the Natural History Museum of Los Angeles County, Section of Birds and Mammals.)

feet in the New Mexico Mogollons. [It snowed, and soon] more snow fell and it kept getting colder . . . Mr. Bailey ran a zone line to the top of the 11,000 foot peak above us, and saw white-tailed deer and followed tracks of a mountain lion through the snow. Down in camp it was cold work writing up notes even with big logs blazing in front of the tent. When the snowstorms had cleared the sky we had glorious days. . . . But soon a second storm began gathering . . . We were not prepared for winter and having no snowshoes, if caught by a storm might have to wade 17 miles through the snow. We decided to go out while we could drive [the horses] out!

"We had come down 4,000 feet in 28 hours, from 9,000 feet at the top of Willow Creek Canyon to 5,000 feet at the foot of the Mogollon Mountains. After rattling down the cold mountain grades we were glad to camp here for a few days work, pitching our tents in a little amphitheater that was warm and still . . . 'The grasshoppers are squeaking up on the hill!' someone called out, and after a moment, the camp man's deliberate voice responded dryly — 'We didn't hear many over on *Willow Crick!*'"

While in New Mexico, Florence also had a chance to observe her favorite hermit thrush and to add it to the known birds of the upper Pecos River, along with ninety-three other new species she identified there. "When we camped in the spruces at 11,000 feet Hermit Thrushes were singing in chorus in such unusual numbers that we called the place Hylocichla Camp, but by August 1 the thrushes had almost stopped singing. On July 23 we found a young bird out of the nest, and from that time on encountered bob-tailed young in the woods until August 15, just prior to our departure for the lowlands. The stomach of a thrush shot contained insects and a few berry seeds, probably strawberry."[10]

Florence deviated from her usual style to write about a human injustice that attracted her attention, the plight of the widow of a small cattle rancher in southwestern New Mexico. She detailed the woman's emotional story of trying to establish a ranch with the threat of Indians a daily terror, only to have her source of water taken by a large cattle company after her husband died. Florence applied the lesson of history repeating itself, commenting that the ill treatment of Indians "— treatment that has caused the murderous outbreaks that have been condemned without a hearing — has been applied to the weak ones of our own race. It is the old story — the oppression of the weak by the self-seeking, unscrupulous strong."[11]

While in the field, they had little time or inclination to think of anything but the day's field notes and the next day's horseback trip. But back in Washington, the Baileys traded dinners by campfire for the social life that his career and her family connections dictated. Among the many who came to see the scientific community in Washington was California botanist Alice Eastwood, who visited her friend Hart and his family.[12] Florence was also happy to see her friend, whose framed photograph hung over Florence's desk. While in Washington, Miss Eastwood attended one reception at the White House with President and Mrs. Roosevelt and another at the home of Alexander Graham Bell. Later Bell's daughter, Elsie May Bell Grosvenor, presided over high tea "at homes" on Thursday afternoons. These were well known as a place to meet distinguished scientific people, and Florence sometimes took her grandnieces to tea there.[13]

When John Burroughs made a rare visit to Washington, he was entertained at a "very cordial" White House luncheon, with Hart among the dozen guests.[14] Burroughs recorded this worthy event in his journal, in the same breath with another day's mention that "I lunched with Mrs. Bailey." Florence and Burroughs had much to talk about. Never a joiner, Burroughs was nevertheless in full sympathy with the Audubon Society efforts to stop the continuing slaughter of birds. Living may have been simpler, but hats weren't. According to one account, a parlor gathering of ladies of the time, "when looked down upon from above, resembled nothing so much as the bird section of a museum of natural history, made up of thrushes, orioles, red-wing blackbirds, the gray mourning dove, the purplish-black grackle, the man-loving wren, and the common pigeon. Even the Shelleyan skylark was taken for a last ride by many a lady of the land, and, thereafter watching from the vantage point of her hat with the all-seeing eyes of the dead, saw her raise funds for missionaries to convert the savages of Africa to the amenities of civilization." Fashion was still calling the shots and bird feathers were still a fast-selling item. Even the new Sears, Roebuck & Company mail order catalog offered "extra large size, fine quality, soft, pliable wings" for fifty cents.[15]

Fifty cents was more than a Biological Survey man received for a day's subsistence in the field, and the stipend ranged down to ten cents a day. This seemed to surprise even the congressional committee when Hart testified in support of increasing his meager budgetary allowance. Wilfred Osgood, a coworker of Vernon Bailey's who had been with him and Hart on the Death Valley expedition, wrote to Fuertes years later, "I am long past the old Biological Survey days with VB and a starvation allowance."[16] But Florence's bird friends didn't even have a starvation allowance, and she kept her pen dipped constantly in the inkwell preparing articles to educate people about live birds and their benefits.

Her interest didn't stop with birds. She also worked for improved public education in the District of Columbia, penning a comprehensive Senate memorial on the subject.[17] Among other things, it urged Congress, which had control over education there, to extend compulsory education beyond the twelve weeks then required. She also urged prevention of child labor abuse, and for working people the expansion of night schools and free lectures.

In addition to their two earlier short trips, the Baileys spent three summers together in New Mexico. Soon they would be off to new territory for the survey. Now that New Mexico had been given as much time as Hart could spare for it, they would spend their fifty cents a day in California the following summer, extending their knowledge of the fauna in lesser-known areas there.

Red-Letter Days, 1907–1908

OCEANSIDE COMMUNITIES around Los Angeles were at their height in the first decade of this century. These were romantic places, such as Venice with its canals. Florence described it as "a resort built in imitation of the Italian city, and fortunately for me temporarily unpopular at the time of my visit."[1] Birds were easier to watch with fewer people around.

Farther south, San Juan Capistrano was already beginning to feel the effects of twentieth-century progress. "While surrounded by a sleepy Mexican village the mission stands on the automobile highway between Los Angeles and San Diego over which whizzing tourist cars toot at all hours, and still worse, twenty rods away the Santa Fe trains whistle and puff and rumble over their tracks."[2] Here too, people were intruding on her birds, but the marshlands were still there. That's more than can be said for 90 percent of them today.

Florence had loved this region since she first visited it as a sickly young woman. This summer of 1907 she enjoyed excellent health and had her husband as a traveling companion. It was another highlight of her western travels, and she titled one of her resulting articles "Red Letter Days in Southern California" (*Condor*, 1917). It celebrated her first real acquaintance with water birds.

Vernon was primarily interested in studying the fauna of the coastal strip and of the alkaline region just east of the coastal mountains of southern California. Before the weather turned too hot, they traveled down the inland side of the mountains. From Palm Springs they headed south to visit her uncle's family at Twin Oaks, and on the way Florence continued to watch the intriguing "palm-leaf oriole," now known as the hooded oriole. Fan palms were being planted in rows along city streets and as decoration for railroad station grounds, to maintain the tropical atmosphere, she theorized. Even with the noise, she found oriole nests only a few yards from the railroad tracks. Her explanation was that the more remote date palms offered no protection from the hot California sun, whereas the wide leaves of the planted fan palms are natural umbrellas.

A workman trimming palms at Hemet saved a fan with a nest attached to it, which she carried east to be photographed. With her typical care, Florence described the nest, "supported on each side by fiber threads sewed through the leaf, and the nest itself, particularly the outer framework, intricately woven of the same fiber. The only lining is of finer threads."[3]

From Twin Oaks the Baileys drove west to the cooler shores of the Pacific. At San Juan Capistrano they were surprised, not by the legendary swallows, but by the opportunity to see white-throated swifts at close range. They were used to seeing them swooping almost out of sight, but here they were nesting right with the swallows in the mission ruins, in spite of the presence of rumbling trains and tooting cars. "Their wild, shrieked-out notes recalled canyons walled with rock in the depths of the mountains and we marvelled that the birds should stop even in passing at such a place as this."[4]

Although most visitors to the ruins are awestruck by the zeal of the early priests and the enormous task of constructing the famous mission, Florence found herself "with one eye to the dim historic past and one eye to the vivid, living, ornithological present." She combined both views in describing her tour. "In looking for the birds' nests we followed down the long colonnades whose beautiful arches with their deep shadows attract the photographers and whose richly tinted old walls afford subjects to rouse the enthusiasm of colorists, but they revealed no ornithological treasures, and a dusky old deserted chapel that was entered proved only the home of the barn owl seen when mousing for her squealing young at bat-hunting time."[5]

From Capistrano they drove east into the mountains. Passing through a cultivated valley, they saw a harvester "drawn by a band of horses, entering fields of straw-colored waving grain, and leaving behind stubble fields and rows of fat grain bags. But in the immediate neighborhood of the alkaline [San Jacinto] lake the soil was too permeated with salt for grain fields." The only signs of human habitation were a ruin and an abandoned house and barn, but far more appealing was the mountain foreground with its "acres of pink abronias, wide stretches of yellow tar weed, and fields of sunflowers with faces turned toward the sun, fields that went well with the fresh, uplifted song of the Meadowlark.

"As the water of the San Jacinto River is now used for irrigation, the lake is only a rain water lake, but at our visit it was about a mile

Nest of a palm-leaf (now hooded) oriole, saved by a man trimming palms in Hemet, California. Florence noted the oriole's preference for the fan palms over the narrow leaves of the date palms, which "offer no protection from the hot California sun." This photograph accompanied her article in Auk, January, 1910. (Courtesy of the Natural History Museum of Los Angeles County, Section of Birds and Mammals.)

long, a typical tule lake, with great stretches of cool-looking dark green tules ten feet high, showing a line of brown heads at the top. At our approach a large flock of Ibises flew from the green walls and from the dotted surface of the lake the nearer Coots and Gadwalls went spattering and splashing off into the sheltering green alleys to begin their talk again when all was quiet. Near the edge of the lake a young Night Heron stood up to its body in water as if half asleep. Three Rails were seen in the tules walking jauntily about with short tails up. Red-winged and Yellow-headed Blackbirds were also flying about among their nests."[6]

A month later they passed the lake again, but this time Vernon had only mammals on his mind. Although Florence longed to stay and study the birds, "we had no time to stop for we were then in search of the kangaroo rats whose tracks and trails were everywhere in the valley." Vernon had work to do at Lake Elsinore, so Florence had a chance to spend some time observing birds there instead, although they had been told that none were there in late July. She quickly found more than two hundred ducks, and in addition through her field glasses identified about thirty white-faced glossy ibises. "As we approached they rose, with a loud *quank, quank,* and circled around in a close flock looking as decorative as figures on a Japanese screen, each bird a segment of a circle with its long extended drooping neck and legs." As she watched the ibises, "another large striking bird appeared on the film of this rare moving picture — a Black-necked Stilt — its black wings raised over its black and white body, as it lit and stood stilted up on its long pink legs."[7]

"The mammalogist," as she generally called Vernon in her magazine articles, was busy with his traps as he attempted to solve a distribution problem of gophers for the local farmers. He took time to bring Florence to see a cinnamon teal's nest discovered when the female burst from it at his approach, and they watched the nest closely for the few days they were there. It was so well hidden that even with her acute vision, Florence had to have it pointed out to her more than once.

Florence took time out from watching the birds to talk about them to the Cooper Club, the West Coast association of ornithologists. She urged them to protect birds through "public intelligence" about their value, discriminating between the harmful and beneficial species, and to include bird study in the schools. "If you can give your children, the children of your state, an abiding interest in birds, by implanting a love of nature in their hearts, you will protect them from many of the world's worst snares and ensure to their old age days of quietness and peace." To do this, she reminded them to study the birds themselves and in that "I can wish you no greater pleasure. From the coast valleys to the crest of the Sierra each beautiful spot that I remember has an added charm from the memory of some bird that gave life and interest to the landscape."[8]

Florence also found much interest in watching the Brewer's blackbirds, common enough in the West but somewhat new to her as an easterner. She had seen them in the mountains of California and New Mexico but found it only a little less than astonishing to find a roost inside a city. Although the Baileys were startled when a "horde" of the birds burst from the trees over their heads one sunset in Redlands, local people hardly seemed to notice them. Unlike some species, blackbirds have been survivors over the years and so common today that few — even birders — pay attention to them. But they continued to fascinate the lady for whom no bird was unimportant, as she aimed to document their little-known life histories.[9]

As she walked down the street, the note of a phainopepla reminded her of Olive Thorne Miller, and later that summer while watching the blackbirds in Pasadena, she visited her new home. Then in her seventies, Mrs. Miller had become so fascinated with the birds and flowers of southern California that her daughter, also a bird lover, had taken her there to live. She built her mother a home "on the outskirts of Los Angeles on the edge of a bird-filled arroyo where rare fruits and flowers ran riot and the cottage — El Nido [the nest] — became embowered in vines and trees."[10]

Mrs. Miller was still writing children's books but was no longer active in field work. She listened with extra delight to Florence's descriptions of her southern California travels, of swifts and ibises, blackbirds and blackheaded grosbeaks, and Mrs. Miller's own favorite bird, the phainopepla. Her daughter helped to found the Bird Lovers' Club of the Southwest Museum, which is still going strong after more than sixty years.[11]

From Pasadena the Baileys returned to the coastal area south of Los Angeles to watch the migrating water birds. To easterners reading the *Condor* (May, 1916), her descriptions of the coastline must have seemed like a fairy tale. "Up the shore the low Santa Monica Mountains could be seen, very ordinary mountains in the strong revealing light of day, but in the glamour of purple haze standing rich and reserved, and, behind a veil of mist, coming under the spell of mystery and magic.

"At sunset the low slanting light illuminated their cliffs and any ships that might be lying at anchor off the long pier of Port Los Angeles, as well as the rigging of boats lying at anchor in the harbor of Venice, where flocks of Gulls gathered, flying about the pier and the sky above;

and one night the light touched up a party of Cormorants sitting statuesquely erect on the edges of a row boat. Then a faint rainbow arched up in the southeast, and soon after, the Gulls disappeared for the night."

Most people, in 1907 as now, go to Venice to watch the ocean or each other. Florence watched "the bird characters of Venice," like the cormorants who had discovered that the fishing was easier in the Venice canals than along shore—and no swells, a ragged boy with a raft pointed out. Together they watched them fishing, diving, and drying their wings on the bank. "When one was on the bank of a canal oiling his feathers one day, a Kingfisher sat watching him as if wondering what manner of bird he might be, but having business of his own soon flew off to a stake out in the marsh." Florence's thoughts returned at that instant to the ongoing battle to protect all birds from their still fashionable headgear fate, and she took a deep breath of inspiration to continue her work.

At low tide the gulls and various shorebirds formed an interesting spectacle. She was amused by the godwits' feeding habits. "As a wave rolled up, combed over and broke, the white foam would chase them in, and as they ran before it, if it came on too fast, they would pick themselves up, open their wings till the cinnamon showed, and scoot in like excited children. But the instant the water began to recede they would right about face and trot back with it . . . As they went their long bills—in the low afternoon sun strikingly coral red except for the black tip—were shoved ahead of them, feeling along through the wet sand, the light glinting from them; and if anything good was discovered deeper, the hunters would stop to really probe, sometimes plunging the bill in up to the hilt, on rare occasions when the tidbit proved out of reach, actually crowding their heads down into the sand."

One aspect of birding that hasn't changed since Florence's day is the problem of identifying immature gulls. They vary not only among species but between years of maturity and then between winter and summer. In addition, they interbreed. Florence noted that the gulls along the beach were mostly immature. "Now and then there was one of the big adult Western Gulls whose snowy head, body, and tail, and dark slaty mantle, were a great satisfaction in the confusion of dingy mottled ones."

She complained to her friend Dr. Joseph Grinnell in Berkeley (no relation to George Bird Grinnell) and received his sympathy, to which she replied, "So young gulls come under the head of [those birds] that no mortal man can tell without a big series [of stuffed specimens] for comparison—to say nothing about the new species which are 'one thing in a north light and another in a south'!"[12]

Gulls were the least of Florence's nightmares about coastal birds, however. Hunting season opened, and just as she stood watching a group of godwits, willets, and one gull, she described in the *Condor* article, "a smart type of city boy appeared, and taking a gun out of a case prepared to shoot my friends. As he was still within city limits I stopped him temporarily by calling his attention to the fact, but I knew it was only a short respite and my only hope for the birds was their apparent recognition of a gun. Two other boys with guns and bags came along later, outside of city limits. At their first shot all but one Surf-bird flew, and at the second shot he fell, flopping distressingly. Before the boy could get him the waves washed him out, out and in, their toy, a limp bundle of feathers; a moment before instinct with life and individuality, a dauntless child of the sea, with power of wing and intelligence to carry him from pole to pole. When the poor wounded bird was picked up its sufferings were prolonged cruelly by the boy's ignorance of the way to kill it.

"And when a man in khaki aimed at one individual, picked it up instantly, and killed it humanely, he stood apart as a legitimate sportsman, one who, like the scientific collector, shoots to kill and considers it a disgrace to maim. But to stone flocks of waders, to shoot scavenger Gulls, and murder tame Cormorants — surely the hunting instinct needs education and regulation! Meanwhile automobiles hurry down to the gun clubs with callow youths and pump guns."

She had her "preach," as she called it in college, and then returned to describing the joys of studying the passers-by in their autumn migrations: brown pelicans and white-winged scoters and her first-ever snow goose, honking its solitary way overhead, an unforgettable moment. "At sunset another time, as I walked home up the beach breathing in the strong ocean air, the only birds in sight were swirling flocks of belated Sandpipers ever resolving ahead of me. . . . And over the gray sea a deep glittering sun path led to a sunset sky that grew and ripened to rich purples — one of the sunsets when a red ball goes down into the Pacific. Long straight lines of deep voiced surf breaking far out at the beck of the moon, following obediently the rhythm of the heavenly bodies . . . How big and simple Nature is in all her processes! How microscopic man becomes viewed in the perspective of the orderly march of the universe! And yet while bird and beast blindly follow the laws Nature has laid down for them and live and die as they must, man alone, mercifully or unmercifully controls their environment, man alone can trace their course from pole to pole and try to read the reasons why. And although he in turn fail to solve the riddles of the Sphinx, he alone, humble student of Nature's laws, waiting in the stillness of the forest or listening in silence to the deep voice of the ocean, moved by the bigness and truth of Nature, can choose to try to keep step in the orderly march of the universe."

The Baileys' orderly march took them on an October train back across the broad country once more to their Washington home. Another winter set in with its days and weeks of writing, working, teaching, planning. Vernon returned alone to New Mexico the following summer, training younger field men like Clarence Birdseye, who went on to gain fame in another field, as the originator of frozen foods. There were no schools or universities to train men for the Biological Survey, and so the senior men were responsible for giving newcomers their training on the job.[13]

It was also during 1908 that Florence's name was memorialized in ornithology by Joseph Grinnell. A new chickadee was identified in the higher mountains of southern California, and he named it *Parus gambeli baileyae* in her honor.[14] Although the trinomial naming system has almost disappeared, a specimen on view at the San Bernardino County Museum in California still bears the subspecies identification. In thanking Grinnell for the honor, Florence commented, "While I have never attempted to do technical work, in the strict sense, I have always tried, to the best of my conscience, to do *true* work, and the recognition of the success of that effort is very grateful. From the side of sentiment, *Parus* has always been one of my favorite birds."[15] It was the only such honor accorded her, but a veritable zoo of subspecies were given names to honor Vernon, including a bobcat, rabbit, bat, wood rat, deer, pocket mouse, pocket gopher, cotton rat, and squirrel.[16]

Florence seemed to find the comforts of her Washington home increasingly more attractive than the arduous camps in the field. Perhaps not. But she stayed home for the next three years, while Vernon continued his annual treks west. Florence had plenty to do in Washington during those years. Noting the dwindling activity in the Audubon Society's bird classes, she took on the challenge of heading the work altogether. She arranged three sections of classes, one for lectures and two for the study of bird skins, with divisions for beginners and advanced students. Widely advertised in the schools, the classes attracted more than a hundred teachers and a hundred more from the general public. The earnest doer had done it again.

Feathered Swimmers of the Prairies, 1909–1916

Florence's brother Hart had always been drawn to the natural beauties and life zone challenges, and, later, to the Indians he found in California. By the time his friend Theodore Roosevelt left the presidential office in March of 1909, Hart was actively considering retirement from the Biological Survey.[1] He wanted to pursue his own research, and a pair of old friends came to his aid. Railroad magnate E. H. Harriman had admired and respected Hart's work ever since he asked the scientist to organize his expedition to Alaska a decade before. After Harriman's death, his widow was approached to support Hart's research in a more tangible way, and the next year she set up a lifetime fund for that purpose. Hart was then free to spend longer periods of time in the West, where he pursued the vanishing California Indians and enjoyed his rustic home in the redwoods north of San Francisco. John Muir often walked to the ferry from his home in Martinez and then to Lagunitas on the other side of the bay, so they could saunter through the forest together.

Even before Hart left Washington, the work of the Biological Survey had begun to shift toward conservation activities and ways to help farmers more.[2] Though important, these projects were of less interest to his pioneer spirit. When he retired, the leadership of the survey went to Henry Henshaw, his friend for almost forty years and the one who had nominated Hart for the post when it was first opened in 1885. Henshaw was well prepared to move up to chief.

Florence continued to serve the efforts of the Biological Survey, including three articles for *Bird-Lore* on specific beneficial birds. Two of these were reprinted by the National Audubon Society as educational leaflets in a series it produced to support the protection of "our economically valuable birds" in the fight against insects that prey upon "our rapidly growing agricultural interests." Today it sounds strange to have the insect diet of the tufted titmouse described as "destroying

After many successes in Washington, Hart tired of politics and sought refuge in northern California, where he lived in a home nestled among the redwoods and tall ferns and continued his study of the vanishing Indian tribes. This photograph, taken late in life, accompanied the memorial to him in Auk, April, 1944. (Courtesy of the Natural History Museum of Los Angeles County, Section of Birds and Mammals.)

Louis Agassiz Fuertes provided this art for Florence's article on the tufted titmouse in Bird-Lore, November, 1913. She stressed that "the Titmice do good" by eating such insect pests as grasshoppers, boll weevils, and scale insects. The National Association of Audubon Societies later reprinted it as an educational leaflet. (Courtesy of the Natural History Museum of Los Angeles County, Section of Birds and Mammals.)

such dangerous enemies of man," unless one knows of the efforts being made then to curb the boll weevils, cutworms, and caterpillars.[3] From that perspective, encouraging the birds sounds more enlightened to many than the chemical efforts being made today.

With the new priorities at the Biological Survey and the first change of chief in its history, naturally the work of others on the staff changed as well. Soon Vernon had a new field assignment: to complete a biological survey of North Dakota, another area little known at the time but one of increasing importance to farmers. This part of the country was not new to Vernon, who had grown up in the great woods of Minnesota. He had done some early field work in North Dakota in 1888 and could see the results of its rapidly changing character. As he noted in his report: "Some of the most desirable native species of both animals and plants are disappearing."⁴ He also noted that water use had changed so significantly with the growth of agriculture that a lake that had a steamboat landing in 1887 had receded two miles from the town since then.

Some of the birds of this country were new to Florence, and she decided to accompany Vernon for the field season and again for a second field season three years later. The result was the longest series of magazine articles she ever published. Over a period of five years, the *Condor* carried seventeen installments.

It is difficult today to envision the consuming interest in North Dakota — or any other state — that would have led her to such extensive writing efforts and would have gleaned for her that much space in an ornithological magazine. However, those were the years of the Great War, and perhaps fewer articles were available to publish. North Dakota was not a "land of enchantment" like New Mexico nor one of "bird-filled arroyos where rare fruits and flowers ran riot" like California, but its very remoteness intrigued her. Of course, she was there and so were new birds, which was interest and purpose enough for Florence. Besides, she was overdue to get out under the open sky again. "Beautiful prairies! How they fill the imagination and free the mind of the escaped city dweller! Miles and miles of prairie with hardly a house in sight, unclouded skies, and strong vivifying sunshine tempered by the cool fresh wind from far away!"⁵

The Baileys stopped in Chicago to discuss with local authorities plans for the North Dakota survey. They spent the time until the next train enjoying the Field Museum and the Art Institute. Then "the Northern Pacific carried us out across the dead level of the old bed of Lake Agassiz and then up over the North Dakota coteau whose gentle morainal swells were left by the ice sheet. The bigness of the great open prairies slowly sinks into your consciousness as hour after hour you look out upon grain fields interrupted only at long intervals by a farm house, or a way station made conspicuous by tall grain elevators."

The train moved too fast for them to recognize many species of birds they saw on the ponds as they passed, but "beating low over the fields was one bird whose identity could not be questioned, the Short-eared Owl, a characteristic bird of the prairie region. Of the anomalous day-hunting owls my experience had been limited to the Burrowing. How I longed to see *flammeus*! My first sight of one had been the other side of the Minnesota line when, on a fence post, a tall bird standing half round shoulderedly peering at us suddenly broke away, flapping off on wide brown wings. What bird-lover does not know the thrill of such a moment! Here was the Short-eared at last! An owl with big round head and slowly flapping wings bound not for dense woods but for the big bare prairie; an owl that seems at first blush as much of a target as an eagle flying freely about in the day time, making its nest and rearing its family safely in the open! Eloquent commentary on the great untenanted prairie!"

Two birds that especially lured Florence there were among the largest, most characteristic, and perhaps generally distributed birds of the prairie region, the prairie hen and sharp-tailed grouse. Yet to her great disappointment, neither was easily seen. However, one day, "when impelled to answer the call of the prairie in spite of the heat that was rousing sore complaints at the farm, I headed for a small clump of cottonwoods that suggested good nesting sites. The three farm dogs reached the trees before me flushing a grouse with pointed tail which flew with beat and soar, several beats and a soar, uttering a low guttural *cluck-uk-uk-uk-ak*. As I stepped from the hot sun into the shade of the cottonwood thicket, the little trees rustled hard with the prairie wind, fanning out coolness, and the dogs made a bolt for the inside of the clump . . . The old Grouse had shown excellent judgment on a hot summer day.

"The Stump Lake wheat farm where I spent part of the summer was east of the hundredth meridian, but its proximity to the arid regions was attested by the alkaline water of the lake and lines of frothy suds along its shores, while partly buried but well preserved bones of buffalo that had come to water from the surrounding prairie were to be picked up along the beaches." How soon we forget.

"In the silver-leaf patches and wild plum thickets back from the shore three birds were especially abundant, the Bronzed Grackle, the Yellow Warbler, and the Clay-colored Sparrow. The dense thickets of wild plum and spiny thornapple make good shelter for the Grackle colonies with their big nests and large nestlings. When the old males are interviewing visitors to their noisy colonies the visitors have an opportunity to examine the bronze of their plumage. To eyes familiar mainly with museum skins an old male standing on top of the thicket in strong sunlight is almost startling."

In this subtle way Florence encouraged her readers to go into the field and study live birds, a familiar theme which she repeated as she worked her way among the sloughs and marshes around the lake. "Would that every bird student could visit them and bring back intimate studies of the birds on their own home grounds!"

Definition of terms was important in this new country. What seemed like "merely black streaks in the prairie" might turn out to be a tule marsh with an interior basin of open water. "According to the width of this basin they may be known locally as marshes or lakes, and many of the so-called lakes are merely wider marshes that one may wade across." On one such marsh — or was it a lake? — Florence experienced another "red letter day long to be remembered . . . At last I was on the famous breeding grounds of the Ducks and Grebes!"

There she was able to list a large proportion of the ducks known to nest locally, and after a week at Lake Elsie she completed the grebe family, for "all but the tiny Mexican species which we found in southern Texas had now been seen in North Dakota." Grebes were one of the birds most commonly used for trimming hats, and Florence put in a word for her feathered friends. "The Eared has the Grebe habit of lying on its side on the water so that its white breast, whose soft silky feathers have been made all too familiar by milliners, gleam far across the water."

She took a rowboat into the marsh, poling her way among the "narrow tule lanes with their dark green walls" especially to see the duck and grebe nests at close view, but always watching for other bird treasures. "When the nose of the boat was snubbed up into a green cul-de-sac three Long-billed Marsh Wren nests were in sight, two old ones and one just begun, pretty domed structures with a round side entrance, woven of brown tules, cat-tail, cane leaves, and grass, with a soft lining of cat-tail down." Even today, not many birders have had such a close look at a marsh wren's nest.

While on foot another day, she relearned an old lesson. "The edge of the marsh was dry and skirted by cow trails, beyond which I made a short essay into the interior, using both hands to part the tules, for their crown of nutlets slap your cheeks with stinging blows as you crowd through them. While the footing was still firm enough to hold, I set up my camp stool and with the tules high above my head looked about my cage. The cool dark green waving rods were interwoven into a dense grill work with meshes so fine that, peer and twist and turn as you might — clumsy mortal — you could only guess at what was happening a foot from your nose! . . . The miniature forest was full of the tantalizing talk and noises of a large invisible population. Ducks quacked so plainly I could see them (with my mind's eye), and heavy-bodied waterfowl went splashing into the water right there ahead of me — I knew just how they were lighting down."

"Looking overhead I could see Swallows and Black Terns skimming along over the top of the marsh, and envied them their advantage. . . . It was too aggravating. I must see! Rising with determination I crowded through the tules and crashed and crackled through the canes. A screeching, thundering railroad train might as well expect to surprise a Hermit Thrush! I had obtruded. Unbroken silence ensued. The moral was all too plain. Would you see? Cultivate a philosophic spirit, be content to sit and listen to the voices of the marsh; let the fascinating, mysterious, bewildering voices encompass you and — hold your peace. Spirits of the marsh — it is their magic forest. Let no mortal intrude."

"But a marsh like a mountain will not be exorcised," so she followed the advice of "one familiar with bogs," as she obliquely referred to Vernon, who also earned her epithet of "the old explorer of bogs." He joined her, "and carefully testing footholds and ordering me to step in his boot prints, led me out to the edge of the open water. . . . At last I had arrived!"

As their first summer there drew to a close, Florence was already eager to return, drawn by the birds seen casually but meriting her further attention, "tantalizing confused memories that rise compellingly again and again and make the call of North Dakota well nigh too strong to resist." So when Vernon was to return three years later, she was ready and eager to climb onboard the train with him.

An unusual disclaimer — for Florence — entered "A Return to the Dakota Lake Region" as she described the lure of water fowl. "Realizing full well the limitations of a woman bent on the study of water birds, I went intending to be satisfied with what came my way, hoping that such casual experiences might in some part supplement the more thorough work of less handicapped field students." Rarely did she consider herself less able than anyone else to pursue her studies! At this point she was remembering the "spirits of the marsh" and the need for help from the old explorer of bogs, but she was still an adventurer at heart. After the train left behind "the beautiful spruce and tamarack swamps of northern Minnesota, the sign *Manitoba Junction* stirred my blood. How good it would have been to follow the straight northward pointing rails that seemed headed for the top of our world!"

While Vernon traveled to Oregon to work, Florence spent most of the summer of 1916 in a small area of North Dakota, concentrating on the lakes of the Sweetwater chain. She was determined to see what was at the center of the marsh, that black streak of open water. Thinking she was well practiced in the art of walking in the marsh, she had given up her "futile rubber boots. Hot and clumsy to walk in when dry, all too heavy when full of water, impossible to withdraw from if stuck in a bog, and difficult to dry out even with the help of a prairie wind and a stove, they were certainly ill-suited to the submerged tenth of North Dakota with which I was struggling. So old shoes, or rubbers tied on over stockings had come to be my substitutes. Leaving the farmhouse . . . I waded out first over the hummocky ground with its short tussocks, then straight out through the dense stand of brown-topped slough grass to the very edge of the Black Streak, although in the rainy interval the grass had grown from shoulder high to over the top of my hat, and the water had deepened from knee to waist high." Once again she found she had moved too quickly, and the open water was deserted when it finally came into view. Undaunted as always, and in spite of the "handicaps" she had foreseen for a woman bent on studying water birds, Florence had once again accomplished what she had set out to do. Even though the birds weren't there, she had reached the black streak. And she had learned another lesson about studying the birds.

In addition to her bird study, Florence was still fond of encouraging young people, including the farmer's young son whose daily return she watched with interest. "In the late afternoons the rattle of old Polly's hoofs would make me look up quickly to greet our little school boy, home again from his daily three mile ride across the prairie. And later, when he had taken a look at his new brother, at the sound of loping feet I would see him again, on a fresh horse, racing bareback down the wheat fields to bring in the cows for the evening milking." Though some on North Dakota farms may still follow a similar routine, it is entirely foreign to most of today's school children, for better or worse.

This young boy also led Florence to past generations and to a sense of Dakota history when his grandparents invited her for dinner. "As the farm-house was torn up by repairs at the moment, a 'cook car' left in the yard by a threshing outfit, a car twenty feet long by ten wide stilted up on four wheels, was used as an emergency dining-room, greatly to my delectation, as it was my first opportunity to examine one. We climbed up the high front steps—taken in before starting on the road that the four horses might be driven from the front door—and as we sat on benches drawn up to the long table fitted to serve twenty or thirty men and I looked with curiosity at the stove at the end of the car and the protected trays for dishes against the walls, the old settlers told interesting tales of the early days on the prairie."

"When they had come as pioneers in 1884, prairie fires were a real danger, it was an easy matter to get lost in the big sloughs with grass standing seven or eight feet high, and buffalo bones strewed the ground. Ox cart trains of Sioux, with squaws and papooses, used to come from Fort Totten to pick up the bones to ship out for fertilizer, and the primitive ungreased wooden carts with wheels five feet high — coming usually in trains of from seven to eleven but once in a train of twenty-eight cars — as the pioneer expressed it, 'squawked so' they could be heard crossing the Belgrade Bridge four miles away. For four or five years after the first settlers came, the Indians kept on 'picking bones,' which gives a slight idea of the hordes of buffalo that once roamed that part of the prairie."

"So too, the Indians, belittled contemporaries of the buffalo, after outliving them and collecting their bones from the prairie, were now, with elaborate care gathered for education at the Industrial School at Fort Totten, at the foot of Sully Hill."

Florence could view the Indians more sympathetically than those early settlers, however. One woman told her that "after the Spirit Lake massacre which she was near she learned the voices of all the birds listening for Indians, for some birds she thought had calls like Indians. Sandhill cranes at a distance were also sometimes taken for Indians. Mirage was common there."

Later in the summer, Florence visited Stump Lake again, looking forward to exploring the marshes from the Ford that her previous host had purchased. But heavy rains had left the countryside "all afloat," including much of the road. The horse and buggy were resorted to, but even the horse had to be pulled from the mire. Even so, she enjoyed her week among old friends "both avian and human." Note which she mentions first.

The season rolled on, and the green wheat fields turned to gold. Threshing machines appeared. One afternoon Florence took the farmer's young schoolboy with her to watch the ducks, first teaching him what to look for. The ruddy ducks were usually close by and easy to identify, especially the drakes with their unmistakable blue bills. On the way home he grinned, "I'm glad I *came*," a remark that Florence deeply appreciated, "as agriculture in the fascinating form of a threshing outfit to watch had threatened to outrival ornithology."

Among the hundreds of "feathered swimmers" Florence now watched were flocks of Franklin gulls resting on the lake. The wheat harvesters told her that they hunted over the bundles of wheat, catching crickets. "One would fly low over the shocks till, apparently, a cricket or a grasshopper caught its eye, when it would suddenly pounce down upon it. A droll sight it certainly was, to see a Gull, a bird associated with the ocean, in the middle of a harvest field sitting on a shock of wheat catching insects!"

Before hunting season opened, a friend took Florence on an automobile trip. As they drove through the wooded hills, the most notable bird they saw was a sandhill crane. She noted that "an old man of the mountains who also saw it, remarked sententiously, 'They used to be lots of 'em, but you don't see many like you uster.' Splendid great birds! May the gods of the hunted preserve their remnant!" They were protected even then, but she knew that they afforded too good a target. Other wildlife had been there too, as well as geese so thick, she was told, "that they hadn't room to light."

Florence returned to her farmhouse residence in time to watch the fall migration of water birds. The countryside had changed seasons. Harvesting was over, and even the small sloughs had dried up and been mowed for hay. Fall plowing was under way, and the Franklin gulls eagerly followed behind the horsedrawn machinery. Hunters followed eagerly too, flushing mallards from the stubble fields. "Evenings, in the golden afterglow, Ducks passed over toward the lake, their flocks suggesting the sound of wind in frosted corn."

One sunset, "the rattle of a Kingfisher made me look up in surprise to find one flying into a tree, as if stopping for the night on his way south." Milliners had finally accepted the fact that legislation prohibited trafficking in feathers, so she could look at this kingfisher and not think about hats. Even so, it was almost time to return east; there was still much work to do in educating people about live birds. "The clear bracing days of a northern autumn" were second only to the resplendent nights, where the heavens had grown "prophetic with northern lights." Florence was drawn in memory back to that starry night of her childhood when her mother wrapped her in a blanket and carried her to the cupola to watch the constellations.

Now the first small flocks of Canada geese flew over the lake, and the farmer's wife graphically described the arrival of the snow geese the autumn before. "She had gone out to the windmill about five o'clock in the afternoon — the fifth of October — and looking north discovered them coming toward the lake. They made a solid phalanx a mile and a half wide, and coming on flew low over the windmill and the barn, passing on to the lake. With keen enjoyment of the memory of the wonderful sight she exclaimed — 'I could see them coming from the east as far as I could see, and could see them going into the west till they were as small as Swallows!'"

But the hunters had driven them off, as the calendar must now drive Florence from North Dakota. "Whatever turn they took the days were days of glory, and although I had to leave for another time that most wonderful ornithological experience, the northern flight of waterfowl, my summer had already had full measure and I left with mental gallery crowded with bird pictures, with pulses quickened by the stirring northern days, with mind swept clear by prairie winds, and with spirit uplifted by memories of gorgeous sunrises and sunsets, of brilliant morning stars, of marvelous star-filled firmaments, and illuminated auroral skies."

12

From Garibaldi to Glaciers, 1914–1919

TWICE AGAIN during the teen years of the century the Baileys went west to specific new field session destinations: in 1914 to coastal Oregon and in 1917 to Glacier National Park.

Florence had been to Mount Hood sixteen years before, but this was the first opportunity the two of them had to return to Oregon's "humid coast," as she titled one article. Florence also traveled inland, at least as far as the famed McKenzie Bridge in the heart of the Cascade mountain range. Few birds live in the forests inland, so that even the more open areas around the bridge did not provide many, but she wrote up what she did find there for two local publications, *Mazama* and the *Oregon Sportsman*, rare diversions for her from the pages of ornithological magazines.[1] The birds of the coast were of more interest to her and led to another long series of articles for the *Condor*, quoted below.[2]

Timbering was already changing the face of Oregon by 1914, when Florence noted the stub of an old spruce. "Dwarfing everything in sight it bore silent testimony to the nobility of the forest that formerly possessed the land. But at the sawmill that the night-watchman guarded an occasional spruce would yet come in, twelve feet through, so large that it had to be dynamited and quartered before it would be gotten into the mill." Today in its second-growth evergreen landscape, Oregon retains much of the natural beauty Florence also admired, especially after summers on the North Dakota prairies and in the Southwest.

"The humid coast of the Northwest appeals to the imagination of the worker from the arid interior not only because of its phenomenal forest growth — its bearded giants towering from one to two hundred feet above an almost impenetrable jungle — but because of the ornithological antitheses that result from the juxtaposition of ocean and forested mountains in northern latitudes. . . . the shore that is strewn with the trunks of headless giants is so close beset by the living forest that the bird student may hear Gulls and Cormorants with one ear and Pi-

In addition to observing the coastal Oregon birds, Florence traveled inland through the thick forests to study along the McKenzie River, already a favorite spot for vacationers and fishermen. (From the collection of the Oregon Historical Society, Negative ORHI 38028.)

leated Woodpeckers and Varied Thrushes with the other." No wonder she accompanied Vernon back there.

They set up headquarters at Garibaldi, a fishing village on Tilla-mook Bay, where "the birds made themselves so much at home that the fishermen had to protect their clams and crab boxes from them. . . . While the Gulls have to be reckoned with in such minor ways, the villages, as the people fully realize, would be uninhabitable were it not for the birds. In the fall the salmon that have come into Tillamook Bay go up the creeks to spawn and when they die are washed down by the high water along the creeks and along the shore, sometimes, as the fisherman assured me, 'you might say by the thousands'; and he added

While Vernon completed his biological survey of Oregon, he and Florence stayed in coastal Garibaldi, traveling there by train from Portland. (From the collection of the Oregon Historical Society, Negative ORHI 15517, Wesley Andrews photograph.)

realistically, 'I've seen the little creeks so thick you couldn't see the bottom.' At this perilous moment the Gulls gather, and acting as scavengers save the day for the villagers."

Then she went into the mountains to observe the birds of the forest. Settling into a camp near the McKenzie River, Florence also observed her surroundings. In her journal she noted that under the big hemlocks she watched a little girl in a red sweater "with her doll, her stove of ferns laid on the ground and her pail and pan, berries and sorrel for the doll's dinner." Although across the continent, Homewood seemed very near, still one of the "links in the chain of the ordered Universe" of which she felt so much a part that summer.

The undergrowth beneath the cool evergreens "grew just high enough for a junco to creep under," and here Florence found a variety of small birds.[3] As she sat quietly observing them near a deserted log cabin, she was sensitive to the other fauna of the forest as well. She wrote in her journal, "When sitting between the trees watching the [brown creeper's] nest, one day, I laid my khaki hat on the moss and leaves beside me and, after awhile, glancing down, was attracted by a slight movement and, on watching closely, discovered a little long-pointed brown nose, followed by the slender brown body of a tiny shrew. It nosed under my hat brim and then explored still farther till, with a dart and a dash, it ran swiftly away."

Nearer to the river itself was a special bird treat, the dipper or water ouzel, so beloved by John Muir in the California Sierra Nevada. Another link in her friendships was David Starr Jordan, who loved Muir's story of the dipper so much that he had read it to his science classes and later befriended Muir as a result.[4] Florence herself had first admired the dipper at Mount Shasta in California when she and Vernon were there with Hart on that expedition sixteen years earlier. Now she had a chance to study it more thoroughly.

"When the ouzel started to swim, it would put its head under the water as if locating something, and then, quivering its wings, disappear altogether, coming up soon after with a long, black-shelled caddice fly larva, the shell of which, as we proved later, is a remarkable mosaic of minute stones. . . . when the bird brought up a grampus (as the larva is known locally), it would shake the long shell till it finally broke open, and, pulling out the yellowish brown larva, quickly swallow it.

"After bringing up and eating several of the larvae, the ouzel picked about in the submerged green mats that suggested sea-weed. Once it stood on a stone green with moss long enough to bring out the strong color contrast of the green and the gray. When walking about over the rocks it would make its droll little courtesies — dip, dip, dip — till you were constrained to speak its name — dipper.

"When it had had a satisfying meal it flew across the river to a stone on the shaded bank, where, in terms of protective coloration, it perfectly pictured its background, for its gray upper parts disappeared in the dark shadow, the lighter shade of its breast toned in with the sun on the rock, and only its light-colored legs were left as slender sticks quite foreign to any bird-like suggestion. But when its profiled bill and head projected into the sun, the bird form was restored."[5]

Florence's allotted days in Oregon included evenings when the cedars like "dark organ pipes stood out against the quiet light of the yellow sunset afterglow." Here she wrote about Screech Owl Johnnie, a tiny fledgling found in a tangle of thorny blackberry vines, where Florence thought his wise mother had safely left him.[6]

Summer ended in the "quiet pillared woods with its sun-touched carpet. As I looked up and up the straight tall pillars, and thought of the noise and heat and clatter, of the sordid crookedness of the world of man outside the forest, how grateful was the penetrating coolness of the dim, sun-crossed aisles!"[7] She turned for a last look at the woods, and then returned to the East.

Florence spent the following summer resting in New Hampshire, near the summer place of her cousin Clint where, as she wrote Hart, "I can go and see the sunsets and hear Hermit Thrushes. Just as we used to at home." She was delighted with Hart's home in the California redwoods. "I love to think of you out watering the ferns and watching Bolinas Ridge." But she still had some old business to attend to in selling some property in New York and clearing her accounts "so that I owe no man nothing!" Vernon, meanwhile, spent the summer in the West, "having a wonderful season with wolves, moose, elk, and bears to burn!" Florence stayed in New Hampshire until October, "as it is the best kind of a place to work and the bracing northern fall will put on the finishing touches of the good summer."

After another summer in North Dakota, the opportunity came for a different assignment—a new government publication. Vernon was to study and write about the mammals, and Florence the birds, of Glacier National Park. They had a variety of travel modes—auto, pack train, and railroad, as well as the usual horseback adventures.[8] For two months they roamed the glaciers and around the lakes of the park, one month of it on a pack trip to the Canadian borderlands of Alberta and British Columbia. Expenses were covered by "a hundred dollar book of coupons for meals and lodging at the hotels and chalets," she wrote Hart; and she was told to telephone for more coupons when they needed them. Spring beauties were blooming with the dogtooth violets, and visions of her little sister's grave at Homewood returned to her thoughts. She thought of Hart too, when she and Vernon found fresh bear sign and elk tracks. The postcard wish hasn't changed at all—"How I wish you could be here with us!"

The mountains invigorated her, and she soon felt she could "ride and climb as well as ever. I am getting stronger every day." While the summer gave Florence a general idea about the breeding birds of the region, she relied on information from others to fill out the year with spring and fall migrant birds and the winter residents. Altogether, the various observers identified almost two hundred species.

One of her sources was a *Forest and Stream* article by longtime friend George Bird Grinnell, published in 1888 shortly after he had started the first Audubon Society and she had just finished at Smith College.

Vernon had additional information for her birds section of the book also, since he had been to the park in 1895 and returned the year after the two of them were there together. On that latter trip he first met Olaus Murie and recognized his potential as a field biologist. In fact, Murie was soon offered a position with the Biological Survey. After a year with the survey in the Olympic Mountains of Washington, Murie went to Alaska to begin his life's work there, first studying the complete life history of the Alaska-Yukon caribou. Olaus Murie and his wife Mardy came under the Baileys' wing when they arrived in Washington as newlyweds a few winters later, after a dogsled honeymoon while Olaus completed some survey work in Alaska.[9]

In 1918 the Baileys' combined efforts at Glacier were published as *Wild Animals of Glacier National Park*. Most of the bird illustrations were from previous publications and included drawings by old friends such as Louis Agassiz Fuertes and Ernest Thompson Seton. In the *Condor* (May, 1919) Joseph Grinnell greeted its publication enthusiastically. "The Baileys are to be congratulated upon their opportunity to inaugurate what must become an increasingly important function of the National Park Service, namely to make known to a large and receptive class of people the wild life resources of national parks. And the National Park Service is to be congratulated upon the good fortune in securing such experienced naturalists to initiate their efforts in getting value out of this asset."

Since this was a guidebook for park visitors, Florence made sure first that her readers knew that birds would even be seen in this seemingly unlikely habitat. "The park with its heavy forest cover and its snow banks and glaciers would seem an unlikely place for birds to spend the summer, as few species care for either deep forests or snow-clad mountains; but while general conditions limit the abundance of birds found within the boundaries of the park, certain local conditions increase their numbers, so that by knowing where to look one may find a richly varied bird population."[10]

Her bird descriptions included new views of the hermit thrush. As if his song weren't exciting enough, here he could be seen among the exhilarating views of the mountain peaks. "The songs heard were, curiously enough, associated with particularly impressive mountain views. On the trail to Iceberg Lake, when we had been slowly climbing up through the dark forest of close-set shaggy firs and spruces, with only an occasional sunbeam lighting up a green fern bed, a patch of lemon yellow lichen, or a clump of magenta Mimulus, suddenly, at a turn, we rode out of the shadowed forest and looked across a great space upon the Swiftcurrent glacier and the noble peak of Grinnell

Mountain. As we gazed, spellbound, at the landscape, over our heads came the thrilling, exalted song of the Audubon hermit, unheard before in the mountains, with its sublime refrain — 'High above you, high above you.' Farther along the trail, when once more we rode out of the shadowed forest for our first inspiring view of the uplifted head of Mount Wilbur and the glacier above Glacier Lake, we were again thrilled by the exalted song with its cool, serene notes — 'High above you, high above you.'"[11]

Florence and Vernon talked so glowingly of Glacier National Park to Hart that they persuaded him to make his first visit there. Returning home to California, he wrote her of the new madrone leaves and the redwoods and oaks at Lagunitas, to which she responded from her Washington, D.C., home. "Give an extra look and enjoy all their beauties twice, for me too! It's good to have so much to remember. I often think if we'd spend more time remembering all the wonderful things that have enriched our lives, we'd forget many of the little worries that destroy our comfort and that of other folks! . . . We have lovely cricket moonlight concerts in our yard o'nights."

In Washington Florence turned her attention to the Audubon Society bird classes with new enthusiasm. The previous year, legislation had finally been passed that prohibited the importation of aigrettes and various other kinds of feathers — the final blow to their use by milliners. But it wasn't done without a fight. Even the venerable John Burroughs, never a fighter, came out for this one battle. He personally signed his name to 450 letters on behalf of the bill, "my last signature as firm as the first," and Mrs. Burroughs even helped fold and stuff them into envelopes.[12] Not satisfied that he had done enough, a month later Burroughs went to Washington with Glen Buck and Ernest Thompson Seton to do his first and only lobbying in the halls of Congress. Another who helped was T. Gilbert Pearson, whose graphic descriptions of the devastation of heron rookeries in his childhood had so impressed Florence. As secretary of the National Association of Audubon Societies, he was backed by its 100,000 members in supporting the bill.[13]

Not everyone was in favor of the bill, but Senator James A. Reed seemed more determined than most to raise the Auduboners' hackles by calling the egrets useless. "The swamp herons' afflictions are doubtless solaced by the thought that it is only a miserable, homely creature, of no use on earth except for one feather, and that its departing agonies must be alleviated by the knowledge that that feather will soon go to glorify and adorn my lady's bonnet."[14]

Just after the Senate debate, two of President Woodrow Wilson's daughters took part in a theatrical performance on behalf of the birds.

Eleanor was chastised in the press by letters from the millinery indus-
try, but one can picture the reaction of the audience, including President and Mrs. Wilson, when they attended "Sanctuary — a Bird Masque"
by George Mackaye. "Miss Eleanor Wilson played Ornia, a bird spirit,
and her sister Margaret sang 'The Hermit Thrush' offstage. Performed
in the sanctuary of the Meriden, New Hampshire, Bird Club, the graceful
allegory in an open-air setting before a well-to-do audience, charmed
the eye and ear. The masque was a poetic plea for bird preservation.
Ornia persuaded the surly plume hunter to cast aside his gun and become a bird lover, much to the joy of a cast of costumed feathered
friends."[15]

Other fashionable ladies were not so easily dissuaded. Customs officials in New York seized a six-hundred-dollar feathered headdress from
one woman, who apparently didn't believe the new law, when she left
the ship from Liverpool.[16] But nothing in the law said that women
couldn't wear feathers once they were in this country, and the black
market demand for them continued, until that too was stopped by a
law in 1922 that required proof of legal importation of wild bird feathers offered for sale. Efforts to counteract the demand included the "Audubon hat" sanctioned by the Audubon Society and advertised shortly
after the 1913 plumage law went into effect. Not only did it sport trim-
mings other than feathers, but it carried a label inside, "Audubon hat:
Save the birds."[17]

Meanwhile, Florence continued her own bird work. Her *Handbook
of Birds of the Western United States* was in its fourth edition. In noting this, *Auk* mentioned that additional material on nomenclature and
books of reference made the book "still more indispensable" and attested to its popularity as well as to increased interest in ornithology.
Two years later, when the book was up to its seventh edition and again
revised, *Auk* noted that "all of these additions tend to bring the work
up to date and give us the very latest information on the birds of the
west, a region in which bird students are increasing at a wonderful
rate, while its avifauna is steadily becoming of greater interest to eastern bird students owing to the increasing travel in the west during recent years."[18]

Bird classes continued at the Audubon Society of the District of
Columbia. Florence added one meeting at her own home because the
students were so eager to go over the collection of skins. She commented that the classes signified a cooperation that was "part of a larger
conscious effort to bring the schools and the people of Washington in
touch with the scientific work centered here, to enable them to profit
by the rare opportunities afforded them."[19] And in turn, the classes

improved the spirit of social service that had long appealed to Florence, by using schools as social centers.

One of the long-time teachers for the society was Professor W. W. Cooke. When he died suddenly, his daughter May gave a large part of his collection of bird skins to the society, enabling it to expand its work even further. May Cooke soon joined the staff of the Biological Survey, becoming the first woman AOU member to acquire institutional affiliation.[20] Professor Cooke's death had a far-reaching effect on Florence, who was called upon to complete an ornithological work that he had started. This developed into her magnum opus, *Birds of New Mexico*. What seemed like a year's project took the next twelve years to publish. Meanwhile, her home was filled with wartime visitors and servicemen friends and relatives traveling through Washington. When Florence was named as a special assistant by the Biological Survey, enabling her to work at its offices, she wrote Hart the good news. "I'm greatly pleased to be *inside* — a *real member* of that estimable organization that my big brother founded!"

During the time Vernon spent in Washington, he also became an instructor in the Audubon bird classes. Florence continued to head its committee for a number of years, still its "guiding spirit." By the end of the decade, children had become increasingly involved through announcements of the classes to the Girl Scouts and Boy Scouts. Of the 250 who signed up one year for the three meetings and two walks, 100 were awarded Audubon Society certificates for perfect attendance.

Working with the Boy Scouts was of particular interest to the Baileys, and Vernon served as a scoutmaster for many years. Educating the young had always been a major priority for Florence as well, and she wrote an article for the *Washington Times* (September 7, 1914), under the column heading, "Truths by Women Who Know," explaining the principles of scout work. Later, in an article for a Boy Scout magazine, she described her observations of the farmer's schoolboy in North Dakota — how he had learned the birds with her help and how she had told him about the Scouts and had written out their law for him. Soon afterward she had found him in the kitchen, "turning the [butter] churn handle with one hand and holding the paper with the [Scout] law on it with the other."[21]

It was good to involve the children in those decisive years of the century's teens, for the young men had other priorities. Those were war years again, and Florence, a child of the Civil War years, shared the "prenatal terror" of war with her fellow Washington hostess, Ellen Slayden.[22] She encouraged support for the War-Camp Recreation Fund by calling on her own travel experience for descriptions.

"'Were you drawn too?' I heard a man at a railroad station brown with uniforms ask commiseratingly of a fresh faced boy in khaki. 'Yes.' And as if answering something in the man's look, the handsome face lit with a smile that went to my heart. 'You might as well die on that side of the water as this!' Superb, light hearted courage of youth! The man turned abruptly, walking away to a window where he stood alone with his back to the crowd. His battles were not so easily won.

"From another village a boy having gone to Canada refused to return for registration, and his family instead of being honored by his response to the call, faced the disgrace of a government investigation. It is not an easy call for all to answer. A boy in uniform took a seat beside me at a theater where war pictures were shown and a Red Cross nurse, raising money to establish more hospitals, told of the wounded she had helped restore to health; and when the pictures of suffering bravely endured moved the audience to tears, the boy bowed his head in his hands.

"Brave lads! With minds holding images of loved ones left behind, of grim battle fields and hospitals ahead of them. They are doing their part. Are we doing ours? . . . In the training camps they have their own engrossing life, but in the off hours, in the communities adjoining them they are among strangers, many of whom are but waiting to exploit them. . . . The army and navy have come to realize this so fully that a War-Camp Community Recreation Fund is being raised to help organize work in the communities adjoining the camps throughout the country, that will reach the million boys and men in training."[23]

The war would soon be over, as all wars eventually are, and lilies of the valley would be picked to decorate the new graves along with the old. At the end of 1918 Florence's dear friend, Olive Thorne Miller, died in California at the age of eighty-seven. At the time she was the oldest member of the AOU, and the group had recognized the fact by sending her greetings at its annual meeting, the month before her death.[24] John Muir was gone, now Mrs. Miller; soon John Burroughs and Theodore Roosevelt would join them.

Florence's health still demanded her attention, and she stayed home the next summer. As she explained to Hart, "I'm really better off here, with a good woman to provide the many and peculiar wants of my mortal frame at this present juncture." Before leaving for North Dakota again, Vernon helped to oversee the bird maps for her New Mexico book, which was—she thought then—nearing completion. They took a short outing together in their tent, camping at the nearby country residence of Mrs. Maynard, who had sung at their wedding almost twenty years before.

Finally, that same summer of 1919, the Homewood property was sold to a local farmer for $6,000. Florence was delighted to see it stay as a farm rather than go to developers her father hadn't liked. The remaining buildings were still filled with family items, and her brother Collins urged her to be sure to collect anything she or Hart wanted. She had already sent Hart all the books she could find that he might use, but she asked him to think again "of the books in the shop, the specimens in the museum, and the wagons in the barn." As for herself, she wanted only the sleigh bells from the old cutter. "I used to love to hear them jingle over the snow."

With her manuscript off to New Mexico for review "at last," and with Vernon returned from the field, Florence had her gall bladder removed that fall and cheerily wrote Hart not to worry. "I am in very good general condition, a husky old dame yet, fit for the fray! The average is only two weeks in the hospital." By December, 1919, she was writing the publication date of the New Mexico book as "1920?" and it's a good thing she added the question mark.

As the next decade opened, with it came a new era of prosperity and the beckoning of new horizons. The Baileys looked toward the horizons of their beloved Southwest, this time Arizona.

13

Feeding Tables for Birds, 1920–1924

THE BAILEYS could hardly wait to head west again, especially to their beloved Southwest. Florence happily accompanied Vernon to Arizona for his winter field assignment there in 1920, after spending the summer season in North Dakota and on the West Coast. Vernon had suffered an apparent heart attack, and they traveled mainly by train with little camping out. Florence wrote to her concerned physician-brother that Vernon was already feeling better and she was sure that if he were careful, "the year out of doors will do him a world of good." The cure of outdoor air had always worked wonders for her, after all.

They went first to sunny California and visited Twin Oaks. Afterward, Florence wrote to Hart about their cousins there, Virginia and Helen, who "have both aged and are working hard." Helen lived absolutely alone, and Virginia was tutoring and ranching. Meanwhile, Vernon's brother Henry had been living alone in Minnesota. She told Hart, "Vernon has worked out a solution to both problems and has sent Henry to Twin Oaks to help the girls with their heavy burdens. He will get him a tractor if that seems best, so that he can make their places more productive and work on other ranches if he has time. Fortunately Helen has been able to get a woman to live with her, so it will be all right for Henry to be there when most needed. . . . we are hoping it will prove happy all around."

They also visited Hart in Lagunitas, and afterward she wrote him again how much she loved his chosen place in California. "It is beautiful and satisfying inside and out—a place to dream of with its views and drives. The only trouble is that for old folks without help it is too hard and for young folks too isolated—for the years are slipping by all too fast."

As the train chugged its way over the December countryside, Florence pondered how much faster the scenery slipped by than when she first traveled west by train some thirty years before. She and Vernon watched the changing life zones outside the window as the train headed up and down mountains, and they talked about a new approach to their assignment. Perhaps because of Vernon's recuperation period, they were to spend five months among the mesquites at the foot of the Santa Rita Mountains in southern Arizona. For Florence, staying in one place for that long "made a bird table seem important; for if they were kept around . . . during the winter, what other interesting migrants might they not tempt to stop in passing during the spring. They were quick to respond to our hospitality . . . the younger [Gambel's, or white-crowned, sparrows] with the brown-striped crowns becoming so tame that they paid little heed to us, some of them even venturing into the tent for food."[1]

When spring arrived, her theory bore fruit. Among the visitors she recorded were a pair of cardinals, "the male a superb bird, with his vivid red plumage and long nodding crest . . . At first they seemed particularly attracted by a cup-shaped section of squash rind kept filled with seed, but soon made themselves at home on the table. The actions of the timid female were an amusing contrast to those of the lordly male. For a long time she was painfully shy in the presence of the flock, usually flying off soon after they appeared, but after three months of association with them she was seen actually making a pass at a usurper.

"A small water cup nailed to the tree by the table was frequented for a time by a Ruby-crowned Kinglet whose size it suited. On the tree above, pieces of suet and bacon rind attracted the black-and-white barred, brown-headed Gila Woodpeckers . . . Among the most regular visitors to the feeding table all through the winter and spring were the Mockingbirds, but while they found some of the food put out to their liking, the water was what attracted them the most, especially as warm weather came, when they were very thirsty. . . . The Phainopeplas, or Silky Flycatchers, the crested males jet black, the females gray, were also thirsty birds."[2]

One of Florence's favorite camp friends was Koo, a roadrunner who named himself by the call with which he announced his presence. He became a regular visitor to share the mice Vernon captured but didn't need for further study, thus supplementing his meager diet until the weather warmed enough to provide his more customary lizards and insects.

"His first appearance in camp was at a truly psychological moment, for not only did our tent contain cages of numerous live rodents which were being studied by the Mammalogist, but a number of white-footed mice which had been caught the night before and were waiting to be

Spending the winter field season in the mountains of southern Arizona, the Baileys studied the local fauna thoroughly. Florence's favorite was Koo, who named himself by his call. The roadrunner quickly discovered that Vernon had a seemingly unending supply of mice, but Koo left when spring called him to other pursuits. The photograph accompanied her article on Koo in Bird-Lore *in 1922. (Courtesy of the Natural History Museum of Los Angeles County, Section of Birds and Mammals.)*

disposed of. So, holding up one of the delectable furry morsels for the alert, long-tailed visitor to see, the Mammalogist invited him to the feast. Being treated like a rational personage, Koo, on seeing the mouse coming through the air toward him, instead of running away, frankly accepted the invitation and started toward the mouse, actually walking up within a few yards of his benefactor for it. But with the prize once in his bill, discretion evidently seemed the better part of valor, for, turning tail, with body and tail held at the swiftest horizontal running level, Koo raced up the slope out of sight."[3]

Occasionally the Baileys made forays from the mountains into the valley bottom to get supplies and mail at Continental, a "bungalow hamlet" of a company experimenting with growing rubber. "It did not take our good neighbor's Ford long to rattle down the nine miles over the stony desert slope past the mistletoe-hung mesquites and catsclaws . . . swerving around sharp turns made to avoid washes from mountain canyons, crossing the terrace where the grotesquely jointed bristling cholla cactus afforded nesting sites for numerous colonies of Cactus Wrens and woodrats and a Cactus Woodpecker's nest had been discovered; down at last to the sight that always brought a thrill, the first of the spectacular giant cactus trees raising their long bare arms stiffly straight toward the sky.

"An old Woodpecker's hole just out of reach was discovered in a stub under the edge of the cottonwood and the Mammalogist proceeded to investigate it. Standing a forked branch against the stub for ladder with a stout stick in the upright fork to prevent his boot from wedging, he climbed up and with a weed stem gently poked down inside the hole, until he recognized the soft touch of feathers. A moment later a long feathered leg was thrust up to drive off the enemy and sharp talons clasped the intruding fingers. So tight was the clasp that when pulled up the long feathered leg was followed out of the hole by its owner, a little, eared Screech Owl. Wanting to examine the hole the Mammalogist handed the handsome little bird to me. While I was admiring the clear black and gray pattern of its soft feathers I inadvertently let its legs slip, whereupon its sharp claws seized my finger, drawing tighter and tighter. 'Straighten its leg,' I was admonished with the explanation, 'when its leg is bent the tendon over its heel draws its claws tight and it can't open them itself; straighten its leg and the claws open.' It seemed quite a worthy experiment to try at the moment and I was soon celebrating my release."[4]

By the middle of March spring came to the Baileys' mountain camp, and the bird migration turned Florence's attention to her new visitors. One of the most spectacular was new to her, and she was surprised at how different it looked, having only seen stuffed specimens before of the "theatrical Painted Redstart, which comes up from Central America just far enough to grace the mountains of Arizona. Unlike the other Warblers it never became common, three being the largest number ever seen at a time; but one was enough to set agog both camp and ranch. Its black plumage which in the sun had the exquisite silken sheen of that of the Phainopeplas might well have been given its strikingly contrasting snowy wing patches and outside tail feathers as well as the appropriately rich carmine breast by the careful hand of an artist deliberately painting a feathered masterpiece."[5]

Then came a surprisingly heavy snow. Some of the birds seemed not to be affected, like the cardinal who had been in full spring song

Even southern Arizona can get snow, as the Baileys discovered that April. Birds flew down the tent's ceiling air hole to escape the sudden storm, giving Florence a close view of a painted redstart, among others. This photograph appeared with her article in Auk, *July, 1923. (Courtesy of the Natural History Museum of Los Angeles County, Section of Birds and Mammals.)*

for some time and "piped up cheerfully as if it took more than an April snowstorm to affect his spirits." One visitor who wasn't used to snow gave Florence a closer view after the storm. "At breakfast time a Painted Redstart after casting his shadow on the tent outside, as he chased after flies suddenly dropped down through the ventilator hole into the tent!"[6]

Among the later migrants toward the end of April was an old friend, though unexpected there. "Our most inappropriate visitor, a Belted Kingfisher, perhaps bound for frozen mountain streams, was discovered . . . perching footlessly over our 'dry wash.' He soon saw his mistake, however, and went rattling up the canyon." She smiled and wished him well. Now that feathered millinery was outlawed, she could begin to forget the association of the kingfisher with that long-time effort and look forward to halcyon days with the birds, free like them from that terror.

Another unexpected event took place when a Gambel's sparrow took a bath in the water pan. "He was the first bird I had seen all winter presuming to use water for that profane purpose. For in that year of drought in the desert both bird and beast were fortunate indeed if they could get enough to drink. The bath was doubtless accounted for by the fact that *gambeli* is a bird of lush mountain meadows threaded with running brooks. Certainly no right-minded desert bird would have been guilty of such shocking wastefulness."

By the time they left camp on the sixth of May, the migration was almost over and the resident species were beginning to nest. "The mesquites which had now come into fresh green leaf were fragrant with yellow tassels. And here and there big cactus flowers were to be seen. The desert was putting on bridal garments."[7]

The coming of the "bridal season" for the birds meant that the winter field season was ending for Florence and Vernon. They headed north for the next summer season in Minnesota near Vernon's home town of Elk River, "back in the land of green things growing!" she wrote to Hart, but there her husband found his quarry unexpectedly difficult. "Vernon came here thinking that the muskrats would be as abundant as when he was a boy but he found that open seasons had so reduced their numbers that it was a question if he could get any. The . . . homemade boat on the lake leaked too badly, but he went to town, got coal tar and canvas and presently had a new canoe! With this he poled and paddled all around the edge of the lake. Nothing worth trapping for was found till near the end of the circuit, when he came to a fresh house and burrowing in with his hand and plunging in his arm he came to the nest warm, and with three silky gray young with their eyes still shut!"

In addition to the baby muskrats to study, Vernon managed to trap four baby beavers. Soon, however, the Baileys were sent east to study beavers in the Adirondacks, and Vernon made elaborate preparations to ship his young charges to the zoo. "We hated to, but Vernon has hardly had an unbroken night's rest since he got them in June and they are so big now that it's very difficult carrying them around from pillar to post. We shipped them in a big dry foods box with two cardboard sleeping boxes, two tin pans of water, two of rolled oats (about 3 lbs.), 4 loaves of bread and bundles of popple, bushmaple, pine, cherry, willow, and hazel all nailed to the walls, besides large and small popple sticks on the walls and in their water pans with the water lilies. They should make the trip in two days and nights." His work to protect the dam builders earned him the title of "Beaver" Bailey among his colleagues.

In her own home country of upstate New York, Florence visited her brother Collins and other relatives, while Vernon explored for beaver. The family cemetery captured her attention, as it had on several occasions and would again, a strong link she maintained with her family's past. Hart never returned to Locust Grove in his later years, however. "Too many ghosts, too many ghosts," he used to say.[8] While Florence was there, one of her nieces was selling off her dairy property. She had suffered a breakdown several years before, and her husband had started to sell it, in Florence's opinion "choosing wisely between his wife and cows," as she wrote to Hart. Besides, the dairy business had faltered after the war demand for powdered milk had killed the sale of fresh milk.

In early October the Baileys returned to Washington, after being away for fifteen months. She described to Hart that furniture had to be moved to its right places, the paperer brought in, coal delivered, and help arranged. "Nothing is really wrong—only time and tide."

It was too late to help with the Audubon bird classes that year, and the pamphlet of the society's history duly notes that they were under someone else's charge "in the absence of Mrs. Bailey."[9] Even so, all of her "meritorious work" now earned for Florence her degree from Smith College, thirty-five years after she had left. On the commencement program in June, 1921, she was listed as a "candidate for the degree of Bachelor of Arts as of the class of 1886." The earnest doer had certainly done it this time, to the quiet applause, no doubt, of the very ones she had thought were making more of their lives than she was when they first left the Northampton campus.

In 1923 the Baileys were on the road again, this time to the lower peninsula of Michigan to help the county agent with muskrats, where Vernon continued his pioneering work on humane live traps, an interest since his childhood days on a Minnesota farm.[10] After many years as a field naturalist, he was even more convinced of the need and value of methods to live-trap animals so they could be moved to a habitat where they were less threatening to agriculture. The days of the buckboard and pack horses were passing, and the railroads were eager to help in developing the land they had acquired in exchange for their rails. The president of the local railroad provided transportation to his farm and to a shipping port so Vernon could meet with officials. Florence detailed the day in an unusually long description to Hart, in which she gave a better clue to the vagaries of travel on the rails than in any of her ornithological outpourings.

"We made the run of 180 miles in a Ford-sedan-railroad-automobile, which has handcar wheels so it runs on the rails. A few miles out the Manager saw a handcar coming and blew his horn with increasing em-

phasis as the distance between us lessened and the gang kept on pump-
ing. When only a few yards away he stood up and made imperative
railroad signals to stop, but it was too late, they couldn't and we couldn't,
and just after I had read in big red letters on the front of the handcar
EXPLOSIVES HANDLE WITH CARE we collided, fortunately not with force
enough to set off the dynamite, but hard enough so the two cars had
to be pried apart with crowbar and shovel! The handcar men, it seems,
had been trying to make a switch so they wouldn't have to lift off the
heavy car and the Manager was trusting them to obey orders and stop
on signal. His only reproof was that they had to allow him to stop a
car that weighed a ton! But all the rest of the day whenever a handcar
appeared in the distance the horn was blown warningly and continu-
ously and we slowed up till the figures were seen scrambling out and
lifting the car off the tracks, which they did with surprising prompt-
ness! And on our return, when we saw the work done by that dynamite we had reason to be thankful that it had not been applied to us!

"The whole run across the state was through woods and the Manager stopped at telephone booths along the way to find out where the
passengers or the freight might be, and several times the Manager gave
Vernon the key and he unlocked switches and let us onto side tracks
before oncoming trains.

"Once when the smoke of a train was discovered all too close ahead
the Manager promptly reversed but the engine heated so it wouldn't
reverse and when we got out to shove it back we shoved it off the
track!!

"But by this time the engine had stopped smoking and the engineer's
head was hanging out of the cab, and when the Manager beckoned,
the whole crew dropped off the train and came running to help us.
Picking up big timbers, they pried us back on the track and soon we
were enjoying the security of the side track. But if you want to know
how small an auto can be you want to look up into the face of a towering locomotive on the same track just ahead! For unlike a handcar,
an auto can't be lifted off the track. And once the switch key wasn't
found at first in its proper pocket.

"On the way home the Manager drove about 30 miles an hour, said
little, and looked frequently at his watch. The passenger was coming.
And when it was a little later he tried to make '2 or 3 extra switches'
before it reached us. A freight was on our heels behind.

"Altogether it was quite a day for a plain housekeeper!"

After the summer in Michigan, although Vernon continued his field
sessions in the West, Florence often remained in Washington. In 1924
Vernon traveled to the Carlsbad Cavern region of southern New Mex-

ico to complete work on his book about animal life there and to take part in the momentous spelunking adventure of the National Geographic Society, of which Hart had been a founder. Although there were national parks in all directions, there were few roads into the cavern area. Its attraction prompted Vernon to note that "the scenic roads of the future will not for long ignore this subterranean wonderland." How right he was! Typical of his mammalogist's view of the universe, Vernon also noted that "to the geologist and mineralogist the graceful, the quaint, the grotesque, the massive secondary rock formations decorating the interior of the cave are of especial interest; but to the biologist the dry and dusty rooms where animal bones and tracks have been preserved for years, and where the bats hang up on the walls or ceilings for their winter sleep, are still more attractive."[11] It is startling to any nonscientist who has experienced the Carlsbad Cavern that anyone could even consider those dry and dusty rooms more fascinating than the geologic formations.

In Washington, Florence turned to some different forms of writing, in addition to her continuing work on the birds of New Mexico. For *Travel* magazine she wrote two stories on the Taos Indians, encouraging people to go to New Mexico to study them "for the purpose of discovering what the finest qualities of the Red Man are." For the *Sunday Star* newspaper, she wrote an article on the Washington National Zoo duck pond to identify what visitors might call "those strange spotted looking ducks."[12] This was in the season when they changed into eclipse plumage—dull coloration to protect them as they molted their wing quills and temporarily retreated to marshes because they could not fly. After describing the process, Florence sent her readers out to the zoo to see for themselves.

Florence and Vernon finished the year by joining to write a book review of *Animal Life in the Yosemite*.[13] Joseph Grinnell was the senior author and at the time director of the University of California Museum of Vertebrate Zoology, which Hart had influenced in its formative years. The book review showed their mutual admiration, since Grinnell had once reviewed Florence's *Handbook*, which he found so useful when it first came out. Although it had been out of print because of a wartime paper shortage, the *Handbook* was on the market again now.

The home the Baileys had built in Washington at 1834 Kalorama Road afforded Florence a comfortable place to stay, and she relished the opportunity to enjoy its comforts more and more. The feeding table she had described for birds in Arizona might as easily apply to her own home. The Baileys' dinner parties were legendary in the scientific community there, as well as among visitors. Just like the Arizona birds, the "flocks" who spent the winter "made a . . . table seem important; for if they were kept around . . . during the winter, what other interesting migrants might they not tempt to stop in passing during the spring. They were quick to respond to our hospitality." Florence's upbringing had trained her well for the role she happily assumed as a Washington hostess, entertaining with a dinner at least once a week. A guest book from the vestibule of their home would list most of the scientific names of the era.

When young brides like Mardy (Mrs. Olaus J.) Murie first came to Washington, they were overwhelmed by it all and awed by their hostess, who introduced them — at a dinner party, of course — to the other Biological Survey members and their spouses. But these young women also recognized a glint of steel in Florence, "a whim of iron," Mardy recalled it. Florence modestly did not talk of her travels, and her young guests knew little of them until later. But when they found out, they could well imagine that her love of birds had been enough to carry her through the rough western terrain many of them were then covering for the first time with their own husbands in the field.

Sixty years later Mardy Murie described her first experience with the Baileys at home. The details she still remembers give evidence of the impression the evening made on the young bride, fresh from the wilds of Alaska. "When Olaus and I, as newlyweds, arrived in Washington in January 1924, the Baileys rather 'took charge' of us; gave us all kinds of good advice about finding an apartment, where to shop, etc., and had a dinner party where we met other members of the Survey and their spouses. The custom back there at that time was that people gave many dinner parties in their homes, and all the families I can remember had a servant — or two. (We ate a lot of roast lamb that winter.) I knew, from Olaus, that Mrs. Bailey had done a great deal of field work out west and in those days all of that would have been fairly rugged. So for me, it was a bit difficult to fit that into the quiet, dignified, very proper silver-haired hostess who was so kind to us but always with very proper dignity."[14]

Mardy also remembered a large party the Baileys gave that winter, "at which Olaus and I were to entertain with some Eskimo stories and Olaus was to do some Eskimo dances. Their home . . . was the typical 3-story row house — dining room and reception room on ground floor, library-living room on second floor, and here is where guests were entertained after dinner. Before the dinner, Olaus and I were up there with the Baileys, talking about just where Olaus would do the dance, and I remember her saying, in her lovely low-key voice which I remember so well — 'Olaus, I have quite a valuable chandelier down below here in the dining room — you won't be bouncing too heavily, will you?' Olaus laughed and replied: 'Oh no, I hop very lightly.' And he did!"

Another friend elaborated on the picture of the Baileys' home. "No one who ever visited that home in the old days will forget it; for it was the home of two devoted naturalists — devoted to Nature and to each other — and every room, every nook and corner, was a testimonial to that devotion — the inviting library and living room on the second floor filled with books and pictures, with warmth and welcome; the octagonal dining room; the fireplaces; the American Indian rugs and baskets the Baileys had collected; Vernon's mammals and humane traps in the basement; the backyard, with its oaks and squirrels (but no cats!). It was a place where many kindred souls foregathered."[15]

Often a hibernating bat could be found in the pocket of an old sweater, hanging in a dark corner, or under an Indian basket in the entryway to the downstairs parlor. At precisely five each evening it awakened and flew upstairs to Vernon's desk, where he would feed it fresh insects collected especially for its dinner, a task assigned to visiting young people on occasion. Florence called the bat Copernicus, because "he flew around the heavenly bodies." A kangaroo rat occupied a well-equipped cage on the library table, and an emerald-tinted lizard lived in a glass bowl on top of Vernon's desk. Like Copernicus, it was fed daily insect tidbits.[16]

One who became as close as family during that period was Douglass Hayes, who worked with Vernon to perfect his humane VerBail trap.[17] He first met the Baileys after his sister published a newspaper article describing her birdwatching activities. Florence invited her to call, and he went with her. He was first struck by the Baileys' collection of artifacts, then later by the scientific journals and books, as well as the resident wildlife like Copernicus. The Baileys called each other "Mr. Dearie" and "Mrs. Dearie," but Hayes's special treat was to hear them greet each other by a songbird's call. "Mr. Bailey whistled a clear and unmistakable reproduction of the song sparrow's musical voice."

Hayes found Florence extremely precise, a trait that sometimes exasperated her husband. One morning when they were scheduled to leave very early on a trip, she made a very late appearance. When Vernon asked about the delay, she replied that she had been putting fresh shelf papers in the pantry. Came the retort, a bit testily, "Oh, Mrs. Dearie, you spoil all the fun!"

Douglass Hayes paid special attention to one painting, a unique showpiece on the panel of the library fireplace, the portrait of a tiger by wildlife naturalist Charles R. Knight. The Baileys had built their house around the tiger picture, which Knight had promised to do for them before the place was actually constructed. The panel seemed to Knight "to give these two splendid friends the greatest amount of satisfaction, and I am wondering what will become of it."[18] Florence bequeathed the painting to the Smithsonian, where it is now permanently deposited in the National Collection of Fine Arts. Actually the mantel itself was dismantled and the whole panel taken, so it was difficult—but not impossible—to trace.

Knight is best known for his renditions of prehistoric animals, although their mutual friend Fuertes once commented that it was a pity Knight painted so few birds because he did them so well. Birds of prey were a passion with Fuertes—"they are what the big cats are to Knighty," who could often be found at the nearest zoo, sharing a supper with the keepers while he painted the felines well past closing time.[19] In fact, while he was painting the tiger for the Baileys, he became such a familiar sight that he overheard one woman say to her friend, "Meet me at the artist," an anecdote he told on himself for years afterward. The tiger he was painting was one of the first on public view in this country, donated to the zoo by a traveling circus when it got too old to perform.[20]

One dinner visitor, impressed by the big fireplace under the portrait, picked up and sacked seventy pounds of Monterey pine cones in California and shipped them to the Baileys to burn in it the next winter. Another survey scientist told a different kind of sidelight on life in the Bailey home. "More at home in the field than in Washington, [Vernon] Bailey's habits were sometimes disconcerting to his wife and their friends. For years he maintained a number of animals in the basement of their Washington home, including kangaroo rats. He advised his wife that these rodents were useful in holding down the resident cockroach population. She was appalled to discover that cockroaches were even present in the premises."[21]

No doubt her whim of iron kept her firm under such circumstances. Besides, if she had fussed, Vernon's standard reply of "oh, pshaw, oh pshaw" would have changed to his more emphatic, "Florence, stop your noise!"[22] Although these interchanges are remembered in kindly terms by visiting relatives, under the ethic of the day they were reserved for "family" and not used (or remembered) in any formal gathering, any more than was their customary "Mr. Dearie" and "Mrs. Dearie." Vernon had other names, collected like mammal specimens. In addition to "Beaver" Bailey, his bulletin on pocket gophers earned him the nickname of "Gopher Jim" Bailey, and Theodore Roosevelt called him "Wolf" Bailey for his work in protecting ranchers from that supposed thief.[23]

Vernon's years of travel in the Southwest left their traces, even in

Washington. Whenever he sat down to dinner, he habitually picked up his plate and blew imaginary grains of sand from it.[24] In deference to the Victorian side of her character, Florence resisted any similar temptation she may have had.

Even so, Florence's young grandnieces who visited thought of her as "quite fussy."[25] Whenever she or Vernon had a cold, for instance, she would put a cloth over the telephone before using it. Perhaps this was a throwback to her early concern about tuberculosis. She wasn't especially fond of the telephone anyway, having little time in her life for such fripperies. When she ended a phone conversation, she simply hung up, without wasting energy on mutual good-byes.

But if the conversation in the library at home reported some favorable trend in conservation or any good incident, that was a different matter. Olaus Murie often watched her switch into rapt attention. Her face would adopt "that keen look, lips slightly parted, her face beaming with a tender exultation, as she would utter one expressive word, 'Good!'" Olaus summed up his impressions. "Here lived a congenial pair of naturalists of the old school, at peace with Nature, and with Mankind."[26]

Whether dining with birds in Arizona or scientists in Washington, Florence and Vernon were always gracious hosts and welcomed one and all.

14

Birds on a Sumptuous Scale, 1926–1933

FOR SEVERAL YEARS Florence had anticipated the publication of *Birds of New Mexico*. It had been a long time in coming, and its actual publication was almost an anticlimax.

Collectors and observers for the U.S. Biological Survey had been working in New Mexico since her brother became first chief of the survey when it began in 1886. Hart had recognized the significance of the diverse habitat of the territory—it was not yet a state—and he assigned his best field man, Vernon Bailey, to work there before the century had turned. Then in 1903 Vernon had returned, this time with his new bride Florence, to do a complete biological survey of New Mexico. Other field men were also involved and spent several seasons there.

But like so many other government studies, the work had never been published for the public. Eventually a member of the survey, Wells W. Cooke, was assigned to write up the bird life of New Mexico, while Vernon was to write up the mammals. Cooke did a tremendous amount of work researching and mapping the routes for everyone who had ever observed birds there. His first entry was for Casteñada, the chronicler for the Coronado expedition in the year 1540, who reported seeing "a very large number of cranes and wild geese" as well as a great many wild turkeys "with great hanging chins."[1] But Dr. Cooke died suddenly in 1916, before he could complete the work. Although Florence worked toward its completion, it gathered bureaucratic dust for another ten years. By then the chief of the Biological Survey was Dr. E. W. Nelson, under whose direction Cooke had begun his project. Nelson had a vested interest in completing that task.

In the intervening years Florence had also spent additional summers with Vernon in New Mexico, continuing her research. She needed no further encouragement to write about birds, but her appointment as a special assistant at the survey gave her a new sense of enthusiasm for her task. Almost every day she rode into the survey offices and worked at a small corner there, piling up references and updating materials that Dr. Cooke had collected. She wrote to Hart, "While Vernon was away I had his desk, and when he came back I took Mr. Murie's, but the other day he appeared on the scene — too happy for words over the new baby — and I went over to the museum to work, and am now enjoying my big brother's desk!" To friends like Doug Hayes, she showed her continuing admiration for Hart by referring to him as GLN — Greatest Living Naturalist.[2] From Hart she had learned well the tricks of the ornithological trade, and she brought with her to the survey offices her own detailed resources, her precious field notes. From these she added her personal observations over the twenty-year span since she had first gone to New Mexico.

Because of her knowledge and interest, the scope of the work was enlarged. The resulting book was the "first comprehensive report on the bird life of the Southwest," as the Biological Survey chief acknowledged in the preface. Florence's contributions were typical of her lifetime of observations: "a study of complete range, descriptions of the birds, their nests, eggs and food, together with accounts of their general habits." Only someone who had known the birds intimately, who had sat there for hours watching them, could have added this kind of information.

When it was suggested that the book be published under joint authorship of Florence and Dr. Cooke, she arched her back: "I only collaborate with my husband."[3] Because of the original material she had provided, the survey backed off and Florence became the sole author, with full credit to Cooke in her introduction.

Writing the book was only half of the problem, however. Publishing it was another matter entirely. It now contained more than 800 pages, plus maps and illustrations. This led one reviewer later to wish that "the publisher had given us a book of lighter weight."[4] It was certainly not a book to be carried in the field. There were twenty-four colored plates of birds, as well as the more common black-and-white renderings either as drawings or photographs, many by friends such as Ernest Thompson Seton, Robert Ridgway, and Olaus Murie. Most of these were from the survey files or had appeared in government publications, in magazines, or in her own *Handbook of Birds of the Western United States*.

The cost to publish such a book was significant, even in the 1920s. Since it was now to be for general reference and not just a specialized government publication, it demanded a different treatment. The government had no budget for such a book, and no publisher could be found.

Finally the New Mexico Department of Game and Fish was approached to help. Much to its credit, that enlightened agency recognized the value of the work that familiar lady had done there over the years. But they too lacked the funds for such a monumental book, so they in turn contacted the State Game Protective Association — now the New Mexico Wildlife Federation, a local group of sportsmen organized like others across the country to protect the diminishing stock of game and their habitat. Although birds were no longer hunted for their feathers, commercial hunting continued unabated. The game protective groups' national arm, the Wildlife Management Institute, was working to correct this. Two of its first directors were C. Hart Merriam and John Burroughs. Today, birders have these concerned early sportsmen to thank for the protected habitats they too enjoy.

Certainly Florence had them to thank. In addition to agreeing to distribute the book through their local groups in New Mexico, they obtained the help of private individuals to underwrite the cost of its publication, to be repaid from sales of the book. The major contributors were Mr. and Mrs. George D. McCreary, Jr., of Silver City, New Mexico, philanthropists from the East Coast, whose generosity also made it possible to carry out another of Florence's convictions about the book. She wanted to keep the cost as low as possible so that more people could use it, and so she insisted that the price be set so that it would cover only the cost of publication. Because it was underwritten privately, this could be done. But even at five dollars, it was beyond the reach of many who wanted it. However, half of the 1,000 copies were sold before the shipment reached New Mexico from the printer in Washington, D.C. In addition to the general printing, a special numbered edition of 350 was leatherbound and signed by the author.

Florence sent Hart weekly reports of her progress while she read the galley proofs and then the page proofs, until she could finally quip, "I'm no longer a 'galley-slave.'" Then it was time to wait impatiently for the book to do its long-awaited work. "May it be to the people what I hope!"

Paul Oehser, a young editor at the survey, was assigned to help in the final process. Like the Muries and others before, the Oehsers had become part of the Bailey family, staying in their large home until they could settle into one of their own and giving Florence company while Vernon was at the Grand Canyon. She was happy to have them there, especially during that busy period on the book. Grace Oehser even did the marketing and planned the meals, which helped Florence immensely. In thanks, she gave Paul one of the autographed leather-

Canadian bird artist Major Allan Brooks, shown here in his studio, completed most of the Birds of New Mexico *illustrations. His technique was described in the* Condor *(July, 1946) by fellow artist/ornithologist Harry Harris: "Probably no artist in history ever practiced such a seemingly impossible method. . . . he began at the tip of the bill and continued on around to encompass the entire form in a single line. . . . He so completely visualized his composition that it was as if he merely traced its outline." (Courtesy of the Natural History Museum of Los Angeles County, Section of Birds and Mammals.)*

bound copies, as well as separate prints of the colored plates from the book.[5]

Most of the original plates were done by Major Allan Brooks, a Canadian bird artist who completed several assignments after Louis Agassiz Fuertes was accidentally killed. Brooks and Fuertes were good friends whose painting styles had grown consciously closer over the years they had worked together as joint illustrators. Like both Fuertes and Charles Knight, Brooks also was an expert at the art of mimicking the calls of birds.[6]

Fuertes had completed only one plate for the book, the Mearns (Montezuma) quail, a favorite in his experience with the Baileys and a fitting tribute to their friendship. He was with Vernon in the Chisos Mountains of Texas in 1900 when he first saw the quail. Vernon described Fuertes at the scene. "One morning at sunrise in our base camp in a gulch . . . a Mearns Quail came and sat on a rock and preened and strutted and spread its hooded crest within four or five feet of his nose. When it had gone he burst out of his sleeping bag and fairly danced with joy as he ran for pencil and paper and worked for an hour on sketches of the quaint bird."[7]

Fuertes also wrote up the experience for an article in the *Condor* that Florence quoted in both her *Handbook* and in *Birds of New Mexico*. "When the Quail also discovered him, as Mr. Fuertes describes it, in his excitement he 'quickened his trot, compressed his plumage, and raised his head to its highest . . . But accompanying this action he displayed his curious crest in a peculiar and striking way. Instead of raising it . . . he spread it out laterally, like half a mushroom.'"[8] The color plate on the facing page in *Birds of New Mexico* was done from a study sketched that dawn.

In this book Florence took a fresh look at the hermit thrush, describing their abundance on Jack Creek, at 11,000 feet in the Pecos Mountains. "From the woods above, below, and around us came their beautiful songs, the first heard in the morning and the last at night. At sunset, as we walked through the cool, still, spruce woods, its pale beards lit by the last slanting rays, involuntarily treading lightly to make no sound, from unseen choristers a serene uplifted chant arose, growing till it seemed to fill the remote aisles of the forest. Sometimes a silvery voice would come from the open edge of the dark forest, where the singer looked far down the mountainside and out over the wide mesa-clad plains – a wide view, the beauty and sweep of which seemed in rare harmony with his untroubled spirit."[9] It was at times like this that Florence remembered her own untroubled spirit as a child walking at sunset with her family in the woods around Homewood, listening to the silvery voice of the hermit thrush.

Florence's own "wide view" now encompassed the completion of this major book, its anticipation very real and very exciting. The *Condor* greeted its publication with a notice in July, suggesting that those interested place advance orders with their fellow member R. T. Kellogg

of Silver City, New Mexico. Kellogg was an avid birder whose observations are among many Florence used in the book. He was a neighbor
of the McCrearys and the one who had encouraged them to underwrite its publication. Kellogg was also the one whom Allan Brooks
first contacted when he arrived in New Mexico to do the illustrations
after Fuertes' death. Kellogg's daughter still lives in the family home
and remembers peering over Brooks's shoulder as he worked on the
painted redstart and red-faced warbler that serve as the frontispiece
in the book. His field specimens lay on the table before him as he worked.
"Their demise had taken place shortly before. His creation so lifelike
the birds seemed almost to fly."[10] Kellogg also helped to sell the book
by going on the road for some time before its publication to stimulate
sales at universities throughout the Southwest.

All of the birding magazines reviewed *Birds of New Mexico* as soon
as it was out that autumn of 1928. *Auk* (January, 1929) recognized its
value as the first "adequate ornithology" of a state other than in the
East or on the Pacific Coast. It also noted how expensive such a publication is and that "we are indebted for a most complete account of
the bird-life of this interesting region while much credit is also due those
who have generously made possible the publication on such a sump-
tuous scale."

Its value went beyond New Mexico, the *Condor* mentioned in March,
1929, because of its usefulness throughout the Southwest. The reviewer
tipped his hat to Florence, whose sections on general habits "permit
the author to depict in her usual happy vein her reactions to the actual
presence and companionship of the birds she loves so well."

In addition to these acclaims of her fellow ornithologists, Florence
received a very special tribute. The AOU elected her a Fellow, the first
woman designated to the "highest honor to which an American ornithologist can attain," as Elliott Coues had expressed it upon his election. Remembering his own election forty years before, Frank Chapman added that "the competition to enter this group, limited to fifty,
was not so keen then as it is now." Florence's election certainly surprised one woman ornithologist. Althea Sherman had just written to
Margaret Morse Nice, "I have said and I believe it, that no woman will
ever be made a Fellow of AOU. In 1912 I was told by a Fellow that
Mrs. Bailey had been nominated, Beebe was justly elected, but think
of Bergtold made a Fellow and Mrs. Bailey not. No, man's nature must
change before a woman is a Fellow."[11]

Florence was increasingly proud of her association with the AOU
and its treatment of women. Three years later she and Althea Sherman
were present when Margaret Morse Nice was elected almost unani-

mously as a Fellow. Florence exclaimed, "This is the very first time any-one has been elected on the first ballot."[12]

The same year, the AOU added another jewel to Florence's tiara, presenting her with its coveted Brewster Medal. In reporting the event to the AOU membership, Vernon's coworker Theodore S. Palmer commented, "this is the first time this medal has ever been given to a woman and the first time for a state list."[13]

Florence's relationship to the Brewster Medal has an intricate history. Its establishment was suggested to the AOU by her friend, Frank Chapman, after the death of William Brewster, another friend, in 1919. It was to be a biennial award for the most important book on birds of the western hemisphere. The medal was designed by Brewster's life-long friend, the sculptor Daniel Chester French, whose works include the Lincoln Memorial in Washington and the Minuteman statue in Concord, Massachusetts.[14] The latter honors those who routed the British in 1776 at "Meriam [sic] corner," where the house of one of Florence's ancestors still stands. Although we think of that battle as "early" in this country's history, Florence points out in *Birds of New Mexico* that birds were first recorded by white men in New Mexico in 1540, "eighty-two years before the first recorded birds were seen in New England."[15]

Not to be outdone by the AOU, the University of New Mexico also praised its adopted daughter by awarding her an honorary LL.D. degree in 1933. The local newspaper merely called her an "ornithologist and author of a volume on New Mexico birds."[16] But then, the recipient of the other honorary degree bestowed that June, Mary Austin, was identified only as a "Santa Fe writer." It had been a long time since they shared the pages of *St. Nicholas* magazine.

Thirty years passed before another book—and the only other, to date—on New Mexico birds was done. When J. Stokley Ligon published his *New Mexico Birds and Where to Find Them* in 1961, he commented that although Florence had not been a contemporary of the earliest ornithologists who pioneered in Southwest field work, she "warrants the title of greatest American woman ornithologist."[17] He described the work of the inseparable team of the Baileys, and he used many of Florence's descriptions of New Mexico birds. By the time Ligon's book was in print, both of the Baileys and Ligon himself had passed on.

In 1928, however, she accepted gracefully the praise for her magnum opus, which seemed the culmination of her dreams. She was very fond of New Mexico, and the territory—now a fast-growing state—held many happy memories of her traveling life with Vernon. Those were important years of helping to identify and describe the fauna of the Southwest for the government, and delightful years of discovery and sharing in the land of enchantment. Vernon's work there had also culminated, with the publication of his *Mammals of New Mexico* in 1932. It is still in use as a field guide and in 1971 was reissued in paperback under the title of *Mammals of the Southwestern United States*.

Adding to her own nostalgic view of New Mexico was Vernon's retirement from the U.S. Biological Survey the summer of 1933, after forty-six years of service. Vernon would be sorely missed at the survey. He was still making new discoveries in the West, such as the buffalo skeletons he had just found in the silt of Oregon's Malheur Lake. But money was tight in Washington (was it ever otherwise?), and the staff had to be cut back. The chief contacted the older men one by one. When Vernon's time came, he felt that he had to give his place to a younger man. Theodore S. Palmer also retired then, after forty-four years. *Auk* urged them to look ahead. "They are both still active in scientific research and we trust that the relief from routine will enable them to pursue more freely the lines of work in which they are so deeply interested."[18]

For Vernon this meant time to pursue his VerBail trap business. He had been to Maine to test them and looked forward to trips to the far West with leisure to work on their application to both small and large mammals. One naturalist recalled meeting Vernon in the field in California "carrying the biggest coyote I ever saw" and pleased with the success of his large trap.[19]

The VerBail traps have had a long history since they were first made in the Baileys' basement. The trap was patented, and the patent was later bought by a large trap company. When the company stopped manufacturing them, C. H. Channing, a bird bander in Washington, took up the challenge, improved the design, and went back to making them in his garage. He never even knew they had come in different sizes, being interested primarily in birds of prey. When he retired, he then taught another young bird bander his skill, and the traps continue to be produced periodically from still another garage. As Channing concluded, "so you see Vernon Bailey is, in essence, still with us."[20]

Yet in spite of being taught so well in the school of nature, Vernon had always felt a little out of place among the professional scientists with their college degrees. He knew that a new era of science had arrived while he had been working out in the field. It was time for the Baileys to move on.

But work was their ethic, and there was still much work to be done. They were ready to move on, but not to move out.

❦ 15 ❦

A Bat and a Beacon, 1931–1948

THE BAILEYS continued their nationwide travels right through the 1930s, and into their seventies. Florence's correspondence with her Smith College Class of '86 picked up again after a long lapse, and she told them of three years' work in one sentence. "Our summers are spent in the field and our winters in writing up our field notes." She expanded on it very matter-of-factly, as though everyone did likewise. "In 1929, we worked in the Grand Canyon; in 1930, on the flood bottom of the Mississippi Wild Life Refuge. In 1931, while Mr. Bailey was in the Sierras, I stayed at his sister's ranch in Nevada — wonderful country."

Wonderful country indeed! That summer of 1931, not only did the Baileys go, but they took with them on the train Collins's two granddaughters, Betty Hone and Florence Merriam, who was named for her grandmother — Collins's wife — and called Floddie. Both girls were of college age. They had grown up in rural New York state, near Homewood. Neither had ever been west, and the excitement of the trip got them up early on the train, visiting and watching the changing scenery outside the windows, as their Auntie Florence had done so many times. Florence herself was always an early riser, like most who are serious about watching birds. The main purpose of the trip was for Vernon to serve as naturalist for a month-long Sierra Club trip into the Yosemite area of the California Sierra. The two girls were to be part of the hiking group. They left the train at Fallon, Nevada, where Vernon's sister, Anna Bailey Mills, still lived with her ranching family. The girls took to their first exposure to western living immediately, racing over the dusty terrain on horseback with their distant cousins.

It had been arranged that Florence would stay with Anna while Vernon and the girls were in California. She didn't feel up to a camping trip, although Floddie recalled that "life with Uncle Vernon had so conditioned her — grabbed her by the brain — to do things with him that

The Baileys in the field, Phantom Ranch, Grand Canyon, 1929. (From the collection of Barbara Hastings McKee.)

[up to this age, at least] she was willing to go along and endure all these outdoor vicissitudes." Betty chimed in, "She was such a gentle person, but she was very determined. Otherwise, she would never have gone as far as she did. Although she had her own scientific ambitions and standards, she never felt that these kept her from taking a back seat for Uncle Vernon and for her famous brother."[1]

Vernon's niece Laura was also to be one of the hikers, and she drove them in the family's Model A over Tioga Pass to Tuolumne Meadows to meet the Sierra Club group. This was no trip for beginners. Participants were expected to hike an average of twenty miles a day. Vernon was then sixty-seven and loved every minute of it, and the campers loved him. He still preferred sleeping on the ground and expected his nieces to do the same, which they did. In fact, when they returned home, they preferred the floor to a bed, at least for a while. Vernon had always been a pied piper, eager to go looking for animals or birds or whatever, with young people always following him so they wouldn't miss any of his constant discoveries in the natural world. Laura, Betty, and Floddie were no exceptions.

Neither Florence nor Vernon was above playing cupid on occasion, as part of their lifelong love of helping young people. Another young hiker on that Sierra Club trip was Carl Youngberg, who taught Floddie to tie trout flies, and she was the one who was hooked. Here was everything she had always dreamed of — the West, a young man paying her every attention, and fishing, her favorite sport. The next year she married him and they returned West. In 1988 she still lived near the California Sierra in a hilltop house surrounded by birds.

Betty too loved the West, but her time there would have to wait. It was just after the Depression, and there were no jobs. Her mother was ill, and that fall the Baileys offered, "Why don't you come and spend the winter with us in Washington? You can type manuscript for Auntie and you can help Uncle with his files down in the basement." And so they did. Betty still considers Florence and Vernon important early role models in her career as a science educator and writer.

On the way home from that trip West, their route took them through New Mexico. Near Taos they visited other cousins, the Goldens. Helen Merriam (not the one from Twin Oaks) had married an Irishman, Peter Golden, who had spirited her off to northern New Mexico to live. When she bore him twin daughters, he named them Eithne and Deirdre after Irish princesses.

At Taos Pueblo, Florence wanted to renew old acquaintances, but they no longer used their Indian names. They had chosen to use Spanish ones that were more acceptable in that changing world. It took a while to find out that Gray Buffalo had died, but she had a happy reunion with Sun Elk. "Helen drove us over to the pueblo and we were much interested to see our old camp man, Sun Elk, now almost venerable looking like the old councillors of the days over twenty-five years ago when we were there," she wrote Hart.

After that trip, Florence corresponded with her young grandniece

One cousin, Helen, settled in Taos, New Mexico, where Florence (seated) visited her family in the early 1930s. Standing (left to right) are Florence's niece Eithne Golden, Elizabeth Hone (another niece, traveling with the Baileys), Helen Merriam Golden, and Florence's nephew Terence Golden. (From the collection of Eithne Golden Sax.)

Eithne Golden, encouraging her interest in becoming a writer. "I am very glad you are trying to help the Mexicans with your stories. Perhaps you can be a second Helen Hunt Jackson. You know what she did for the Indians. . . . We don't want to get sentimental about any race, but we do want people to understand their best qualities, and we also want to bolster their virtues, keep them from imitating the low grade people who gather around them and keep them true to the best standards of their ancestors."

That Christmas Florence sent the Goldens a package. On Eithne's gift she attached a note. "I have often seen beautiful thoughts and eager enthusiasms in your eyes and so am sending you a little Diary to preserve them. It would be a pity to lose them. Something suggested by your studies, some fine or heroic trait that appealed to you, changing colors and lights and shadows on the mountains, the glories of sunset— a thousand thoughts worth preserving. . . . You get the idea. Be putting down the foundation for your future stories and books. Live and work with a purpose. And keep in your heart the purpose to make the world sweeter and better and stronger for your having lived. Help. Write me as you would talk to me."

Florence also passed on a family tradition to the two Golden girls. She mailed them the old mythological star atlas that had been her mother's—their great-grandmother's—which had helped "in finding my way about in the sky," so they too could enjoy that lifelong pleasure of hers.

Both Florence and Vernon took pleasure in correspondence. In addition to his continuing relationships with coworkers from the Biological Survey, Vernon also kept in touch with many of the Boy Scouts he had led in Washington. One of those was Kermit Roosevelt. Another was Edwin McKee, who went on to become a National Park Service ranger at the Grand Canyon.

One summer the Baileys brought another niece, Barbara Hastings, west to drive their car. On the way they stopped at Mammoth Caves in Kentucky so Vernon could do some field work. Besides collecting a few bats, he kept one live in his coat pocket for several days, showing it to interested people "with a little lecture on bats," Barbara recalled. In the evenings she helped him make up study skins of bats, mice, chipmunks, whatever he had trapped the previous day or night. He always carried a canvas bag of dry oatmeal to bait the traps. Florence was always there, but very quietly in the background. It was the role she chose to play throughout her life. Once at the Grand Canyon, she collected material for her next book, guided around by young Edwin McKee,

The Baileys went west one summer driven by a niece, Barbara Hastings. While at the Grand Canyon, she met a ranger who later became her husband. Feeding deer on the North Rim, she posed for Vernon and the photograph appeared in Florence's last book, Among the Birds in the Grand Canyon Country, *in 1939.*

Vernon's former Boy Scout. Barbara later became his wife, with a little help from a doting aunt and uncle.

This was Florence's kind of country. She wrote Hart about Phantom Ranch in the bottom of the Grand Canyon. "Strange too it seems to hear an aeroplane and look up from our big creek to see one flying over us! The migrants are pausing by our door now, through the fragrant mesquites. It is exciting to see the new ones, day by day. This is a thoroughfare — strings of mules — pack trains going both ways and tourists going and coming. Just how we'll manage all this zoo and Barbara do all the trapping and skinning while Vernon makes his Kaibab trip, remains to be seen! I have my hands full with birds and notes."

The next week, on mules and pack horse with Edwin McKee, they moved camp. With their typical simplicity of style, they adapted well to the small cabin. It was sheltered from the weather and "with a big table to write on, plenty of nails to hang things on, and shelves for all our supplies. Vernon made a broom out of half of an agave stem and a piece of burlap and Barbara soon had the house in perfect order — with nails for each member of the family. The cots we took outdoors to put our sleeping bags on and a campfire was stoned up in front of the house for cooking."

The tourist scene hasn't changed much in the intervening half-century. "Strings of saddled mules are brought up every morning and young men and maidens and some gray headed patriarchs clad in protecting bluejeans swallow their breakfast and cheerfully sally forth — returning at night — some young girls weary and dejected, holding onto their saddle horns significantly." The Kolb brothers had a stone house, which still stands on the south rim, where they lectured every afternoon on their trips down the Colorado. The last one had been an attempt to rescue a man and his wife who were drowned. "I hear that the Kolbs say they will never go again, which sounds like common sense to me." Florence never was much for water outings.

Another new friend that summer was identified in her resulting book only as "the young ornithologist." Randolph (Pat) Jenks was a young volunteer worker at the canyon whose interest in birds attracted him to Florence and her to him. He added several birds to her Grand Canyon list, including one at Phantom Ranch, where he was awakened "by the beautiful shrill call of the canyon wren."[2] Vernon taught him how to prepare and label bird specimens, and soon Pat had the largest scientific collection of such skins in Arizona. With his early interest inspired by the Baileys and later encouraged by Joseph Grinnell, Pat also described a new Arizona subspecies of the golden-crowned kinglet.

Some years later, while surveying the Indians' ancient sacred salt trail into old Mexico, Pat honored his ornithological friend Florence by attaching the name Bailey Crater to an unmapped volcanic formation sacred to local Indians. Since it was not within the U.S. borders, however, the name was never officially registered. It lies south of Organ Pipe National Monument in the Pinacate Mountains, which were described in an *Arizona Highways* article. "Few come to this place, but all remember the ground. The black rocks blasted across the horizon by volcanos now drink the desert sun. Craters open to the heavens and swallow the sky. . . . No one lives here now. But all imagine this place."[3] Florence may never have seen her crater, but it was part of her beloved Southwest and that's what counted. She treasured Pat's letter to her telling of his naming Bailey Crater.

The summer passed in pleasant study, Florence quietly observing the birds while Vernon more vigorously explored both rims of the canyon. In August Vernon went with a field party from the University of Arizona to San Francisco Mountain near Flagstaff, but Florence wrote Hart that she had decided "it would be too strenuous for me to keep up with a lot of young folks so I am going with Barbara and her brother back to Grand Canyon to wait." They went into town for a short vacation from camp — mail, a shower, and dinner — and then they returned with renewed appetites for the simple life, where "the sincere uplifted notes of the hermit thrush rang out through the stillness, seeming to interpret the far view in terms of human life — free of all belittling earthly influence, urging a far, serene view of life."[4]

Later they moved into the lodge, where a visiting "reptile man" gave Vernon a chuckwalla who liked to eat dandelions on the windowsill of their room. Florence chuckled to Hart, "we came near not having our room made up yesterday on his account, but when the chambermaid saw me come in she said she'd come while I was there!"

Florence turned her attention to other wildlife as well. She was intrigued by the two forms of gray squirrel at the canyon, the Abert's on the south rim and the Kaibab on the north. As she watched the Abert's bury pine cones, she recognized the value of this activity in distributing the pine seeds and later wrote up her discovery for the *Journal of Mammalogy*. Vernon was interested in the unusual Kaibab squirrel with its tufted ears. A young nature artist named Will Osborn visited the Baileys in Washington with their mutual friend, Betty Lee, whose geologist father Vernon had accompanied into the Carlsbad Cavern with the National Geographic expedition. When Vernon learned that Will had photographed the Kaibab squirrel, he delightedly asked if he could include the photo in his article for an upcoming issue of the same journal. This honor encouraged the young naturalist in his wildlife inter-

The unusual Kaibab squirrel caught the attention of both Vernon Bailey and a young naturalist named Will Osborn, who took this photograph. When Will met Vernon in Washington later, Vernon asked if he could use the photo for an article he was writing. The young naturalist saved this copy of the resulting issue of the Journal of Mammalogy, May, 1928. *(From the collection of Will Osborn.)*

ests, and he later helped Frank Chapman to mount a major exhibit called "Birds and Man" at the American Museum of Natural History in New York. He later became a major influence in Audubon work and environmental protection in Arizona, where he still lives and observes nature.

From chuckwallas to cupid was all fair game to the Baileys. And once they had played matchmaker, Florence often went on to encourage the newlyweds to start a family. She had married late and had suffered several miscarriages. She always regretted not having children herself, but loved to mother anyone she could bring under her wing.

Time and again they helped young people — especially upcoming young naturalists — to find jobs, even housing them when need be. When Floddie found that she couldn't attend Smith College as she had hoped, Auntie Florence and Uncle Vernon happened to be visiting her and her mother at Collins's family home. The Baileys asked her to come to Washington, go to George Washington University, and stay with them. She was delighted, and that very night her mother packed her trunk, and she left with them for a visit that extended to the California Sierra Club trip. "It was the beginning of a wonderful career in Washington for four years, living with Auntie and Uncle and seeing a lot of Uncle Hart and Aunt Elizabeth. I did some printing for Uncle Hart later on his maps. We went to all kinds of marvelous scientific lectures, and to the National Geographic Society meetings. In my last year of college Auntie Florence was proofreading *Birds of New Mexico*. She was about 65 at the time. It seemed marvelous to me that she had written such a volume with so much scientific information and knowledge." Floddie described her Auntie at that time as "rather tall and willowy, with beautiful white hair and snapping brown eyes, quite bird-like in fact." Vernon is remembered at that time by one friend as being more like a lizard. "I always thought when he died he could just dry up in a corner."

Florence was still giving dinner parties, and Floddie recalled the preparations. "Those were quite gala affairs. No liquor, of course. No drinks before dinner. I don't even remember whether they had orange juice or anything. But I know that we sat down and there was no wine served, just water on the table. I think she did have coffee later. Uncle Vernon and she never drank coffee. In fact, they didn't even drink tea. For breakfast they drank hot water. But Auntie would get her table all set by four o'clock in the afternoon, with a beautiful damask cloth — I used to help her put it on — and her best silver and crystal."[5]

Florence and Vernon finished the work for his book on *Cave Life of Kentucky* about this time as well. He had done most of the survey work two years before. From her notes and those of others in the area, Florence contributed a chapter on some of the birds of the Mammoth Cave region.

When Vernon retired from the Biological Survey, the Baileys had decided to build a home at Twin Oaks, carefully set north and south by the North Star, so they could go out on the piazza to look at the sky and see Orion before going to bed. They asked Vernon's brother Henry, who was still living at Twin Oaks, to construct it in addition to his help to cousin Helen. Helen didn't drive, and Henry took her everywhere. That led to some local confusion, which Helen was quick to straighten out. Once when they entered a restaurant together and the hostess asked a waitress to seat the couple, Helen snorted, "we are *not* a couple."⁶ She still retained the independence of her youth that had led to her newspaper commendation for killing a wildcat.

Electricity was just coming to the Twin Oaks Valley, a welcome addition. The next summer it also reached Hart at Lagunitas five hundred miles up the California coast, and Florence was delighted to hear that Hart was putting it into his house. "It is my private feeling that old folks who have done their jobs in life are entitled to take things easy."

While their house was being completed, Florence and Vernon tried to pack up their life in Washington. Florence resigned from the AOU Committee on Bird Protection, even though she was the only woman to serve on a standing committee. The chairman was loath to let her go, not only because of her fine work but also because he felt that she would not be seriously isolated through residence in Southern California. She also sent books and magazines to the University of New Mexico, which had so recently honored her work. "It is hard dentistry (extraction) letting some of the books go," she wrote to Hart. Meanwhile, Vernon turned over his collection of bird skins and specimens to the Audubon Society.

Florence also unpacked that trunk of long-ago memories we all keep in the attic, even if it's only a room in our thoughts. She considered distributing many of her treasures to growing nieces for their offspring and then decided to treasure them a while longer, choosing instead to bequeath them in her will. Ruth, her precious china-headed doll, saw the sunlight again but briefly before being packed away until another day.

She mused a lot in that attic of her thoughts, remembering and writing about the joys of growing up at Homewood. The seasons of her life had turned like the world around her, and those "home woods became a true home woods to linger in, a place of cool delights, a greenwood of subtle lights and shadows; of homecoming birds in spring, of songful nesting birds in summer; a place of mystery and magic under the silver moonlight of summer nights; a joyous place to glory in under the flamboyant colors of autumn; a new hushed world to rest in under the soft white mantle of winter."⁷ Her own mantle of white hair was as soft as this hushed world of memories, and she nodded it quietly as she went back to making the decisions of the day.

They moved only what they still used to their little retirement home in Twin Oaks, where they lived for about a year. The first few months in the Southland were a treat. "I don't know how I'll ever get across a street [back in Washington] when I get there. . . . The flowers and bushes are coming out now. The wild peony and red fuchsia are beautiful — the blue 'lilac' [ceanothus] best of all. . . . It is a great blessing to be able to live out of doors all winter. We have our dinners out now. It would be hard to go back and be snowbound. And that awful traffic! Let's *all* stay in California the year round." Hart had decided that long ago, and it was Florence herself who soon felt otherwise.

In spite of the new picture window with "the best views of the valley," they soon found that Twin Oaks was not like the bird-filled arroyo of Pasadena where her friend, Mrs. Miller, had spent her last days. Vernon was a desert rat at heart, but Florence had grown more accustomed to creature comforts. When their Washington house didn't sell, they decided to return to it; and so they spent their remaining years mostly in their Washington home with nighthawks nesting on the roof. They returned to Washington in time for the national meeting of mammalogists to see the talking film of "Mr. Murie's elk . . . it is admirable," she wrote to Hart.

Once back in the city, they found much to do in helping people — and animals. Florence turned again to her writing, completing her book on the Grand Canyon for the National Park Service. Vernon finished one of the largest of his many books, *The Mammals and Life Zones of Oregon.* Then with Douglass Hayes's continuing help, he concentrated on perfecting his VerBail humane trap, which was by then being marketed. In fact, Florence wrote to her Taos grandniece Deirdre that "the Business Manager gets a sheaf of letters in response to our ads every day."

Vernon had been doing more than marketing, however, and was especially pleased to be the Director of Conservation for the American Trappers Association (ATA). Their new constitution included a new direction, which Florence wrote Deirdre was "an astonishing attempt to be as 'humanitarian as they can.' It is a long step in the right direction that should be followed by abolition of the steel trap."[8] The ATA featured "Wolf" Bailey in a cover photo on their magazine and reported that "At 72 years young, Mr. Bailey can outstep a lot of us and outthink most of us. Has field-worked in every state in the Union . . . has worked consistently to perfect traps and research better trapping methods."[9]

Vernon invented both a beaver trap for the Biological Survey, which became widely used in restocking operations, and the so-called foot-

As retirement changed their life-style, the Baileys posed for this photograph out-
side their home in Washington, D.C., about 1935. (From the collection of Florence
Merriam Youngberg.)

hold trap. This consists of a "chain, released by a spring, [that] catches
and holds without breaking the leg of the animal caught in it."[10] He
received prizes from the American Humane Association for both in-
ventions.

The following winter Florence wrote to Eithne, "the trees are getting

For New Year's in 1936, Florence sent a picture "from the four of us, three little foxes — one poking his nose up a soft sweater sleeve — and their foster grandmother, Auntie Florence." (From the collection of Eithne Golden Sax.)

bare now, their leaves almost gone. They are a delight with their bright fall colors but when those are gone you seem to know the *real* trees. How their characters stand out! Some seem to have grown without plan, others — great oaks — to have achieved by hard struggle, their big branches twisted and gnarled, but in the end pointing up to the sky. You seem to gain strength for life by looking at them as you pass."

Florence also sent Eithne and her twin sister Deirdre a copy of the new Girl Scout and Boy Scout handbooks, the latter for them to read and then save for their brother Terence. She sent them other books as well, describing the best use for each. Eithne had been studying Italian,

In 1940 Vernon, proud of his accomplishments in developing a humane trap, sent his picture with his own notation. "Gray Fox taken out of VerBail Trap with bare hands and carried home in my arms, not hurt nor scared but glad to go home when released. A happy Christmas from Uncle Vernon." (From the collection of Eithne Golden Sax.)

and so Florence sent her Dante. "Your knowledge of the language will help you in studying Dante. An engraving that we had at Homewood framed archwise has two figures – the white-robed figure of Dante's Ideal above his black-robed figure, she with upraised hand pointing him to Paradise. It is good to remember as woman's influence on man. Someday you may make it the text of a story."

As the year 1936 got under way, Florence learned of the planned celebration at Smith College. She sent greetings of "a royal 50th reunion to all who go." She wasn't going because she and Vernon were planning what would be their final trip across country to California, and all of her energy went to that. The main purpose was for Vernon to test his traps, and he was busy making them when she wrote the trip's plan to Hart. "Betty [Hone] is going with us to help with the driving. We start on the Lincoln Highway, skip Chicago (Betty will see the [World's] Fair on the way back) and St. Louis with its sleeping sickness. Our first address will be Santa Fe, General Delivery. Helen [Golden] writes that we can get a house for $3 a month, so if the coyotes are in a coming-on mood we may take advantage of it. Then we go to the Grand Canyon auto camp or such. We find that a pension is quite different from a salary, and the simple life becomes most alluring. Don't worry, we're gypsies and old timers, and mean to take a great deal of comfort for the rest of our days."

It was a monumental trip, with three cars crossing the continent together. By then Betty was an elementary school science teacher, and one of her students had given her a flying squirrel, which she had kept as a pet. Vernon assured her she could bring Chibuba along, and so she did. Most of the time it slept in Florence's hatbox, and every night they would let it out. If they were in a motel room, it would run to a curtain rod and fly across the room. At the California border inspection point, Betty was terrified that they wouldn't let her pet cross. The inspector was very dubious because flying squirrels were on his list of undesirable rodents, and besides, he had just been called to task for admitting a wolf that had subsequently escaped from its owner's car during an accident. But Vernon's assurances and Betty's insistence that she was returning immediately and would take the squirrel quickly out of the state finally won him over, and the three cars drove on with Chibuba unconcernedly asleep in the hatbox.

Florence capsulized the trip for her Smith College friends. "We stopped at the Grand Canyon and encountered a cyclonic storm in the dust bowl when lights were necessary. New Mexico and Arizona gave us fossil forests, the prehistoric ruins of Mesa Verde, Mexican adobes and Indian pueblos. We drove through Laguna and Zuni, lunched at the foot of the Enchanted Mesa [near Acoma Pueblo in New Mexico], saw Acoma in the distance and stopped near Taos, the queen of the pueblos. . . . The party left us in California in our home cabin where forty years ago I wrote 'A-Birding on a Bronco.' Here we enjoyed the fruit, the animal neighbors and the wonderful views of mountains and sky. Best of all to carry home in memory was the dark peak with uplifted head seen against the peaceful evening sky."

Betty remembers parts of that trip vividly, such as the visit they made to the Goldens near Taos.[11] They spent some time there to give the young cousins time to get acquainted, the Baileys hoping that Betty's interest in science would rub off on the twin girls. Vernon went walking in the hills nearby, and the twins were urged to go. But their faces were already set toward artistic careers, and the treatment didn't take. Even so, the cousins have remained friends ever since.

Betty also remembers that on that trip Vernon took her to meet Ernest Thompson Seton, or tried to. When they reached the gate to his ranch, Vernon looked at the ground — a usual practice for the naturalist wherever he went — and quietly commented, "Oh, he's not home." Betty couldn't figure out how he knew, until he explained. A wolf always leaves his sign and then scratches three times as he passes through his territory. Seton had left three scratches by the gate post so that those who knew him would know he had passed through and was gone.

Another memorable stop for Betty on that trip was camping out in Monument Valley. "All three cars made it through the rocky ford across the San Juan River. We made overnight camp at the base of some of the tall red buttes. As usual, Uncle wanted to explore and perhaps set a few mouse traps. As usual, we followed. Auntie stayed behind. Looking back toward camp from a shoulder of a tall butte, I could see Auntie quietly sitting on her folding campstool, enjoying the view, her white head a beacon at the foot of those great sandstone monuments." Almost fifty years later, it was an image that Betty still treasured.

When the Baileys returned to Washington after that long summer trip, Florence found another valley. She told her Smith College classmates that she "came near entering 'the Valley of the Shadow.' Looking ahead I realized as never before how much remains to be done before darkness falls — how many lives there are to help . . . Now that I have come back into the sunshine, the memory still spurs me on."

Florence continued to correspond with her young grandnieces. Deirdre wrote to her from college as she looked toward a teaching career, and Florence responded enthusiastically. "I'm glad to see that you are getting points on what a good teacher should do — better keep a notebook for your first year of teaching. You could begin with *'Make them work.'*

As a help to that end—'*Make them like me,*' which goes a step further —'*like them,*' which means an earnest study of their personality, for after all if we go deep enough we will find something good to like in most everybody. 'Don't be unreasonable'—you see I'm finding how many texts *you* are finding for your future teaching."

Florence put more meaning than perhaps she knew into the closing words in one letter to Hart. "The West seems near to us with our nieces just out by the sunset we have been watching from our little cabin among the hills." As the sunset of her own life deepened, she continued to become more aware of just how near it was.

A few months later she continued her encouragement to Deirdre, still using an example from nature as her guide. "After living with Uncle Hart and Uncle Vernon where files are matters of daily living, it's no wonder that the old adage, 'a place for everything and everything in its place' is deeply ingrained in my mind, as well as in my housekeeping and literary work. For a teacher it is equally important. How could she keep Anna Ames waiting to recite while she pawed over a woodrat's nest of papers to find her composition or her records? You can multiply instances. The mental habit of orderliness—the classifying mind is needed as a foundation for generalizations."

Florence was her own best example once again, and she was still putting to use her classifying mind as she continued her ornithological writing efforts. Glacier National Park talked of revising her and Vernon's 1918 book, but the money didn't materialize and the revision was shelved. But the next year, 1939, her last book, *Among the Birds in the Grand Canyon Country*, was published by the National Park Service. Florence was still up to her old tricks. In the introduction, she encouraged her readers as she always had: "Whatever one's especial or scientific interest may be in the birds of the canyon country, there is much more. In telling the story of our enriching summer, my hope has been not only that old interests be quickened and the pleasures of the way be enhanced but that to those with seeing eyes and listening ears may come the deeper satisfactions underlying bird study in the inspiring setting of the Grand Canyon."

The reviews of its publication also had a familiar ring to them. "Only by living in it, camping in it, and repeatedly visiting it at different times and seasons, as the author has done, may one form a real acquaintance with this extraordinary region and its animal life. . . . The [birds] along the way are charmingly written of, so the reader easily imagines that he himself is making the transit."[12] At seventy-six, Florence could still wow her audience.

She found that health was a time-consuming priority in her life, but by summer she was ready to get outdoors again. Vernon had new traps to try, and they spent three months back in their favorite Adirondacks, repeating the trip the following summer. She enjoyed it to the fullest. World War II was then raging in Europe, and its effect was not lost on her, although she kept it in her own perspective when writing to her Smith College class. "I never realized before the full beauty of the rich blue sky with its encircling, ever-changing snowy clouds. And at night, the peace of the star-filled canopy of the heavens. Is that not what we need to remember above all in these terrible days of man-made disasters? Let us raise our eyes to the heavens above us." When this country became involved, she helped out by knitting. A friend, she wrote to her cousin Helen Golden, "dragged me through two child sweaters, but now I am making squares to be sewed into an afghan for use in a shelter." She never had been one to enjoy plain sewing.

About this time Florence sent Eithne a single sheet titled "Rules for a Perfect Lady," through which she encouraged the best of her own Victorian upbringing.

> Cultivate repose of manner.
> Never touch your nose, except with a handkerchief. It is a goodly feature but suppose it were a red protuberance from too much attention!
> Don't scratch your scalp. If it itches, wash your hair.
> Hands are made for work, not calisthenics at table.
> Do not hang your arm over your chair. Sit with spine $\perp$ not $\langle$.
> Don't be sloppy.
> Take a course in voice culture. Modulate your tones.
> Eliminate Carlyle's "higgling, whiffling, ackenation." In a word, train yourself to be a gentlewoman.
> You are so beautiful that I want you to trim off all the excrescences and be your very best possible self.

Eithne doesn't recall her reaction at the time, but the rules were significant enough that she saved that letter and quickly produced it in discussing her beloved Auntie Florence fifty years later. Uncle Vernon would merely sniff when Florence gave advice. "You can't rule the universe, Mrs. Dearie."[13]

While Florence was busy transmitting her idea of one's "best possible self," Vernon was busy transmitting his own ideas of another sort. He had taken on the presidency of the Audubon Society of the District of Columbia and also continued to work on his humane traps. Florence accompanied him to test them whenever she could. Otherwise, she continued her quiet life in Washington. In September of 1940 the *Condor* paid a simple tribute to the Baileys by publishing their photographs, captioned modestly, "Florence Merriam Bailey and Vernon

Bailey, far known for their long time devotion to the study of birds and mammals."

The Baileys were later listed among the forty-nine "notable couples in science before 1940." These were rarities in the scientific world, for it had long been thought that married women couldn't hold a professional job and be an adequate wife and mother. Florence never exhibited any indication that she felt inadequate to her joint tasks in life. In fact, in addition to birds she also continued her interest in social welfare through membership in various organizations and through serving on the board of managers for the Working Boys' Home in Washington.[14]

Eithne visited the Baileys in Washington, where Florence took her to art galleries to improve her cultural appreciation. Vernon went along to the Freer Gallery, with little interest in its offerings until he saw a vase with animals on it. He rattled off the Latin name for one, then corrected himself, "No, that's a badger." His words still ring in Eithne's ears, having made more of an impression than the "uplifting" statues Florence pointed out, using her favorite word.

Vernon still occasionally visited the familiar offices of the Biological Survey. One day he poked his head in the door where a meeting was in progress, and the director invited him in. "There are some field men here I want to meet you. What can you tell them about procedures?" Vernon shrugged. "I've always tried to cut through the red tape." Forty years haven't dimmed that memory for Victor Scheffer, one of the field men sitting in that meeting. Visiting scientists also continued to seek out the Baileys, and dinner parties were still a part of their lives. Scheffer, among others, remembers meeting Vernon at Sunday dinner. As a zoologist, Scheffer was also interested in Hart, who was visiting Washington at the time, but Hart—then eighty-six—was out that day. Scheffer has objected to the epithet that has been applied to Hart as the last of the naturalists, but prefers to think of him as "among the first of the environmentalists. He surely understood that every environment on earth is a language that is continually telling of the past and the present and (if one listens carefully) is predicting the future."[15]

During this decade, national thinking about federal lands was shifting from specific uses such as national forests or parks or wildlife refuges to multiple uses. This meant rethinking how existing federal lands were used, and Vernon occasionally took part in the associated field work. On one such expedition to a game management area in Virginia, Vernon, then seventy, impressed the younger men with his stamina in climbing to the top of that wild and remote area. But his lifelong practice of note taking in the field made even more of an impression on Arnold Nelson, who learned a valuable lesson that day. Whenever the group stopped to rest, Vernon was busy writing up notes. "The message he gave me was – don't trust to your memory too long, write it down *now*."[16]

By 1942 the Baileys had been married forty-two years. In March of that year Hart died in California. Two months later, Vernon succumbed to pneumonia. Edward Preble eulogized in the next issue of *Nature Magazine*, "It is particularly fitting that our Association should mourn his passing, for he was co-author, with his wife, of the leading article in [our] first number . . . This joint authorship was symbolic of the Bailey household, for their married life of more than forty years has been an object lesson worthy of a pair whose entire lives have been governed by the principle of 'working together,' and working for others, whether in natural-history studies, or in any field – social, educational, or humane – that called for cooperative effort."

Preble continued, "Vernon Bailey was, perhaps, best known as a mammalogist, but he was also a practical ornithologist of the outdoor type, and had a field knowledge of the plants of the country that many a botanist might well envy. His knowledge of the geography of the West was, I believe, unsurpassed. There have been few years, during the past five decades, that did not find him traveling, by some method, through desert, forest, mountain trail, or river valley. His memory of places visited was the most exact that I have ever known. He added to a genius akin to that of the Indian for memory of topographic details the broad geographic viewpoint of the cultivated scholar. With all these various fields of interest, advanced by a tireless energy, Vernon Bailey has accomplished much. He had no need for the time-consuming amusements that so many crave, for with his interest and enthusiasm in all Nature's products, including his fellow-man, he was always busy, and all his work was play."

Florence may have been devastated to lose both her beloved husband and her beloved brother so close together, or perhaps age shielded her from the full impact. She left no comments. She was comfortably settled in her familiar home of forty years, with a faithful maid of twenty years and two "paying guests" who were longtime friends.

She spoke in her last several letters to the Smith College group of taking brisk walks daily, as well as vitamins A, B, C, and D. Even though past eighty, she felt in better physical condition than in many long years. It was not winter in her heart, but spring. "We have had an unusual [autumn] season here – the leaves on the trees are almost as perfect as in Spring and the grass in our yard is as green."

Frank Chapman had made a similar analogy in his later years to express how "the present slips from us with growing rapidity, but the

By 1940, memories abounded for Florence Merriam Bailey, along with pictures. This one shows her in front of her heirloom dresser, still in the family today, surrounded by pictures of her nieces and nephews. (From the collection of Florence Merriam Youngberg.)

birds are ever with us." Using their beloved hermit thrush as his textbook, he commented that "as his silvery voice rings through the woods we are young again. No fountain of youth could be more potent." The veteran naturalists whom he had in mind "were old in years only. Their hearts were young. The earth was fair; plants still bloomed, and the birds sang for them. There was no idle waiting here; the days were all too short. With what boyish ardor they told of some recent discovery; what inspiration there was in their enthusiasm!"[17] The enthusiasm of earth's springtime remained in Florence's heart, and the birds still sang for her as well.

In the autumn of 1947 she sat often in the sunny study of her Washington home, wrapped in her favorite red kimono with the black braid trim, and watched the trees start to turn outside the window. On October 8 she addressed a final letter to her Smith College friends, just a few months before her death. The letter was only two lines long. "Yes. All is well with me. I am living in my own home and enjoying it."

She always did enjoy living.

Notes

ALL QUOTATIONS not otherwise attributed are by Florence Merriam Bailey. Her name is abbreviated FMB in the notes below. If quotations of published material are not identified in the text, they are shown below as: FMB, a partial title, and the year (since her bibliography is chronological). Her personal quotations are primarily from her unpublished letters to C. Hart Merriam, which are identified only in the text. This small collection is filed chronologically as the Florence Merriam Bailey Papers (82/46) at the Bancroft Library, University of California at Berkeley. Also from this collection are quotations from her field notes, her Autobiographical Notes, brief selections she copied from the journals her father kept, and the two letters quoted to Joseph Grinnell; these are cited below as FMB Papers, Bancroft Library.

Information from relatives and friends through personal communication with the author is identified in the text wherever practical. Where it is identified only in these notes, the name is followed by "pers. comm." to indicate personal communication.

INTRODUCTION

1. Paul Brooks, "Painter as Naturalist," p. 88.
2. Gilbert White, *Natural History of Selbourne and Observations on Nature*, introduction by John Burroughs, p. xvii.
3. James Lovelock, *Gaia*, p. 59.
4. Henry Chester Tracy, *American Naturists*, p. 262.
5. Stephen Jay Gould, "Only His Wings Remained," p. 10.
6. Paul Brooks, *The House of Life: Rachel Carson at Work*, p. 34.
7. William H. Goetzmann, *Exploration and Empire*, p. xi; William H. Stickel, pers. comm. Dr. Stickel "came along one generation too late to have known Mrs. Bailey," but while he was a graduate student he attended a Mammal Society meeting where Vernon Bailey was present. Vernon "made a point of introducing him-

self to each of us young folks and saying how glad he was to see so many fine young people coming along in mammalogy. I have been to many meetings of various sorts, but I never knew anyone else who was warm, confident and friendly enough to do that."

8. Dorothy Middleton, *Victorian Lady Travellers*, p. 3.

9. Orlando Romero, *Nambé—Year One*, p. 141.

1. Babe in the Woods, 1863–1882

1. These were years that she later described in Autobiographical Notes for her brothers' children. Quotations throughout the remainder of this chapter on her childhood are all from those notes in the FMB Papers, Bancroft Library.

2. Cited in Eve Merriam (no relation), *Growing up Female*, p. 81.

3. R. W. B. Lewis, *Edith Wharton: A Biography*, p. 35.

4. Mrs. Alice Tucker of Victoria, Australia, pers. comm. She was so intrigued by the history of her fan that she later wrote it up for the *Bulletin* ([Summer, 1986]: 24–26, with photograph) of the Fan Circle International.

5. Elizabeth Horner and Keir B. Sterling, "Feathers and Feminism in the 'Eighties,'" p. 20.

6. "The Birds' Friend," p. 282. "Collecting specimens" is a euphemism for shooting birds and then mounting them for scientific collections, either for one's own or for one of the rapidly growing public museums. Shoot it first and ask questions later was the accepted process for studying wildlife at the time.

7. FMB Papers, Bancroft Library.

8. Knowlton Mixer, *Old Houses of New England*, p. 260; G. Byron Bowen, *History of Lewis County*, p. 258.

9. Charles Henry Pope, comp., *Merriam Genealogy in England and America*, p. 321.

10. C. Hart Merriam, "The Biological Survey—Origin and Early Days—A Retrospect," p. 39.

11. Harold D. Carew, "Merriam, the Naturalist," p. 32; Richard A. Bartlett, *Great Surveys of the American West*, p. 72.

12. William H. Goetzmann and Kay Sloan, *Looking Far North: The Harriman Expedition to Alaska, 1899*, p. 9; Goetzmann, *Exploration and Empire*, p. 331.

13. Keir B. Sterling, *Last of the Naturalists: The Career of C. Hart Merriam*, p. 17.

14. Elizabeth Longford, *Eminent Victorian Women*, p. 62.

15. Carew, "Merriam, the Naturalist," p. 34.

16. Alma Chesnut, "Vernon Bailey: A Nobleman," p. 229.

17. Edward A. Preble, "Vernon Bailey Passes," p. 329.

18. Chesnut, "Vernon Bailey," pp. 229–30.

19. Charles L. Camp, "C. Hart Merriam" (obituary), p. 284.

20. Sterling, *Last of the Naturalists*, p. 4.

21. Elliott Coues, *Key to North American Birds*. Coues called himself a "shotgun ornithologist," as opposed to what he called an "opera-glass ornithologist," as FMB became, according to his biographer, Michael Brodhead, who added: "Still

he was sympathetic to the conservationist cause and quite supportive of women in natural history" (pers. comm.).

22. "Florence Merriam Bailey," *Town and Country Life*, p. 12.

23. "Official Circular No. 12," p. 1.

2. College-bound Special, 1882–1885

1. Henry Wetherbee Henshaw, "Autobiographical Notes," p. 58.

2. Sterling, *Last of the Naturalists*, p. 47.

3. Quoted in Paul Brooks, *Speaking for Nature*, p. 208.

4. Ibid.

5. Lewis, *Edith Wharton*, pp. 34–35.

6. Cited in Garrett Hardin, *Nature and Man's Fate*, pp. 102, 36.

3. Bonnets and Burroughs, 1886–1887

1. John Burroughs, *Wake-Robin*, pp. v–vi.

2. Z. M. Talbot and M. W. Talbot, "Obituary: C. Hart Merriam," p. 546.

3. Brooks, *Speaking for Nature*, p. 6.

4. Burroughs, *Wake-Robin*, p. xiii.

5. Robert Henry Welker, *Birds and Men: American Birds in Science, Art, Literature, and Conservation, 1800–1900*, p. 201.

6. Robin W. Doughty, *Feather Fashions and Bird Preservation*, p. 16; Harry A. Kersey Jr., *Pelts, Plumes, and Hides*, p. 76.

7. A. Ward, "Home Life at Smith College," p. 162.

8. Doughty, *Feather Fashions*, pp. 41, 87.

9. George Bird Grinnell, *The Passing of the Great West: Selected Papers of George Bird Grinnell*, ed. John F. Reiger, p. 3; Frank M. Chapman, *Autobiography of a Bird Lover*, p. 32.

10. Grinnell, *Passing of the Great West*, p. 22.

11. FMB, "How to Conduct Field Classes," 1900, p. 83; FMB, "Our Smith College Audubon Society," 1887, p. 175.

12. Doughty, *Feather Fashions*, pp. 64–65.

13. Ibid., pp. 81–82.

14. FMB, "Our Smith College Audubon Society," 1887, p. 176.

15. Ibid., p. 177.

16. Ibid., p. 175.

17. Ibid.

18. Ibid., p. 177.

19. Clara Barrus, *The Life and Letters of John Burroughs*, pp. 279–80.

20. Clifford Johnson, *John Burroughs Talks*, pp. 121–22.

21. Edith Jordan Gardner, "The Days of Edith Jordan Gardner," p. 4.

22. FMB, "Our Smith College Audubon Society," 1887, p. 178; Celia Thaxter, "Woman's Heartlessness," p. 13.

23. John Burroughs, "Letter to the Editor," p. 22.
24. FMB, "Fifty Common Birds . . . ," 1887, pp. 258–59.
25. Ibid., 1889, p. 49.
26. "Audubon Note Book," 1887, p. 189.
27. Lewis, *Edith Wharton*, p. 52.

4. EASING THE BURDEN, 1886–1893

1. Florence Merriam Youngberg, pers. comm. Mrs. Youngberg is the grand-daughter of Florence's older brother Collins.
2. Robert Ridgway, *The Hummingbirds*, p. 256.
3. Sterling, *Last of the Naturalists*, p. 66.
4. Wallace H. Elliott, *History of San Diego County*, p. 71.
5. Notice of opening school at Twin Oaks, March 23, 1891, Archives of the San Diego (California) Historical Society.
6. FMB Papers, field notes, Bancroft Library.
7. Ibid.
8. Ibid.
9. Ibid. The author is preparing Florence's unpublished manuscript of this visit for publication during the Washington state centennial, just a hundred years after Florence was there.
10. Doughty, *Feather Fashions*, p. 98.
11. Aaron Clark Bagg and Samuel Atkins Eliot, *Birds of the Connecticut Valley in Massachusetts*, p. xx.
12. FMB, *Birds Through an Opera Glass*, 1890, p. 187.
13. Welker, *Birds and Men*, p. 190.
14. FMB, "Olive Thorne Miller," 1919, p. 271.
15. FMB, "Mrs. Olive Thorne Miller," *Auk*, 1919, p. 164.
16. FMB, "Olive Thorne Miller," *Condor*, 1919, p. 70.
17. Ibid., p. 71.
18. Middleton, *Victorian Lady Travellers*, p. 6.
19. Clinton L. Merriam diaries, June 9, 1888, May 26, 1893, and May 28, 1893.
20. Elizabeth Hone, pers. comm. Dr. Hone is the granddaughter of Florence's older brother Collins.
21. FMB, *My Summer in a Mormon Village*, 1894, pp. 5, 39–40.
22. Ibid., p. 21.
23. Ibid., pp. 21–22.
24. Ibid., p. 47.
25. Ibid., p. 48.
26. Ibid., p. 164.
27. Ibid., pp. 163–64.
28. Ibid., pp. 26–27.
29. Ibid., p. 46. Helen Hunt Jackson had died, comparatively young, of cancer, so FMB felt a sense of the double tragedy in losing both her mother and this fellow crusader.

30. Ibid., pp. 65–72, passim.

31. Ibid., pp. 170–71.

5. BIRDS AND BRONCOS, 1893–1894

1. Isabella Lucy Bird, *A Lady's Life in the Rocky Mountains*, p. 23.

2. Edward A. Ross, "Amos Warner," pp. 197–98.

3. Susanna Bryant Dakin, *The Perennial Adventure: A Tribute to Alice East-wood, 1859–1953*, introduction by John Howell.

4. "Valleys of St. Mark," *San Diego Union*, January 1, 1894.

5. Roger Tory Peterson used the same scene from *The Merry Wives of Windsor* in his European guide, dedicating it to "our long suffering wives": "She laments, sir. Her husband goes this morning a-birding" (John C. Devlin and Grace Naismith, *The World of Roger Tory Peterson*, p. 122). See also Harriet Kimbro [Kofalk], "Roger Tory Peterson and Florence Merriam Bailey," pp. 5–6.

6. FMB, *A-Birding on a Bronco*, 1896, pp. 3–4.

7. Ibid., pp. 1–2.

8. Ibid., p. 5.

9. Ibid., pp. 121–22.

10. Ibid., pp. 31–33.

11. Ibid., p. 170.

12. Ibid., p. 107.

13. Ibid., p. 193.

14. Ibid., p. 17.

15. Ibid., p. 67.

16. Ibid., pp. 140–41.

17. Ibid., p. 139.

18. Burroughs, *Wake-Robin*, p. 126.

19. FMB, *A-Birding on a Bronco*, 1896, pp. 151–52.

20. R. N. Goodwin, letter printed in *California Rancher*, February, 1957.

21. "Miss Helen Merriam . . . ," in *San Diego Union*, October 3, 1881.

22. FMB, *A-Birding on a Bronco*, 1896, pp. 125–29, passim.

23. Ibid., p. 218.

24. Ibid., pp. 219–20.

25. C. Hart Merriam, "Biological Survey," p. 42.

26. Horner and Sterling, "Feathers and Feminism," p. 20; Hone, pers. comm.

27. Margaret W. Rossiter, *Women Scientists in America*, p. 95.

6. NESTING TIME, 1893–1899

1. William Henry Hudson, *Osprey; or, Egrets and Aigrettes*, p. 5.

2. Doughty, *Feather Fashions*, p. 14; Ellen Maury Slayden, *Washington Wife*, p. xiv.

3. Barrus, *Life and Letters of John Burroughs*, p. 336.

4. FMB, "The Nesting Habits of *Phainopepla nitens* in California," 1896, pp. 38–43.

5. J. A. Allen, "Miss Merriam's 'A-Birding on a Bronco,'" p. 107; Brooks, "Painter as Naturalist," p. 88; Mary Fuertes Boynton, ed., *Louis Agassiz Fuertes, His Life,* p. 11.

6. Brooks, "Painter as Naturalist," p. 88; Welker, *Birds and Men,* p. 190; Frank M. Chapman, "Citizen Bird" (review), p. 414.

7. Robert McCracken Peck, *A Celebration of Birds: The Life and Art of Louis Agassiz Fuertes,* p. 46.

8. J. A. Allen, "Recent Literature," p. 337.

9. Sterling, *Last of the Naturalists,* p. 112.

10. Ibid.

11. Doughty, *Feather Fashions,* pp. 81–82.

12. Barrus, *Life and Letters of John Burroughs,* p. 313.

13. Peter Matthiessen, *Wildlife in America,* p. 168; Welker, *Birds and Men,* p. 205.

14. FMB, report, in William Dutcher, "Report of Committee on Bird Protection," 1898, p. 110.

15. FMB, "How Our Birds Protect Our Trees," 1898, pp. 11–12.

16. Paul H. Oehser, "Florence Augusta Merriam Bailey," p. 83.

17. FMB, *The Bird Classes of the Audubon Society of the District of Columbia, 1898–1912,* 1912, p. 3.

18. FMB, "Clark's Crows . . . ," 1899, pp. 46–47.

19. FMB, report, in "Report of the AOU Committee on Protection of North American Birds," 1899; Frank M. Chapman, "Louis Agassiz Fuertes, 1874–1927," p. 366.

20. FMB, report, 1899, pp. 58–60.

21. Hone, pers. comm.

22. Brooks, *Speaking for Nature,* p. 158; Frank M. Chapman, editorial, *Bird-Lore,* February, 1899, p. 28.

23. FMB, "Our Doorstep Sparrow," 1899, 20–23.

24. Carew, "Merriam, the Naturalist," p. 31.

25. T. S. Palmer, "In Memoriam: Clinton Hart Merriam," p. 131.

26. Boynton, ed., *Louis Agassiz Fuertes,* p. 15; David Starr Jordan, *Days of a Man,* p. 297.

27. Goetzmann and Sloan, *Looking Far North,* pp. 20–21.

28. Jeanie Maury Patten, "Report of the Audubon Society of the District of Columbia," p. 173.

29. Slayden, *Washington Wife,* p. 7.

30. FMB Papers, field notes, Bancroft Library.

31. Sterling, *Last of the Naturalists,* p. 72.

32. Hone, pers. comm.

33. FMB to Youngberg, pers. comm.

34. Peter J. Schmitt, *Back to Nature: The Arcadian Myth in Urban America,* pp. xv–xxiii, quoted in Doughty, *Feather Fashions,* pp. 31–32.

35. *In American Fields and Forests.*
36. John Burroughs, "Bird Enemies," in *Signs and Seasons,* p. 235.

7. MEETING SPRING HALFWAY, 1900–1901

1. American Association of University Women (hereafter, AAUW), *Hats, History and Hemlines,* p. 5.
2. Doughty, *Feather Fashions,* p. 149.
3. Brooks, *Speaking for Nature,* p. 201; Doughty, *Feather Fashions,* pp. 110, 85.
4. FMB, Autobiographical Notes, Bancroft Library.
5. "Homewood."
6. FMB, "How to Conduct Field Classes," 1900, p. 84.
7. *Bird-Lore,* October, 1900, p. 151.
8. Foreword; Paul H. Oehser, pers. comm. Mr. Oehser and his wife were protégés of the Baileys in Washington, D.C. As a young editor on the staff of the Biological Survey in the 1920s, Oehser helped with the final production of FMB's major book, *Birds of New Mexico.* He spent a long career as an editor at the Smithsonian Institution and wrote a history of the Smithsonian.
9. Grace Gallatin Seton-Thompson, *A Woman Tenderfoot,* pp. 57, 63. She was Ernest's first wife. They parted company because both wanted to pursue writing careers.
10. Ibid., p. 118.

8. A BIRD IN THE HANDBOOK, 1900–1902

1. Vernon Bailey, "Into Death Valley Fifty Years Ago," pp. 3–4.
2. Ibid.
3. Ibid.
4. Sterling, *Last of the Naturalists,* p. 105.
5. Chesnut, "Vernon Bailey," p. 231.
6. Boynton, ed., *Louis Agassiz Fuertes,* pp. 57, 58.
7. Peck, *Celebration of Birds,* p. 111.
8. Vernon Bailey, *Animal Life of the Carlsbad Cavern,* p. 130.
9. Chapman, "Louis Agassiz Fuertes," p. 368.
10. Welker, *Birds and Men,* p. 205.
11. Frank M. Chapman, "What We Can Do for Our Members," p. 202; FMB, "Bird Study," 1900, p. 645.
12. Sterling, *Last of the Naturalists,* p. 243; Chesnut, "Vernon Bailey," p. 229.
13. FMB, *Bird Classes,* 1912; Rossiter, *Women Scientists in America,* p. 276.
14. Goetzmann, *Exploration and Empire,* p. 435.
15. FMB, *Handbook of Birds of the Western United States,* 1902, pp. 471–72.
16. Paul H. Oehser, "Florence Merriam Bailey: Friend of Birds," p. 153.
17. "Editorial," p. 204.

18. Paul H. Oehser, "In Memoriam: Florence Merriam Bailey," pp. 22–23.
19. Paul Brooks, "Birds and Women," p. 89.

9. ENCHANTED BIRDLAND, 1903–1906

1. Elliott S. Barker, pers. comm. Dr. Barker served New Mexico as a naturalist and game warden for his entire career until he died at almost one hundred years of age. He wrote his twelfth book at the age of ninety-six. Because he knew the land as well as its people, he was well aware of scientists working in the field there, including the Baileys, although they never met personally.
2. FMB, "The Yellow Pines of Mesa del Agua de la Yegua," 1910, p. 181.
3. FMB, *Bird Classes*, 1912, p. 4.
4. AAUW, *Hats, History and Hemlines*, p. 6.
5. *Condor*, September, 1904, p. 137.
6. FMB, *Birds of New Mexico*, 1928, pp. 24–25.
7. Oehser, "In Memoriam," p. 22.
8. See FMB, "The Yellow Pines of Mesa del Agua de la Yegua," 1910, and "A Drop of Four Thousand Feet," 1911.
9. The artist was Bert Phillips, who had arrived in Taos just five years before with a fellow artist, E. L. Blumenschein, thus beginning what became a thriving art colony there.
10. FMB, "Additional Notes on the Birds of the Upper Pecos," 1904, p. 363.
11. FMB, "Memories of a Frontierswoman," 1910, pp. 744–47.
12. Carol Green Wilson, *Alice Eastwood's Wonderland*, p. 106.
13. Youngberg, pers. comm.
14. Barrus, *Life and Letters of John Burroughs*, p. 336.
15. David L. Cohn, *The Good Old Days*, pp. 329–30, 337.
16. Sterling, *Last of the Naturalists*, p. 261; Boynton, ed., *Louis Agassiz Fuertes*, p. 264.
17. FMB, *Some Needs of Public Education in the District of Columbia*, 1905.

10. RED-LETTER DAYS, 1907–1908

1. FMB, "A Populous Shore," 1916, p. 100.
2. FMB, "White-throated Swifts at Capistrano," 1907, p. 169.
3. FMB, "The Palm-Leaf Oriole," 1910, pp. 33–35.
4. FMB, "White-throated Swifts at Capistrano," 1907, p. 169.
5. Ibid., pp. 170–72.
6. FMB, "Red Letter Days," 1917, pp. 155–56.
7. Ibid., pp. 156–57.
8. FMB, "Talk to Cooper Club," 1904.
9. FMB, "A Brewer Blackbird Roost in Redlands," 1916, p. 95.
10. FMB, "Mrs. Olive Thorne Miller," 1919, p. 168.

11. Bess M. Hoffman, pers. comm. Mrs. Hoffman wrote the history of the group, now known as the Southwest Bird Study Club. At this writing, she has been a member for almost fifty years.

12. FMB Papers, Bancroft Library.

13. Oehser, "Florence Merriam Bailey: Friend of Birds," p. 154; Sterling, *Last of the Naturalists*, p. 88.

14. Oehser, "In Memoriam," p. 26; Oehser, "Florence Augusta Merriam Bailey," p. 83.

15. FMB Papers, Bancroft Library.

16. Don Bloch, "Men Who Have Given Their Names," p. 282.

11. Feathered Swimmers of the Prairies, 1909–1916

1. Sterling, *Last of the Naturalists*, p. 280.

2. Ibid.

3. T. Gilbert Pearson, ed., *Portraits and Habits of Our Birds*, foreword; FMB, "The Tufted Titmouse," 1913, p. 396.

4. Vernon Bailey, *A Biological Survey of North Dakota*, p. 3.

5. Quotations in the remainder of the chapter are from her *Condor* articles, 1915–20.

12. From Garibaldi to Glaciers, 1914–1919

1. FMB, "Birds of River, Forest and Sky," 1916, and "Notable Birds of McKenzie Bridge," 1916.

2. This and subsequent quotations are in FMB, "Birds of the Humid Coast," 1917.

3. FMB, "A Home in the Forest," 1916, p. 229.

4. Linnie Marsh Wolfe, *Son of the Wilderness: The Life of John Muir*, p. 198.

5. FMB, "Birds of River, Forest and Sky," 1916, pp. 1–2.

6. Ibid., p. 7; FMB, "Screech Owl Johnnie," 1916.

7. FMB, "A Home in the Forest," 1916, p. 233.

8. FMB, *The Wild Animals of Glacier National Park: The Mammals by Vernon Bailey, the Birds by Florence Merriam Bailey*, 1918, p. 103.

9. Victor B. Scheffer, *Adventures of a Zoologist*, p. 43; see also Margaret E. Murie, *Two in the Far North*.

10. FMB, *Wild Animals of Glacier National Park*, 1918, p. 104.

11. Ibid., p. 196.

12. Barrus, *Life and Letters of John Burroughs*, p. 187.

13. Doughty, *Feather Fashions*, p. 98.

14. Ibid., pp. 87–88.

15. Ibid., pp. 131–32.

16. Cohn, *The Good Old Days*, p. 341.

17. *Bird-Lore,* 1915, p. 400.

18. Witmer Stone, "Mrs. Bailey's 'Handbook of Birds of the Western United States'" (separate reviews of 4th and 7th editions, in 1915 and 1917).

19. FMB, *The Bird Classes of the Audubon Society of the District of Columbia, 1913–1922,* 1922, p. 8.

20. Marianne Ainley, "The Involvement of Women in the American Ornithologists' Union," p. 7.

21. FMB, "Prairie Boys," 1916.

22. Slayden, *Washington Wife,* p. 14.

23. FMB, "Our Part," 1917.

24. FMB, "Mrs. Olive Thorne Miller (in Memoriam)," 1919, p. 163.

13. FEEDING TABLES FOR BIRDS, 1920–1924

1. FMB, "An Arizona Feeding Table," 1922, p. 474.

2. Ibid., pp. 474–77.

3. FMB, "Koo," 1922, p. 260.

4. FMB, "An Arizona Valley Bottom," 1924, pp. 423–31.

5. Ibid.

6. FMB, "Notable Migrants Not Seen at Our Arizona Bird Table," 1923, p. 401.

7. Ibid., p. 408.

8. Youngberg, pers. comm.

9. FMB, *Bird Classes,* 1922, p. 6.

10. See Vernon Bailey, "Humane Traps" and "Our Fur Bearing Animals." See also "Humane Traps," in *Literary Digest.*

11. Bailey, *Animal Life of the Carlsbad Cavern,* pp. 1–4, passim.

12. FMB, "Poetic Children of the Pueblos," 1924, and "Red Willow People of the Pueblos," 1925; FMB, "Season of 'Eclipse' in Zoo Duck Pond," 1924.

13. FMB, "Grinnell and Storer on 'Yosemite Animal Life,'" 1924.

14. Margaret E. Murie, pers. comm. Mardy Murie is certainly the grande dame of the conservation movement in America and has been honored with the two most prestigious awards in the environmental movement: the Audubon Medal and the Sierra Club's John Muir Award. She was the first woman graduate of the University of Alaska, in 1924. The Baileys served as early mentors for both her and her husband Olaus, a well-nown naturalist.

15. Oehser, "FMB: Friend of Birds," p. 154.

16. Youngberg, pers. comm.

17. Douglass Hayes, pers. comm., and quotations following.

18. Charles R. Knight, letter to Paul Oehser, quoted in Oehser, "In Memoriam," p. 24.

19. Peck, *Celebration of Birds,* pp. xi, 77.

20. Youngberg, pers. comm.; Sybil E. Hamlet, pers. comm. Ms. Hamlet is the historian of the National Zoological Park in Washington, D.C.

21. Sterling, *Last of the Naturalists,* p. 114.

22. Hone, pers. comm.

23. Chesnut, "Vernon Bailey," p. 229.

24. Sterling, *Last of the Naturalists*, p. 114.

25. Hone, pers. comm.

26. Olaus Murie, letter to Paul Oehser, pers. comm.

14. BIRDS ON A SUMPTUOUS SCALE, 1926–1933

1. FMB, *Birds of New Mexico*, 1928, p. 16.

2. Hayes, pers. comm.

3. Youngberg, pers. comm.

4. H. S. Swarth, "The Birds of New Mexico" (review), p. 82.

5. Oehser, pers. comm.

6. Peck, *Celebration of Birds*, p. 25; Hamilton M. Laing, "Allan Brooks, 1869–1946," p. 435.

7. Quoted by his daughter, Mary Fuertes Boynton, in her book, *Louis Agassiz Fuertes*, p. xvi.

8. Louis Agassiz Fuertes, "With the Mearns Quail in Southwestern Texas," p. 114.

9. FMB, *Birds of New Mexico*, 1928, p. 572.

10. Nancy Kellogg Hansen, "Ornithologists I Have Known – Ralph Todd Kellogg, 1876–1940."

11. Chapman, *Autobiography*, p. 9; Althea Sherman, letter to Margaret Morse Nice, Margaret Morse Nice Papers, Archives of the Cornell University Libraries.

12. Quoted in a letter from Althea Sherman to Margaret Morse Nice, May 30, 1932, Margaret Morse Nice Papers.

13. Theodore S. Palmer, "Brewster Medal."

14. Brooks, *Speaking for Nature*, p. 148.

15. FMB, *Birds of·New Mexico*, 1928, p. 1.

16. "Graduation of 119 Graduates at the University," *Albuquerque Journal*, June 6, 1933.

17. J. Stokley Ligon, *New Mexico Birds and Where to Find Them*, p. 11.

18. "Notice," *Oregon Historical Society Quarterly*, p. 89; "Notes and News," *Auk*, p. 468.

19. Prof. Roland Case Ross, pers. comm. Dr. Ross was a California naturalist from the 1920s on. He was in his nineties when he died in 1987.

20. Peter Bloom, active in the California Condor Project, provides the traps primarily to licensed bird banders working with owls; C. H. Channing, pers. comm. Mr. Channing was a bird bander for many years. A government brochure on live-trapping wild hawks spurred his interest in the VerBail trap. When he retired, a Wisconsin bander purchased his remaining stock and using one of the traps banded the first great gray owl ever banded in that state. Mr. Channing sent the author his one remaining VerBail trap with instructions to "BE CAREFUL!" when opening the box. He taught not only Peter Bloom to make the traps "but also the men at

the Bird Banding Lab at Patuxent, Maryland." Justly proud of his accomplishments, he signed the letter, "Verbailily yours."

15. A Bat and a Beacon, 1931–1948

1. Youngberg, pers. comm.; Hone, pers. comm.
2. FMB, *Among the Birds in the Grand Canyon Country*, 1939, p. 39.
3. Charles Bowden, "The Sierra Pinacate," p. 40.
4. FMB, *Among the Birds in the Grand Canyon Country*, 1939, p. 180.
5. One of the delights of researching was being served supper at Betty Hone's retirement apartment, when we ate with some of FMB's tableware that Betty had inherited. Another delight was when Floddie Youngberg unpacked FMB's china-headed doll Ruth and dressed her in fresh clothes to show me.
6. Eithne Golden Sax, pers. comm. Mrs. Sax is the granddaughter of Florence's older brother Collins; Youngberg, pers. comm.
7. FMB, Autobiographical Notes, Bancroft Library.
8. Deirdre Golden Katz, pers. comm. Mrs. Katz is the granddaughter of Florence's older brother Collins.
9. "Our Director of Conservation," *Trapper*, April, 1937, p. 2.
10. "Bailey, 78, Noted Naturalist, Vernon," *New York Times*.
11. Hone, pers. comm., and quotations following.
12. J. A. Allen, "Mrs. Bailey's 'Among the Birds in the Grand Canyon Country.'"
13. Sax, pers. comm.
14. Rossiter, *Women Scientists in America*, p. 143; Oehser, "FMB: Friend of Birds," p. 83.
15. Scheffer, *Adventures of a Zoologist*, p. 8.
16. Arnold L. Nelson, pers. comm. Mr. Nelson joined the staff of the Biological Survey in 1931, when "Vernon and Florence Bailey were 'senior' naturalists" there. Recognizing the difficulties of obtaining firsthand information now, he kindly provided his own "tiny glimpse into their lives," delighted with the opportunity this book presents for others to "rediscover the contributions of Florence Bailey in spreading the good news about the natural world. Long before the time of the feminist movement, she was demonstrating that there was a place for a woman devoted to field work and writing on natural history." Nelson recognized that "her world was much larger than that of a professional ornithologist. In her writing, she was often thinking of the not-so-well-trained amateur naturalists — the enthusiastic beginner."
17. Tracy, *American Naturists*, p. 198.

Bibliography

Chronological List of Works by Florence Merriam Bailey

Letters, Class of 1886, 1886–1947. Smith College, Northampton, Massachusetts (unpublished).

Letters to C. Hart Merriam, 1872–1938. Bancroft Library, University of California, Berkeley (unpublished).

1885

"An Appeal to Women." *Watertown* (N.Y.) *Times*, November 4.

1886

"Fall Hats." *Turin* (N.Y.) *Gazette*, September 29.

"Fashion and Law." *Boonville* (N.Y.) *Herald*, September 30.

"French Milliners and Bird Murder." *Evening Star*, Washington, D.C., October 2.

"French Milliners or Conscience." *National Eagle*, Claremont, N.H., October 2.

"A Plea for the Birds." *Watertown* (N.Y.) *Times*, September 25.

1887

"Our Smith College Audubon Society." *Audubon Magazine* 1:175–78, signed "From Behind the Scenes."

"Why Not Have a Christmas Tree?" *Boonville* (N.Y.) *Herald*, December 24, signed "The Children's Friend."

1887–1888

"Hints to Audubon Workers." *Boonville* (N.Y.) *Herald*, July 14, 1887–February 16, 1888.

"Hints to Audubon Workers: Fifty Common Birds and How to Know Them." *Audubon Magazine*, 1:108–13, 132–36, 155–59, 181–85, 200–204, 224–26, 256–59, 271–77; 2:6–12, 34–40, 49–53.

1889

"Our Winter Birds." *Popular Science.*

1890

Birds Through an Opera Glass. Boston: Houghton Mifflin.
"Interesting Nesting Sites of a Winter Wren." *Auk* 7:407.
"Orie." *St. Nicholas* 17 (June): 662–66.
"Was He a Philanthropist?" *Auk* 7 (October): 404–407.

1891

"Our Piazza Boarder." *American Agriculturist*, August, pp. 449–50.
"A Pair of Robins." *Congregationalist*.

1894

My Summer in a Mormon Village. Boston: Houghton Mifflin. (Available on microfilm from Research Publications, Inc., New Haven, Conn., 1976, under History of Women, 3807.)
Observation Blank, National Science Club.

1895

Biographical Sketches. In Frank M. Chapman, *Handbook of Birds of Eastern North America*, 1895, pp. 245, 304, 314, 317, 324, 382.

1896

"Around Our Ranch-House." *Observer*, 7 (January): 1–5.
A-Birding on a Bronco. Boston: Houghton, Mifflin.
"How Birds Affect the Farm and Garden." *Forest and Stream* 47 (August 8, 15, 22): 103–104, 123–24, 144–45. (Reprinted as a separate item by Forest and Stream Publishing.)
"Nesting Habits of *Phainopepla nitens* in California." *Auk* 13 (January): 38–43.
"Notes on Some of the Birds of Southern California." *Auk* 13 (April): 115–24.
"A Sensible Hummingbird." *Our Animal Friends* 23 (February): 133–34.
"The Snowbird at Home." *Observer* 7:499–502.
"A True Observer (Mrs. Olive Thorne Miller)." *Observer* 7:291–95.
"The Ways of the Red-heads." *Observer* 7:287–90.

1897

"Trade Rats and Coyotes." *Forest and Stream* 2 (January): 5.

1898

"Are You Feeding the Birds?" *By the Wayside* (Wisconsin and Illinois Audubon Societies) 1 (November 20): 1–2.
Audubon Calendar, January.
"Balder and Scrap." *Congregationalist*.
Birds of Village and Field. Boston: Houghton Mifflin.
"Birds on Bonnets." *Oak Leaves* (Students Association of Michigan Women's Seminary, Kalamazoo) 9 (September–October): 1–3.

"How Our Birds Protect Our Trees." *Arbor Day Annual* (New York State Department of Public Education), May 6, pp. 11–12.
"Introduction." In Mrs. L. W. Maynard, *Birds of Washington and Vicinity*. Washington, D.C., pp. 1–18.
Report in William Dutcher, "Report of Committee on Bird Protection." *Auk* 15 (January): 110–14.
"This and That." *Congregationalist*, June 23, p. 915.

1899

Report in "Report of the AOU Committee on Protection of North American Birds." *Auk* 16 (January): 55–63.

1899–1900

"Clark's Crows and Oregon Jays on Mount Hood." *Bird-Lore* 1 (April, 1899): 46–48; 2 (June, 1900): 72–76.
"Our Doorstep Sparrow" (in "For Young Observers"). *Bird-Lore* 1 (February, 1899): 1, 20–23.

1900

Audubon Calendar, June.
"Bird Study." *Chautauquan*, Chautauqua Literary and Scientific Circle Round Table, ch. 30, pp. 644–45; ch. 31, pp. 86–87, 196–97.
"How to Conduct Field Classes." *Bird-Lore* 2 (June): 3, 83–87.
"The Spring Migration of Birds." *St. Nicholas* 27 (May): 644–45.

1902

Handbook of Birds of the Western United States. Boston: Houghton, Mifflin (eleven editions published, including four revisions, to 1935).
"The Scissor-tailed Flycatcher in Texas." *Condor* 4 (March): 30–31.

1903

"The Harris Hawk on His Nesting Ground." *Condor* 5 (May): 66–68.
"A Sierra Nighthawk Family." *Bird-Lore* 5 (March–April): 43–45.

1904

"Additional Notes on the Birds of the Upper Pecos." *Auk* 21 (July): 349–63.
"Additions to Mitchell's List of the Summer Birds of San Miguel County, New Mexico." *Auk* 21 (October): 443–49.
"A Dusky Grouse and Her Brood in New Mexico." *Condor* 6 (July–August): 87–89.
"Scott Oriole, Gray Vireo, and Phoebe in Northeast New Mexico." *Auk* 21 (May): 392–93.
"A Swallow and Flycatcher Feud" (field note). *Bird-Lore* 6 (March–April): 68.
"Talk to Cooper Club" (unpublished notes, n.d., circa 1904).
"Twelve Rock Wren Nests in New Mexico." *Condor* 6 (May): 68–70.

1905

"Breeding Notes from New Mexico." *Condor* 7 (March): 39–40.
"1904 Report." Working Boys' Home and Children's Aid Association of the District of Columbia.
"Notes from Northern New Mexico." *Auk* 22 (July): 316–18.
"Scaled Partridge at Pueblo, Colorado." *Condor* 7 (July): 112.
Some Needs of Public Education in the District of Columbia. Memorial to Congress, Executive Council, Public Education Association of the District of Columbia. Washington, D.C.: Government Printing Office.

1906

"Nesting Sites of the Desert Sparrow." *Condor* 8 (September): 111–12.
"A Nest of *Empidonax difficilis* in New Mexico." *Condor* 8 (September): 108.

1907

"White-throated Swifts at Capistrano." *Condor* 9 (November): 169–72.

1910

"An Irrigated Ranch in the Fall Migration." *Condor* 12 (September): 161–63.
"Memories of a Frontierswoman." *Outlook* 95 (July 30): 744–47.
"The Palm-leaf Oriole." *Auk* 27 (January): 32–35.
"The Red-headed Woodpecker." *Bird-Lore* 12 (March–April): 86–89. (Reprinted as Educational Leaflet No. 43, National Association of Audubon Societies.)
"Wild Life of an Alkaline Lake." *Auk* 27 (October): 418–27.
"The Yellow Pines of Mesa del Agua de la Yegua." *Condor* 12 (November–December): 181–84.

1911

"A Drop of Four Thousand Feet." *Auk* 28 (April): 219–25.
"Haymakers of the Rock Slides." *Forest and Stream* 76 (April 8): 530–31.
"The Oasis of the Llano." *Condor* 13 (March–April): 42–46.

1912

Bird Classes of the Audubon Society of the District of Columbia, 1898–1912. Washington, D.C.: ASDC.
"Birds of the Cottonwood Groves." *Condor* 14 (July–August): 113–16.

1913

"The Tufted Titmouse." *Bird-Lore* 15 (November–December): 394–97. (Reprinted as Educational Leaflet No. 71, National Association of Audubon Societies.)
"With Asio in the Greenwood." *Bird-Lore* 15 (September–October): 285–90.

1914

"Boy Scouts of America." *Washington* (D.C.) *Times*, September 7.

1915

"A Family of North Dakota Marsh Hawks." *Bird-Lore* 17 (November): 431–38.

1915–1916

"Characteristic Birds of the Dakota Prairies." *Condor:* "I. In the open grassland," 17 (September–October): 173–79; "II. Along the lake borders," 17 (November): 222–26; "III. Among the sloughs and marshes," 18 (January, 1916): 14–21; "IV. On the lakes," 18 (March): 54–58.

1916

"Birds of River, Forest and Sky." *Mazama* 5 (December): 41–47.

"Black-headed Grosbeaks Eating Butter" (in "From Field and Study"). *Condor* 18 (September): 20.

"A Brewer Blackbird Roost in Redlands." *Wilson Bulletin* No. 95, pp. 51–57.

"Dick, the Sandhill Crane." *Bird-Lore* 18:355–56.

"Feeding the Birds." *Oregon Sportsman* 4 (January): 22.

"For the Boys Who See." *Trail* (Washington, D.C.) 1:29–30.

"A Home in the Forest." *Bird-Lore* 18 (July): 229–33.

"Hummingbird's Home." *Home Prog.* 5 (May): 409–11.

"Meeting Spring Half Way." *Condor* 18 (July): 151–55; (September): 183–90; (November): 214–19.

"Notable Birds of McKenzie Bridge." *Oregon Sportsman* 4 (April): 96–98.

"A Populous Shore." *Condor* 18 (May): 100–10.

"Prairie Boys." *Trail* (Washington, D.C.) 2 (November): 7–8.

"Screech-Owl Johnnie." *Bird-Lore* 18 (September): 306–10.

1917

"Birds of the Humid Coast." *Condor:* "I. Fishermen," 19 (January): 8–13; "II. The center of a compressed nesting area," (March): 46–54; "VI. In the bracken," (May): 95–101.

"Our Part." *Utica* (N.Y.) *Press*, November 8.

"Red Letter Days in Southern California." *Condor* 19 (September): 155–59.

1918

Wild Animals of Glacier National Park: The Mammals by Vernon Bailey, The Birds by Florence Merriam Bailey. Washington, D.C.: Government Printing Office.

1918–1920

"A Return to the Dakota Lake Region," *Condor:* "I. Back to the sweetwaters," 20 (January): 24–37; (March): 64–70; "II. Birds of the unbroken prairie," (May): 110–14; "III. Among old friends," (July): 132–37; "IV. The grebe of the silvery throat," (September): 170–78; "V. From the bridge over the coulee," 21 (January, 1919): 3–11; "VI. The coulee of the meadows," (May): 108–14; "VII. The gem of the sweetwaters in cove and shore," (July): 157–62; (September): 189–93; (November): 225–30; 22 (January, 1920): 21–26; (March): 66–72; (May): 103–108.

1919

Autobiographical Notes. (Unpublished; one version at the California Academy of
   Sciences, San Francisco, dated December; another, n.d., at Bancroft Library,
   University of California, Berkeley.)
"Mrs. Olive Thorne Miller" (in memoriam). *Auk* 36 (April): 163–69.
"Olive Thorne Miller" (in memoriam). *Condor* 21 (March): 69–73.

1922

"An Arizona Feeding Table." *Auk* 39 (October): 474–81.
Bird Classes of the Audubon Society of the District of Columbia, 1913–1922.
   Washington, D.C.: ASDC.
"Cactus Wrens' Nests in Southern Arizona." *Condor* 24 (September): 163–68.
"Koo." *Bird-Lore* 24 (September–October): 260–65.

1923

Birds Recorded from the Santa Rita Mountains in Southern Arizona. Berkeley:
   Cooper Ornithological Club.
"Fifteen Arizona Verdins' Nests." *Condor* 25 (January): 20–21.
"Johnny and Paddy, Two Baby Beavers," by Vernon Bailey and Florence Merriam
   Bailey. *Nature Magazine*, January, pp. 1–7.
"Notable Migrants Not Seen at Our Arizona Bird Table." *Auk* 40 (July): 393–409.

1924

"An Arizona Valley Bottom." *Auk* 41 (July): 423–32.
"Christmas Thoughts of the Birds." *Every Child's Magazine*, December, p. 282.
"Grinnell and Storer on 'Yosemite Animal Life,'" by Vernon Bailey and Florence
   Merriam Bailey. *National Parks Bulletin* No. 42, National Parks Association,
   December 25.
"Poetic Children of the Pueblos." *Travel* 43 (August): 23–26.
"Season of 'Eclipse' in Zoo Duck Pond." *Sunday Star*, Washington, D.C., August 3.
"Some Plays and Dances of Taos Indians." *Natural History* 24:84–95.

1925

"The Fauna and Flora of California." Pp. xlii–li in *Rider's California*. New York:
   Macmillan Co.
"Red Willow People of the Pueblos." *Travel* 45 (September): 10–13+.

1928

Birds of New Mexico. Santa Fe: New Mexico Department of Game and Fish.

1931

"Plumage of the Black Swift." *Murrelet* 12 (March): 2, 55.

1932

"Abert Squirrel Burying Pine Cones." *Journal of Mammalogy* 13 (May): 2, 165–66.
"Plumage of the Black Swift Once More." *Murrelet* 13 (January): 1, 22.

1933

"Birds." In Vernon Bailey, *Cave Life of Kentucky Mainly in the Mammoth Cave Region*. Notre Dame, Ind.: Notre Dame University Press. (Reprinted from *American Midland Naturalist* 14 [September, 1933]: 385–635.)

"Pages from the Merriam Family History for the Children of Helen Merriam Golden" (unpublished).

"Pages from the Merriam Family History for the Children of Lyman Lyon Merriam" (unpublished).

1934

"Birds of the Southwest." *Nature Magazine*, February, pp. 76–80+.

1939

Among the Birds in the Grand Canyon Country. Washington, D.C.: Government Printing Office.

SECONDARY SOURCES

Ainley, Marianne. "The Involvement of Women in the American Ornithologists' Union." In Keir B. Sterling and M. G. Ainley, *A History of the American Ornithologists Union*. In press.

American Association of University Women, Orcas Island (Washington) Branch. *Hats, History and Hemlines*. N.d. (circa 1970s).

"Audubon Conference." *Bird-Lore*, November–December, 1900.

Bagg, Aaron Clark, and Samuel Atkins Eliot. *Birds of the Connecticut Valley in Massachusetts*. Northampton, Mass.: Hampshire Bookshop, 1937.

Bailey, Vernon. *Animal Life of the Carlsbad Cavern*. Baltimore: Williams and Wilkins, 1928.

––––––. *A Biological Survey of North Dakota*. North American Fauna No. 49. Washington, D.C.: Government Printing Office, 1926.

––––––. "Humane Traps." *Nature Magazine*, February, 1934, pp. 88+.

––––––. "Into Death Valley Fifty Years Ago." *Westways*, December, 1940.

––––––. *Mammals of New Mexico*. North American Fauna No. 53. Washington, D.C., 1931. Republished as *Mammals of the Southwestern United States*. New York: Dover Publications, 1971.

––––––. "Our Fur Bearing Animals." *National Humane Review*, July, 1940, pp. 6–9.

––––––. "Platform of American Trappers Association." *Trapper*, April, 1937, pp. 3+.

––––––. "Where the Grebe Skins Come From." *Bird-Lore*, February, 1900, p. 34.

"Bailey, 78, Noted Naturalist, Vernon" (obituary). *New York Times*, April 23, 1942.

Barrus, Clara. *Life and Letters of John Burroughs*. Boston: Houghton Mifflin, 1925.

Bartlett, Richard A. *Great Surveys of the American West*. Norman: University of Oklahoma Press, 1962.

Bird, Isabella Lucy. *A Lady's Life in the Rocky Mountains*. 1879 (originally titled *Journey to Truckee*). Rpt., Norman: University of Oklahoma Press, 1960.

"Birds and Women" (editorial). *Osprey*, April, 1900, p. 124.

"Birds' Friend, The." *Every Child's Magazine*, December, 1924, pp. 282–83.

Bloch, Don. "Men Who Have Given Their Names." *Nature Magazine*, May, 1938, pp. 280–83.

Bowden, Charles. "The Sierra Pinacate." *Arizona Highways*, November, 1984, pp. 40–45.

Bowen, G. Byron. *History of Lewis County* [New York]. Board of Legislators of Lewis County, 1965.

Boynton, Mary Fuertes, ed. *Louis Agassiz Fuertes, His Life*. New York: Oxford University Press, 1956.

Brewster, William. "Two Corrections." *Auk*, October, 1893, p. 365.

Brooks, Paul. "Birds and Women." *Audubon*, September, 1980, pp. 88–97.

———. *The House of Life: Rachel Carson at Work*. Boston: Houghton Mifflin, 1972.

———. "Painter as Naturalist." *Sierra*, March–April, 1983, pp. 88–91.

———. *Speaking for Nature*. Boston: Houghton Mifflin, 1980.

Burroughs, John. "Letter to the Editor." *Audubon* 2, 1888, p. 22.

———. *Signs and Seasons*. Boston: Houghton Mifflin, 1886

———. *Wake-Robin*. Boston: Houghton Mifflin, 1904.

Camp, Charles L. "C. Hart Merriam" (obituary). *California Historical Society Quarterly* 21, no. 3 (1942): 284–86.

Carew, Harold D. "Merriam, the Naturalist." *Touring Topics*, October, 1929, pp. 31–34+.

Chapman, Frank M. *Autobiography of a Bird Lover*. New York: Appleton-Century, 1933.

———. *Birds and Man* ("a guide to the exhibit illustrating the relations between birds and man"). Guide Leaflet Series, No. 115. New York: American Museum of Natural History, 1943.

———. "Louis Agassiz Fuertes, 1874–1927." *Bird-Lore*, September–October, 1927, pp. 359–68.

Chesnut, Alma. "Vernon Bailey: A Nobleman." *Nature Magazine*, October, 1929, pp. 229–32.

Cohn, David L. *Good Old Days*. New York: Simon and Schuster, 1940.

Coues, Elliott. *Key to North American Birds*. Estes and Lauriat Publishers, 1882.

Cutter, William Richard, ed. *Genealogical and Family History of Northern New York*. New York: Lewis Historical Publishing, 1910.

Dakin, Susanna Bryant. *Perennial Adventure: A Tribute to Alice Eastwood, 1859–1953*. Introduction by John Howell. San Francisco: California Academy of Sciences, 1954.

Devlin, John C., and Grace Naismith. *The World of Roger Tory Peterson*. New York: New York Times Books, 1977.

Doughty, Robin W. *Feather Fashions and Bird Preservation*. Berkeley: University of California Press, 1975.

Elliott, Wallace W., and Company (publishers). *History of San Diego County*. San Francisco, 1883.

"Florence Augusta Merriam Bailey." *Woman's Who's Who of America, 1914*. New York: American Commonwealth, 1914, p. 66.

"Florence Merriam Bailey." *Town and Country Life*, n.d. (1930s), p. 12.

Fuertes, Louis Agassiz. "With the Mearns Quail in Southwestern Texas." *Condor,* September–October, 1903, pp. 113–16.

Gardner, Edith Jordan. "The Days of Edith Jordan Gardner." Unpublished manuscript in the Stanford University Archives, 1961.

Goetzmann, William H. *Exploration and Empire.* New York: Alfred A. Knopf, 1966.

Goetzmann, William H., and Kay Sloan. *Looking Far North: The Harriman Expedition to Alaska, 1899.* New York: Viking Press, 1982.

Goodwin, R.N. Letter in *California Rancher,* February, 1957.

Gould, Stephen Jay. "Only His Wings Remained." *Natural History,* September, 1984, p. 10.

Grinnell, George Bird. *Passing of the Great West: Selected Papers of George Bird Grinnell,* ed. John F. Reiger. New York: Winchester Press, 1972.

Halliday, Anna. *Golden Wedding, 1819 and 1869.* Syracuse, N.Y.: George W. Silcox, 1869.

Hansen, Nancy Kellogg. "Allan Brooks — Bird Artist, 1869–1946" (unpublished).

———. "Ornithologists I Have Known — Ralph Todd Kellogg, 1876–1940" (unpublished).

Hardin, Garrett. *Nature and Man's Fate.* New York: New American Library, 1959.

Harris, Harry. "An Appreciation of Allan Brooks, Zoological Artist: 1869–1946." *Condor,* July–August, 1946, pp. 145–53.

Henshaw, Henry Wetherbee. "Autobiographical Notes." *Condor,* March, 1920, pp. 55–60.

"Homewood" (real estate flyer). Privately published, n.d. (circa 1900).

Horner, Elizabeth, and Keir B. Sterling. "Feathers and Feminism in the 'Eighties.'" *Smith College Alumnae Quarterly,* April, 1975, pp. 19–21.

Hudson, William Henry. *Feathered Women.* 1893. Rpt., London: Royal Society for the Protection of Birds, 1902.

———. *Osprey; or, Egrets and Aigrettes.* London: Royal Society for the Protection of Birds, Leaflet No. 3, 1902.

"Humane Traps." *Literary Digest,* September 26, 1936, pp. 31–32.

In American Fields and Forests. Boston: Houghton Mifflin, 1909.

Jackson, Helen Hunt. *Ramona.* 1885. Rpt., New York: Avon Books, 1970.

Johnson, Clifford. *John Burroughs Talks.* Boston: Houghton Mifflin, 1922.

Jordan, David Starr. *Days of a Man.* Yonkers-on-Hudson, New York: World Book, 1922.

Jordan, Virginia Merriam. Unpublished tape interview, San Marcos (California) Historical Society.

Kersey, Jr., Harry A. *Pelts, Plumes, and Hides.* Gainesville: University Presses of Florida, 1975.

Kimbro (Kofalk), Harriet. "The Birds and Bees in Twin Oaks: Visit of a Naturalist in 1889." *Journal of San Diego History,* Spring, 1985, pp. 76–85.

———. "'A Genuine Western Man Never Drinks Tea': Gustavus French Merriam's Letters from Kansas in 1860." *Kansas History,* Autumn, 1985, pp. 162–75.

———. "Roger Tory Peterson and Florence Merriam Bailey." *Bird Watcher's Digest,* July–August, 1984, pp. 5–6.

Laing, Hamilton M. "Allan Brooks, 1869–1946." *Auk,* July, 1947, pp. 430–44.

Lakeview Center for the Arts and Sciences. "Charles Robert Knight, 1874–1953." Peoria, Ill., 1969.

Lewis, R. W. B. *Edith Wharton: A Biography*. New York: Harper & Row, 1975.

Ligon, J. Stokley. *New Mexico Birds and Where to Find Them*. Albuquerque: University of New Mexico Press in cooperation with the New Mexico Department of Game and Fish, 1961.

Longford, Elizabeth. *Eminent Victorian Women*. New York: Alfred A. Knopf, 1981.

Lovelock, J. E. *Gaia: A New Look at Life on Earth*. London: Oxford University Press, 1979.

Matthiessen, Peter. *Wildlife in America*. New York: Viking Press, 1959.

Maynard, Mrs. George Colton. *Birds of Washington*. Washington, D.C.: n.p., 1898.

Merriam, C. Hart. "The Biological Survey—Origin and Early Days—A Retrospect." *Survey* (United States Biological Survey), March, 1935, pp. 39–43.

Merriam, Clinton L. Unpublished diaries in the New York State Historical Society Archives.

Merriam, Eve. *Growing Up Female*. Garden City, N.Y.: Doubleday, 1971.

Merriam, Frances. *Twin Oaks Valley—Then and Now*. San Marcos, Calif.: privately published, 1972.

Middleton, Dorothy. *Victorian Lady Travellers*. New York: E. P. Dutton, 1965.

Miller, Olive Thorne. "Popular vs. Scientific Ornithology" (letter to editor responding to William Brewster's "Two Corrections," October 1893). *Auk*, January, 1894, pp. 85–86.

———. "The Study of Birds—Another Way." *Bird-Lore*, October, 1900, pp. 151+.

"Miss Helen Merriam . . . ," *San Diego Union*, October 3, 1881.

Mixer, Knowlton. *Old Houses of New England*. New York: Macmillan, 1927.

Murie, Margaret E. *Two in the Far North*. Anchorage, Alaska: Alaska Northwest Publishing, 1957.

"Notes and News" (on Vernon Bailey's retirement). *Auk*, October, 1933, p. 468.

"News and Comments" (notice of Vernon Bailey's finding buffalo bones). *Oregon Historical Society Quarterly* 32 (1932): 89.

Notice of Opening School at Twin Oaks, March 23, 1891. Archives of the San Diego (California) Historical Society.

Obituary (of Florence Merriam Bailey). *Audubon Magazine*, January–February, 1949.

Oehser, Paul H. "Florence Augusta Merriam Bailey." In Edward T. James, ed., *Notable American Women*. Cambridge: Harvard University Press, 1971.

———. "Florence Merriam Bailey: Friend of Birds." *Nature Magazine*, March, 1950, pp. 153–54.

———. "In Memoriam: Florence Merriam Bailey." *Auk*, January, 1952, pp. 19–26.

"Official Circular No. 12." *Memorabilia of Smith College, 1874–1888*. Northampton, Mass.: Smith College, October, 1885.

Osgood, Wilfred H. "C. Hart Merriam." *Biographical Memoirs*. Washington, D.C.: National Academy of Sciences, 1947, pp. 1–57.

Palmer, T. S. "In Memoriam: Clinton Hart Merriam." *Auk*, April, 1954, pp. 130–36.

———. "Vernon Orlando Bailey: Obituary." *Auk*, July, 1947, pp. 502–503.

Pearson, T. Gilbert, ed. *Portraits and Habits of Our Birds*, vol. 7. New York: National Association of Audubon Societies, 1928.

Peck, Robert McCracken. *A Celebration of Birds: The Life and Art of Louis Agassiz Fuertes*. New York: Walker, 1982.

Peterson, Roger Tory. *A Field Guide to the Birds* (east of the Rockies). Boston: Houghton Mifflin, 1934.

Pope, Charles Henry, comp. *Merriam Genealogy in England and America*. Boston: Charles H. Pope, 1906.

Preble, Edward A. "Vernon Bailey Passes." *Nature Magazine*, June–July, 1942, p. 329.

Ridgway, Robert. *The Hummingbirds*. Washington, D.C.: Smithsonian Institution, 1892.

Romero, Orlando. *Nambé—Year One*. Berkeley, Calif.: Tonatiuh International, 1976.

Ross, Edward A. "Amos Warner." *Stanford Sequoia*, January 26, 1900, pp. 197–98.

Rossiter, Margaret W. *Women Scientists in America*. Baltimore: Johns Hopkins University Press, 1982.

Scheffer, Victor B. *Adventures of a Zoologist*. New York: Charles Scribner's Sons, 1980.

Seton-Thompson, Grace Gallatin (Mrs. Ernest). *A Woman Tenderfoot*. New York: Doubleday, Page, 1900.

Sherman, Althea. Unpublished letters to Margaret Morse Nice, in the Margaret Morse Nice Papers, Cornell University Libraries, Ithaca, N.Y.

Slayden, Ellen Maury. *Washington Wife*. New York: Harper & Row, 1962.

Sterling, Keir B. *Last of the Naturalists: The Career of C. Hart Merriam*. New York: Arno Press, 1977.

Strom, Deborah, ed. *Birdwatching with American Women*. New York: W. W. Norton, 1986.

Talbot, Z. M., and M. W. Talbot. "Obituary: C. Hart Merriam." *Science*, May 29, 1942, pp. 545–46.

Thaxter, Celia. "Woman's Heartlessness." *Audubon*, 1887, pp. 13–14.

Tracy, Henry Chester. *American Naturists*. New York: E. P. Dutton, 1930.

"Valleys of St. Mark." *San Diego Union*, January 1, 1894.

Ward, A. "Home Life at Smith College." *Car Window*, January, 1883, pp. 162–71.

Welker, Robert Henry. *Birds and Men: American Birds in Science, Art, Literature, and Conservation, 1800–1900*. Cambridge, Mass.: Harvard University Press, 1955.

White, Gilbert. *Natural History of Selbourne and Observations on Nature*. 1789. Rpt., introduction by John Burroughs, New York: D. Appleton, 1895.

Who Was Who in America, vol. 2. Chicago: A. N. Marquis, 1950.

Wildlife Management Institute. Washington, D.C.: Wildlife Management Institute, n.d. (circa 1980).

Wilson, Carol Green. *Alice Eastwood's Wonderland*. San Francisco: California Academy of Sciences, 1955.

Wolfe, Linnie Marsh. *Son of the Wilderness: The Life of John Muir*. Madison: University of Wisconsin Press, 1945.

Zahniser, Howard. "In August, Florence Merriam Bailey." *Nature Magazine*, August, 1936, pp. 71+.

⸻. "Obituary: Vernon Orlando Bailey." *Science*, July 3, 1942, pp. 6–7.

SELECTED LIST OF NOTICES, REVIEWS, AND MENTIONS

"Abridgments of Some Current Literature Relating to West Coast Birds" (on "Palmleaf Oriole"). *Condor*, July, 1910, p. 138.

"Additional Notes on Birds of the Upper Pecos" (review). *Condor*, September, 1905, p. 146.

"Additions to Mitchell's List of the Summer Birds of San Miguel County, New Mexico" (notice). *Condor*, September, 1905, p. 146.

Allen, G. M. "Mrs. Bailey's 'Among the Birds in the Grand Canyon Country'" (review). *Auk*, January, 1940, p. 140.

Allen, J. A. "Merriam's Biological Survey of Mt. Shasta" (review by editor). *Auk*, January, 1900, pp. 73–74.

⸻. "Miss Merriam's 'A-Birding on a Bronco'" (review by editor). *Auk*, January, 1897, pp. 107–108.

⸻. "Miss Merriam's 'Birds of Village and Field'" (review by editor). *Auk*, April, 1898, pp. 206–207.

⸻. "Mrs. Bailey's 'Handbook of Birds of the Western United States'" (review by editor). *Auk*, January, 1903, pp. 76–78.

⸻. "Recent Literature" (review of "How Birds Affect the Farm and Garden" by editor). *Auk*, October, 1896, pp. 337–38.

"Audubon Note Book," *Audubon*, 1887, p. 189.

"Audubon Note Book," *Audubon*, 1888, p. 86.

"Audubon Note Book" (letter on "The 'Magazine' as an Educator"). *Audubon*, 1888, p. 130.

"Bailey, Florence Augusta Merriam" (biographical note on *Penthestes gambeli baileyae*). *Condor*, September, 1928, p. 266.

"Bailey, Mrs. Florence Merriam" (photo and caption). *Condor*, September, 1904, p. 137.

"*Bird-Lore* for 1900" (editorial). *Bird-Lore*, December, 1899, p. 202.

"Birds of New Mexico" (editorial note). *Condor*, July, 1928, p. 257.

"Birds of Village and Field" (review by WAJ). *Osprey*, April, 1898, p. 105.

"Birds of Washington and Vicinity" (review). *Bird-Lore*, February, 1899, pp. 26–27.

"Birds Recorded from the Santa Rita Mountains in Southern Arizona" (review). *Condor*, November, 1923, p. 223.

Brewster, William. "Birds through an Opera Glass" (review). *Auk*, October, 1889, p. 330.

Chapman, Frank M. "Birds of New Mexico" (review by editor). *Bird-Lore*, March–April, 1929, p. 135.

⸻. "Citizen Bird" (review). *Auk*, October, 1897, pp. 413–14.

⸻. (Editorial mention of FMB in first issue) *Bird-Lore*, February, 1899, p. 28.

————. (Editorial note). *Bird-Lore*, November–December, 1903, p. 204.

————. "Handbook of Birds of the Western United States" (review by editor). *Bird-Lore*, November–December, 1902, pp. 200–201.

————. "What We Can Do for Our Members." *Bird-Lore*, November–December, 1900, p. 202.

Commencement Program. Smith College, Northampton, Mass., June 14, 1921.

"Editorial" (on *Handbook of Birds of the Western United States*). Bird-Lore, November–December, 1903, p. 204.

"Editorial Notes and News" (on *Birds of New Mexico*). *Condor*, July, 1928, p. 257.

"Editorial Notes and News" (of North Dakota and Texas observations). *Condor*, September, 1916, p. 206.

Fisher, Walter K. "Handbook of Birds of the Western United States" (review). *Condor*, January, 1903, pp. 21–22.

"Graduation of 119 Graduates at the University." *Albuquerque* (N.M.) *Journal*, June 6, 1933.

Grinnell, Joseph. "The Animal Life of Glacier National Park" (review). *Condor*, May, 1919, pp. 131–32.

"Mainly Personal" (review of *Handbook of Birds of the Western United States*). *New York Times Saturday Review of Books and Art*, December 6, 1902, p. 180.

"New York [Audubon] Society" (mention). *Bird-Lore*, February, 1899, p. 31.

"Notes and News" (on "How Birds Affect the Farm and Garden"). *Auk*, October, 1896, p. 351.

"Notes and News" (on Vernon Bailey's retirement). *Auk*, October, 1933, p. 468.

"Notes and News" (photographs of Florence Merriam Bailey and of Vernon Bailey). *Condor*, September, 1940, p. 267.

Palmer, Theodore S. "Brewster Medal." *Auk*, January, 1932, p. 52.

Patten, Jeanie Maury. "Report of the Audubon Society of the District of Columbia." *Bird-Lore*, October, 1899, p. 173.

"Receives Medal for 'Birds of New Mexico.'" *Survey* (United States Biological Survey), October 31, 1931, p. 125.

"Sixteenth Congress of the American Ornithologists' Union." *Auk*, January, 1899, pp. 51–55.

"Sketch and Portrait." *Bird-Lore*, March, 1916, pp. 142–44.

Stone, Witmer. "Mrs. Bailey on 'Birds of the Mammoth Cave Region'" (review by editor). *Auk*, January, 1934, pp. 109–10.

————. "Mrs. Bailey's 'Birds of New Mexico'" (review by editor). *Auk*, January, 1929, pp. 125–27.

————. "Mrs. Bailey's 'Handbook of Birds of the Western United States'" (4th ed., review by editor). *Auk*, January, 1915, p. 115.

————. "Mrs. Bailey's 'Handbook of Birds of the Western United States'" (7th ed., review by editor). *Auk*, July, 1917, p. 350.

Storer, Tracy I. "Handbook of Birds of the Western United States" (review). *Condor*, March, 1915, p. 105.

Swarth, H. S. "The Birds of New Mexico" (review). *Condor*, March, 1929, pp. 82–83.

Index

No Woman Tenderfoot was composed into type on a Compugraphic digital phototypesetter in ten and one-half point Palatino with two points of spacing between the lines. Electronic input was supplied by the author, then massaged and typeset by Metricomp, Inc. The book was designed by Jim Billingsley, printed offset by Thomson-Shore, Inc., and bound by John H. Dekker & Sons. The paper on which the book is printed is designed for an effective life of at least three hundred years.

TEXAS A&M UNIVERSITY PRESS : COLLEGE STATION